Collins

INTERNATIONAL PRIMARY ENGLISH AS A SECOND LANGUAGE

Teacher's Guide 1

HarperCollins
PUBLISHERS
200

William Collins' dream of knowledge for all began with the publication of his first book in 1819.

A self-educated mill worker, he not only enriched millions of lives, but also founded a flourishing publishing house. Today, staying true to this spirit, Collins books are packed with inspiration, innovation and practical expertise. They place you at the centre of a world of possibility and give you exactly what you need to explore it.

Collins. Freedom to teach.

An imprint of HarperCollins*Publishers*
The News Building
1 London Bridge Street
London
SE1 9GF

Browse the complete Collins catalogue at
www.collins.co.uk

10 9 8 7 6 5 4 3 2 1

978-0-00-821360-2

British Library Cataloguing in Publication Data

A catalogue record for this publication is available from the British Library.

Publisher Celia Wigley
Commissioning editor Karen Jamieson
Series editor Karen Morrison
Managing editor Sarah Thomas
Editor Alexander Rutherford
Project managed by Tara Alner
Edited by Tracy Thomas
Proofread by Zoe Smith
Cover design by ink-tank and associates
Cover artwork by Milly Teggle
Internal design by 2hoots publishing services and QBS Learning
Typesetting by 2hoots publishing services and QBS Learning
Illustrations by QBS Learning and Beehive Illustration Agency
Production by Lauren Crisp

Printed and bound by CPI Group (UK) Ltd, Croydon, CR0 4YY

All exam-style questions and sample answers have been written by the author. In examinations marks may be given differently.

Text acknowledgements

The publishers gratefully acknowledge the permissions granted to reproduce copyright material in the book. Every effort has been made to contact the holders of copyright material, but if any have been inadvertently overlooked, the Publisher will be pleased to make the necessary arrangements at the first opportunity.

HarperCollins*Publishers* Limited for: Artwork from *Time for School* by Wendy Cope, illustrated by Mike Phillips, text © 2013 Wendy Cope. Artwork from *Fox and Stork* by Simon Puttock, illustrated by Milly Teggle, text © 2013 Simon Puttock. Artwork from *Bob's Secret Hideaway* by Tom Dickinson, illustrated by Jimothy Oliver, text © 2014 Tom Dickinson. Artwork from *Jack and the Beanstalk* by Caryl Hart, illustrated by Nicola L. Robinson, text © 2013 Caryl Hart.

p79 song What's in the bag? by Karen Press, reproduced with permission; p80 song The colour purple by Karen Press, reproduced with permission.

Photo acknowledgements

The publishers wish to thank the following for permission to reproduce photographs. Every effort has been made to trace copyright holders and to obtain their permission for the use of copyright materials. The publishers will gladly receive any information enabling them to rectify any error or omission at the fi rst opportunity.

(t = top, c = centre, b = bottom, r = right, l = left)

Cover & p1 Milly Teggle

PCM12 1b lineartestpilot/Shutterstock, PCM12 4 TAW4/Shutterstock, PCM16 tr Angorius/Shutterstock

CONTENTS

Introduction

About the *Collins Cambridge Primary English as a Second Language* course

The *Collins Cambridge Primary English as a Second Language* course is specifically written to fully meet the requirements of the Cambridge Primary English as a Second Language curriculum framework, and the material has been carefully developed to meet the needs of young English learners and teachers in a range of international contexts.

The material at each level is organised into nine topics, each divided into three related units. The activities in each unit are introduced and explored in context so that language is developed and learnt in meaningful and familiar contexts related to learners' interests and what they may be learning in other school subjects.

The course materials are supplemented and enhanced by printable and downloadable resources, including photocopiable (printable) master sheets for support and extension of classroom-based activities (you can find these on pages 87–120 of this Teacher's Guide) and Audio recordings to model pronunciation, develop listening skills and add interest and excitement to learning.

Components of the course

For each of Stages 1–6, as detailed in the Cambridge Primary English as a Second Language curriculum framework, we offer:

- a full-colour, highly illustrated, magazine-style **Student's Book** with integral reading texts
- a write-in **Workbook** linked to the Student's Book and clearly referenced in the teaching guidelines
- this comprehensive **Teacher's Guide** with clear instructions for using the materials in a flexible and clearly differentiated way
- free-to-download **Audio** recordings of key texts, songs and listening activities.

Approach

The course is designed with flexible and interactive learning at its heart but it follows a consistent approach.

- Generally, lessons will start with a warm-up session in which the teacher leads the class into the unit either by linking back to previous learning or by engaging in some other activity to hook their attention and interest.
- This is followed by a whole class teaching session to introduce vocabulary and model language structures to be used in the unit.
- Once the basics are covered, the teacher then selects from the differentiated activity bank to suit the needs of each class. These activities can be done in small groups or pairs, but they can also be used as whole class activities if that is what the teacher wants to do.

The Teacher's Guide is the central element of the course. It provides a detailed and structured script for teaching the core vocabulary and language structures to the whole class, as well as the bank of differentiated activities (marked triangle, circle and square) which provide different levels of challenge for learners. The teacher can select from the activities in the bank, to suit the level of English among learners and to meet the needs of particular groups or classroom contexts. It is not intended that learners should work through all of the activities in the Teacher's Guide, but rather that teachers should select according to the needs of the learners. If teachers try to complete *all* activities listed in the triangle, circle and square sections of the activity banks in the Teacher's Guide, they will find in some cases quite similar activities pitched at a slightly higher level of challenge, and this would be too repetitious, so teachers should select activities according to the need and ability level of learners. This way, the materials within this course are truly flexible and can be tailored to each class, and learner.

The suggested activities relate to, and use, the magazine-style Student's Book (which contains the stimulus, or 'input', for learners, in the form of varied reading texts, scene pictures, picture-dictionary-style pages and photographs for discussion).

The suggested activities in the activity bank also provide ideas for using the Workbook which enable learners to consolidate and apply what they have learnt, and to relate what they are learning both to the environment in which they live and beyond, to other contexts.

Much of the learners' work is conducted in pairs or small groups in line with international best practice. The tasks and activities are designed to be engaging for learners and to support teachers in their assessment of learner progress and achievement.

Throughout the course, there is a wide variety of learning experiences on offer. The materials are organised so that they do not impose a rigid structure, but rather allow for a range of options linked to the learning objectives. The materials are therefore truly flexible and can be adapted to suit a range of learning contexts.

Differentiation

Differentiation is a key element of second language teaching and learning so it forms a key element of the support and teaching ideas in this Teacher's Guide.

Fluency levels are likely to vary from learner to learner. The triangle, circle and square symbols indicate what learners at varying levels might be expected to manage. The triangle indicates what can be expected of almost all learners. The circle indicates what might be expected of most learners with some support, and the square indicates what level of achievement might be expected from more able and confident learners. Levels will vary, as some learners may find some topics more interesting and/or easier. Similarly, some may excel at speaking activities rather than written ones.

Using the Teacher's Guide

The Teacher's Guide offers detailed guidance for covering each topic.

The topics are designed to cover approximately three teaching weeks. The teacher knows their class and context best, so they should feel free to vary the pace and the amount of work covered each week to suit their circumstances. The course has been designed to be totally flexible and allow for speeding up and slowing down.

At the start of each of the nine topics, a full list of learning objectives is provided. The main focus objectives covered in the topic are underlined for planning purposes.

In addition, a summary of the grammar and language structures covered in each topic is provided for reference. This summary is for teacher information only. The structures and grammar detailed here will be taught in context and modelled for learners to use.

Each of the units has a clear structure, with:

- a list of resources
- suggestions for introducing the unit
- lead-in ideas
- ideas for introducing vocabulary and language structures to the whole class
- a differentiated activity bank for each unit. Activities are grouped in sections according to lower-, mid- and higher-level challenge (**triangle** activities for lower-level challenge; **circle** activities for mid-level challenge; **square** activities for higher-level challenge).
- suggestions for a plenary wrap-up session at the end of the unit
- ideas for informal assessment activities.

Student's Book

The Student's Book offers a colourful and attractive set of stimulus (or 'input') materials to introduce vocabulary and match the language structures being taught. The book follows a magazine-style design with strong visual appeal for maximum enjoyment and engagement. The following features are found at all levels:

- A range of fiction and non-fiction text types, including stories, poems, play scripts, information texts and transactional texts are provided to use as a starting point for contextualised learning.
- Instruction rubrics are kept short and simple, allowing more space on the page for the visuals and the text. Traditional-style language exercises are kept off the Student's Book pages, so that it doesn't feel like a textbook.
- 'Let's talk' and 'Let's think' bubbles are included on the pages, with questions to prompt personalisation of the topic, and to introduce higher-order cognitive skills, no matter how young learners are or how fluent they are in English.

Workbook

The Workbook is clearly linked to the Student's Book pages. The activities here contain structured spaces for learners to record answers. The activities can be used as classroom tasks, for homework or for assessment purposes. The completed workbook tasks give the teacher an opportunity to check work and give written feedback and/or grades. Learners have a consolidated record of their work and parents can see what kind of activities learners are doing in class.

Online resources

The Audio recordings for the course are available online as a free download. You can access these at Collins.co.uk. These resources can be downloaded, stored offline and used to support the activities as needed.

Sounds and letters

At Stage 1, learners could potentially have no previous knowledge of the English alphabet. If this is the case, teachers should spend time at the start of the course focusing on the alphabet, the names of the letters and the sounds the individual letters make, until learners are confident with this activity and are able to recognise the names and sounds of the letters.

Handwriting

Handwriting is not taught explicitly in this course, although the following objectives are implicitly covered in the activities and supporting notes in the Teacher's Guide:

1Wa1 Hold a pen/pencil in a comfortable and efficient grip

1Wa2 Form higher and lower case letters of regular size and shape

1Wa3 Write letters and words in a straight line from left to right with regular spaces between letters and words.

We recommend that teachers choose a structured and suitable course for teaching handwriting skills at Stage 1. *Collins Primary Focus: Handwriting*, by Sue Peet, is a useful resource for this as the series progresses from the introduction of fine motor movements, through cursive styles at the early stages, progressing to different handwriting styles, calligraphy and links to computer fonts at higher levels.

Personal dictionaries and journals

It is useful for learners to have a hardcover notebook that they use to make a personal dictionary and for independent writing (journaling). You can decide at which point to start these, but even emergent readers and writers can keep a journal. Make sure each learner has a book and allow them to decorate the cover as they like. They should write the letters of the alphabet (upper and lower case) at the tops of the first 26 pages. They can then write down any new words they learn to spell and draw pictures to help them remember the meanings. Insert a tab after the alphabet pages and use the rest of the book for independent writing. Research shows that encouraging emergent writing is a good way of improving literacy skills. At first, learners will draw and scribble. You can ask them to tell you about their drawing and write the words for them. They will then move to letters and letter-like symbols and you can ask them to tell you what they mean. The next development steps are often the writing of beginning sounds, or just the writing of a single letter, which to the child represents the overall prominent sound of that word (also called the 'salient sound'). For example, writing 'k' for 'like', because that's the sound that is most distinct when the child says the word. As they write more and more, their spelling and expression generally improves. There is a very good article about this in the journal *The Reading Teacher*, which you can access online, by Sonia Q. Cabell, Laura S. Tortorelli, and Hope K. Gerde (May 2013). *How Do I Write…? Scaffolding Preschoolers' Early Writing Skills* (*The Reading Teacher*, 66(8), pp. 650-659).

Assessment in primary English

In the *Collins Cambridge Primary English as a Second Language* course, assessment is a continuous, planned process that involves collecting information regularly about learner progress and learning, in order to provide constructive feedback to both learners and parents and also to guide planning and the next teaching steps.

The Cambridge Primary English as a Second Language curriculum framework makes it clear what learners are expected to learn and achieve at each Stage. Our task as teachers is to assess whether or not learners have achieved the stated goals using clearly-focused, varied, reliable and flexible methods of assessment.

In the *Collins Cambridge Primary English as a Second Language* course, assessment is continuous and in-built. It applies the principles of international best practice and ensures that assessment:

- is ongoing and regular
- supports individual achievement
- provides feedback and encouragement to learners
- allows for integration into the activities and classroom teaching, by combining different assessment methods, including observations, questioning and formal and informal tasks
- uses strategies that cater for a variety of learner needs in the classroom (language, physical, emotional and cultural), and acknowledges that learners do not all need to be assessed at the same time, or in the same way
- allows for, and prepares learners for, more formal, summative assessment including controlled activities, tasks and tests.

In Stage 1 of the course informal assessment ideas are included within this Teacher's Guide, at the end of each unit (the **Quick check** feature). In addition, an end-of-year Review Activity is included as photocopiable masters on pages 121–123, with ideas for how to administer it on page 77. There is also an informal assessment page in the Workbook, for each topic. These can be used in the same way as all the other activities in the classroom.

More formal testing in the form of progression tests begins in Stage 3. No formal assessments (tests or examinations) are required at Stages 1 or 2.

High-frequency sight words for Stage 1

a	dad	I	no	to
all	do	in	of	up
am	don't	is	on	was
and	father	it	said	we
are	for	like	see	want
at	get	look	she	went
big	go	me	small	yes
can	going	mom	the	you
can't	has	mother	they	
come	he	my	this	

Subject words

Number words from *one* to *ten*

Colour words: *red*, *green*, *yellow*, *blue*, etc. (Used in context and with support.)

Size words: *big*, *small*, *long*, *short*, *thick*, *thin*, *full*, *empty*, *more*, *less*, *lots*, *same*, *different*

Instruction and question words

Who? Where? How many? What?

write, *tick*, *cross*, *find*, *match*, *point to*, *choose*, *copy*

Topic 1 Our school

Overview

This topic allows you to introduce basic vocabulary and knowledge of English phonemes while assessing the prior knowledge of learners in your class. There are opportunities to integrate language lessons with other subjects in the curriculum, such as art and music. Vocabulary and concepts are developed using familiar objects at school and by encouraging learners to express themselves using whatever knowledge they already have. Learners are encouraged to participate enthusiastically in activities to develop confidence.

Pages 155-160 in the Workbook provide additional practice for learners who are learning to recognise and write the letters of the alphabet and number words in English. These activities can be used as necessary and according to the needs of your class. The pages should be completed in stages, rather than all at once. Here are some examples of activities:

The alphabet

Give learners some lower-case letters of the alphabet. Write the letters on the whiteboard and let learners find and trace the letters in their Workbooks. You could give a sequence of letters, or you could group the letters according to handwriting development.

Do the same with capital letters. For example, write the names of some learners in the class on the whiteboard. Ask learners to find the capital letter in their Workbooks and then trace it. Alternatively, write some lower-case letters on the board and let learners find the matching upper-case letters to trace in their books.

A bit later in the year, let learners draw pictures of things that begin with each letter of the alphabet.

Numbers

Learners first trace the numerals for handwriting practice. Later, when they are learning to associate the number words with the numerals, let them trace one or two words at a time.

Shapes

Learners can trace the names of the shapes when they learn the names. Let them trace one or two names at a time.

Units in this topic

Unit A: What's your name?
Unit B: In my classroom
Unit C: What I do at school

Teaching focus

- 1Rg1 Recognise, identify, sound and name the letters of the alphabet.
- 1Rg2 Recognise, identify, sound, segment and blend phonemes in individual words.
- 1Uf1 Use imperative forms of common verbs for basic commands and instructions.
- 1Uf2 Use common present simple forms [positive, negative, question] to give basic personal information.
- 1Ug1 Use common singular nouns, plural nouns [plural 's'] and proper names to say what things are.
- 1Ug4 Use possessive adjectives to describe objects.
- 1Ug14 Use, with support, a simple picture dictionary.
- 1Ug17 Write familiar words to identify people, places and objects.
- 1Ut1 Use the questions *What colour is it? What now?*
- 1Ut2 Use determiners *a, the, this, these* to indicate what/where something is.
- 1Ut3 Use interrogative pronouns *which, what, where* to ask basic questions.
- 1Ut4 Use demonstrative pronouns *this, these* to indicate things.
- 1Ld4 Understand a limited range of short, basic, supported classroom instructions.
- 1Lg2 Recognise the sounds of phonemes and phoneme blends.
- 1Lg3 Recognise the names of letters of the alphabet.
- 1S1 Make and respond to basic statements related to personal information.
- 1S2 Ask questions in order to find out about a limited range of personal information and classroom routines.
- 1S3 Use a limited range of basic words, phrases and sentences related to classroom objects, activities and routines.
- 1S4 Respond to basic questions on classroom and daily routines.
- 1S5 Use words and phrases to describe people and objects.

Language patterns

Grammar summary for teachers:

- **Verb 'to be':** This is an irregular verb which is the basis for many sentences. The different forms of the verb (*is, am, are*) are high-frequency words. Do not teach the grammar, but use repetition to teach this structure.
- **Possessive adjectives:** These are words such as *my, your, his, her, our, their*. The words are used before nouns. Example: *This is **my** book.*
- **Determiners:** These are words such as *a, the, this* and *these.* The words are used to indicate what something is or where it is. *A* and *this* are used with singular subjects, *the* can be used with both singular and plural subjects, and *these* is only used with plural subjects.
- **Imperative forms:** The imperative forms of verbs are used to give instructions. The infinitive form of the verb is used, without the preposition *to*. The imperative is used at the beginning of instructions. The negative *Do not/Don't* can be added to the instruction, before the verb. Examples: *Stand up. Do not/Don't talk. Wash your hands.*

Unit A What's your name?

Resources and materials

- Student's Book pp. 4–5
- Workbook pp. 4–7
- Audio files: Audio 1; Audio 2
- Photocopiable Masters (PCMs) PCM 1; PCM 2
- A name tag for yourself and for each learner in the class
- A poster with letters of the alphabet
- Prompt cards with letters of the alphabet

Key vocabulary

my, his, her, name, is, this, that, teacher

(+ names of learners in class)

Lead-in ideas

(select as appropriate)

- Introduce yourself to the class, using the structure: *Hello. My name is ______. I am a teacher.*
- Teach learners any song about greetings or names. Sing or chant using actions. Learners can sit in a circle to sing, turning to face the person as his/her name is mentioned. The song *Hello* (**Audio 1**) is a good example.

Script for the lesson

Introducing vocabulary

Start with the letters of the alphabet. Use pages 4–5 in the Student's Book. Let learners say which letter names they know, and read through them all with the class. Say the letter names at this stage. Reinforce the letter names in English by asking learners to find and name objects starting with different letters. Point out that each letter can be written as a capital and a small letter using the text as an example (but do not focus too much on this).

Use the name tags to introduce the names of all learners in the class. As you hand out the cards, say the name and greet each learner.

Sounds

Revise and teach sounds in the context of the topic. Focus on the initial sounds of the names of learners in this unit. Ask learners to identify the initial sounds and to match names that have the same initial sounds. Remember that letters in the English alphabet can have different sounds, for example, *A* can sound like 'ah' in names like *Ali* or 'ay' in names like *Adrian*. You may want to return to pages 4–5 in the Student's Book to teach some letter sounds.

You can also choose a few names that are easy to decode – Consonant-Vowel-Consonant (CVC) words such as *Sam, Ali* and *Ban*, for example – and help learners to read the whole names. Most learners will, however, learn to recognise their own names as sight words.

Introducing structures

Teach learners how to introduce themselves and others using these structural patterns:

Hello./Hi./Good morning./Good afternoon.

What's your name? My name is ______. I'm ______.

What's her name? Her name is ______.

What's his name? His name is ______.

Teach *This is ______* and *That is ______* by pointing first at a learner who is closer to you and then at a learner who is sitting further away from you.

Previous knowledge

Learners may already be familiar with the alphabet and with some letter sounds from literacy lessons in their first language.

Possible areas of difficulty

Some letter sounds may be the same in other languages, but others will be different. Help learners to pronounce letter sounds correctly in English. Rhymes and songs play an important role in teaching learners pronunciation and intonation in a second (or third) language.

Some learners will confuse *this* and *that* in the beginning and it may be difficult to explain the difference. Focus on pronouncing the words correctly and model the correct use until learners get used to the difference.

Activities

Select from these activities depending on the level of challenge needed for different learners, interest levels and what you have time to include. Supplement these with additional activities of your own and/or digital activities from the online resource.

▲ **1.** Learners work in groups. Give each learner a name card. Learners take turns to introduce themselves (*My name is ______.*) and then ask the learner sitting next to them a question (*What's your name?*).

▲ **2.** Work with the whole class. Call up one learner at a time and say: *This is ______.* Then clap the syllables in the learner's name. (Example: *Na/ta/sha*)

▲ **3.** Learners find the letters in their names in the alphabet in activity 1 in the Workbook. They colour in the letters and write their names. Some learners may know that they should start their names with capital letters. This is not the focus of the activity, but allow learners to do this if they can.

▲ **4.** Learners draw a picture of themselves and write their names in activity 2 in the Workbook. This time, encourage them to use capital letters to start their names.

▲ **5.** Revise or teach beginning sounds, using the names of learners in the class. Hold up letters of the alphabet and ask questions. (Example: *Whose name begins with M?*)

▲ **6.** Teach further possessive adjectives *his/her* in sentences. (***Her** name is Maryam. **His** name is Pedro.*) Write the words on the board or use prompt cards to teach these high-frequency words.

▲ **7.** Learners complete activity 3 in the Workbook to consolidate their understanding of *his/her* and to help them recognise the words as high-frequency words.

▲ **8.** Give learners copies of **PCM 1**. They cut out the names and then arrange the names according to beginning sounds.

● **9.** **Link to mathematics*. Make a name wall with the names of learners in the class. Each learner writes his/her name on a piece of paper and pastes it on the wall, under the letter of the alphabet with which their name begins. When this is complete, count the names under each letter and talk about the results.

Here is part of a wall as an example:

A	B	C	D	E	F
Anna Ali	Bella		Daria Don Diego		F
2	1	0	3	0	1

● **10.** Teach the structures *This is______, That is ______* using names of learners in the class.

● **11.** Learners work in groups. They use name cards and prompt cards with the structures *This is ______* and *That is ______* to make sentences. They read the sentences aloud.

● **12.** Teach a traditional rhyme with names. **Audio 2** is a good example. You could start with the traditional rhyme and then change the names to the names of learners in the class. Learners act the rhyme as they repeat it.

■ **13.** Learners work in pairs. They draw a picture of their partner and show it to the class. As they work, walk around and ask them which letter each name begins with. Learners make oral sentences about their pictures. (*This is Anna/my friend. Her name is Anna. Her name begins with A.*)

■ **14.** Write some short names (CVC names such as *Sam, Ted, Pon, Liz, Ben*) on the board and help learners to decode the names. Explain, if you have not done so already, that we always start names with capital letters.

(Note: If learners are unsure about the difference between capital letters and lower case letters, you should teach this difference now.)

■ **15.** Learners draw a picture of a friend in their Workbook (activity 4) and complete a sentence about the friend. If they are able to do so, they can say (or write) another sentence about their friend.

Wrap-up plenary

Talk about how we use capital letters to write the first letters of our names. Then find out what learners know about their names. Do they know what the names mean? Are the names traditional, or do they have cultural significance? Give an example: *Her name is Katherine. Katherine means 'pure and strong'. Her grandmother's name is also Katherine.* This can be done in another language if necessary at this stage.

Quick check

1. Hold up a selection of name cards or point to cards on the name wall you made. Ask learners to identify and say the initial sounds in each name.
2. Give learners **PCM 2**. They copy the first letter of each name in the spaces provided and then write or say another name with that beginning sound.

Unit B In my classroom

Resources and materials

- Student's Book pp. 6–7
- Workbook pp. 8–12
- Audio files: Audio 3; Audio 4
- Photocopiable Master (PCM) PCM 3
- A collection of pictures of classroom objects, with labels or prompt cards to match
- Labels for common objects in the classroom
- Prompt cards or a poster with all the letters of the alphabet
- Prompt cards: *his, her, This is* ______. *That is* ______.
- Paper and crayons for drawing

Key vocabulary

whiteboard, table, desk, chair, pen, pencil, book, crayon, eraser, ruler, glue, scissors, paper, bin, computer, bag, lunchbox

Lead-in ideas

- Revise beginning sounds of words using the letters and pictures on pages 4–5 of the Student's Book. Say the name of each thing pictured and ask learners to say what sound the beginning letter makes.
- Play a game of 'I spy' with the class to assess how much they know about the names of classroom objects and initial sounds. (Example: *I spy something that begins with a 'buh'.*) Ask the questions yourself and see who can respond. Start with simple words, such as *book, desk, table, board, computer*. (You could use page 7 of the Student's Book for this activity.)

Script for the lesson

Introducing vocabulary

Use real classroom items and labels or prompt cards to teach or revise the names of common classroom objects. Turn to page 6 of the Student's Book. Read through the story with the class or listen to **Audio 4** and teach them the names of the objects shown on the desk. Let them play the game themselves using available classroom objects.

Sounds

Revise and teach sounds in the context again, this time focusing on the initial sounds of classroom objects. Ask learners to identify the initial sounds and to match objects that have the same initial sounds.

Introducing structures

Teach the structures *This is a* ______ and *These are* ______ using classroom objects.

Introduce simple plural forms (*books, bags, rulers*) naturally as you teach the structure *These are* ______.

Previous knowledge

Some learners will be familiar with some classroom vocabulary.

Possible areas of difficulty

Some learners may have difficulty pronouncing the end sound 's' in plural words and the 'th' sound in *this, that* and *these*.

The use of a determiner (a/an) with singular nouns may be confusing at first, which is why it is important to teach simple structures to use with nouns.

Activities

Select from these activities depending on the level of challenge needed for different learners, interest levels and what you have time to include. Supplement these with additional activities of your own and/or digital activities from the online resource.

▲ 1. Teach the names of common classroom objects using prompt cards and real items. Read the words and match them to the objects. Then read each word aloud again and invite learners to match the words to the objects.

▲ 2. Say the names of objects in the classroom. Let learners identify each object by pointing to it or touching it.

▲ 3. Revise beginning sounds using classroom objects. Hold up objects and ask learners to say the name. (Example: *What is this? A book. It begins with 'buh'.*) Write the words on the board as you do this and circle the first letters of the words to help learners make the connection between the sound and the letter of the alphabet.

▲ 4. Learners can complete activity 1 in the Workbook, in which they write the beginning sounds of words to match classroom objects.

▲ 5. Learners can complete activity 2 in the Workbook, in which they match words and pictures of classroom objects.

▲ 6. Learners can complete activity 3 in the Workbook, in which they identify initial letters of words, which name classroom objects.

▲ 7. Work with groups. Put a selection of classroom objects in a bag. Let learners take turns to put their hands in the bag and identify an object without looking at it. They say the name and then take the object out of the bag to see if they are correct. Ask the class to work out a scoring system for the game.

● 8. Introduce learners to a simple picture dictionary (for example, *Collins First English Words*) if you feel they are ready for this. Use page 7 of the Student's Book and then use any appropriate picture dictionary that you have available. You could use a monolingual English dictionary or a very simple bilingual dictionary. These dictionaries are usually arranged in themes, so look for a theme about school. Let learners look at the pictures and read the words. Explain that the words are arranged in order, like in the alphabet they have learnt.

9. Read or reread the story *A Game* in the Student's Book on page 6. Talk about the pictures first and let learners identify classroom objects in the pictures. Then read the story aloud and let learners follow. Do some word recognition activities using the words in the story. For example, hold up a prompt card with the word 'book'. Ask learners what the beginning letter is. Then let them find the word 'book' in the story.

10. Play a game with groups of learners. Put 8–10 objects on a table. Let learners say the names of the objects and then cover the table. Learners have to remember and say the names of all the objects on the table. (This game is sometimes called 'Kim's game'.)

11. Learners draw pictures of things they use in the classroom. They write the name of each item under the picture. Then they arrange the pictures according to the beginning letters. They can do this on a word wall or on sheets of paper.

12. Teach *This is a* ______ and *These are* ______ using prompt cards and real objects in the classroom. Help learners to form lots of simple sentences with these structures.

13. Give each learner some paper. Learners draw pictures of things they use in the classroom. Then, working in pairs, they talk about what they have drawn, using the structures *This is a* ______ and *These are* ______.

14. Learners find words in a word search puzzle in activity 4 in the Workbook and then trace the words in activity 5.

15. Read or reread, or sing an alphabet song that you know. You could use **Audio 3**. Learners can perform the song with actions.

16. Workbook activity 6. Learners join the letters of the alphabet in the correct order to find out where the girl is going.

17. Learners work in pairs or small groups, using copies of **PCM 3**. They cut out the words and use them to make as many simple sentences as they can. They read the sentences to their groups or partners.

Wrap-up plenary

Sing the Alphabet Song with learners again. Explain that the letters all have names, but that the letters also have different sounds. If there are learners in the class who have started to read and write other languages with different alphabets (for example, Greek or Russian), let them share what they know about other alphabets.

Quick check

Play the 'I spy' game again with groups of learners. Let them take turns to think of objects beginning with different letters. The person in the group who guesses correctly gets the next turn.

Unit C What I do at school

Resources and materials

- Student's Book pp. 8–9
- Workbook pp. 13–17
- Audio files: Audio 3; Audio 5; Audio 6
- Photocopiable Master (PCM) PCM 4
- Prompt cards or a poster with all the letters of the alphabet
- Prompt cards with basic instructions (examples: *Sit down. Open the door. Close your book.*)

Key vocabulary

sit, stand, open, write, read, find, put, go, walk, run, jump, skip, play, hop

Lead-in ideas

- Teach learners a song or rhyme about school activities and routines. *This Is the Way We Go to School* (**Audio 5**) is an example that can be chanted and acted out (total physical response) or sung in groups with movements. You can make up additional verses for this song.

Script for the lesson

Introducing vocabulary

In this lesson the focus is on understanding verbs which give instructions. Repeat these instructions often until learners are familiar with them. Use actions to show what you mean to help learners understand.

Sounds

Continue to teach and revise initial sounds as learners acquire new vocabulary. Ask learners to identify initial sounds in texts and songs that you sing or read together.

Introducing structures

Teach a series of short, basic instructions that learners will need to understand in class. Use the imperative forms of common verbs. You can introduce a few negatives as well. For example: *Sit down, please. Stand up. Go to the door. Open your books. Take out your crayons. Put up your hand. Don't run. Wash your hands.*

Look at the pictures on page 8 of the Student's Book. Talk about what learners do at school. Have some learners mime the things they do at school, for example, *read, write, paint* and let the others say the verb.

Introduce the present simple tense to discuss classroom activities. Use verbs with the pronoun *I* and *we* to do this. You do not need to explain the rule about adding an '-s' with third person subjects at this stage.

Previous knowledge

Instructions in their mother tongue should be familiar to learners by this stage.

Possible areas of difficulty

Some learners may not yet have developed good listening skills and may, therefore, struggle to follow instructions. Some of the suggested activities below will help learners to develop these skills.

Activities

Select from these activities depending on the level of challenge needed for different learners, interest levels and what you have time to include. Supplement these with additional activities of your own and/or digital activities from the online resource.

▲ **1.** Teach learners a few new instructions each day. Give each instruction and demonstrate what you mean or use gestures. Repeat the instructions clearly and often.

▲ **2.** Write a few of the verbs you have taught on the board or on prompt cards. Let learners identify and repeat the initial sounds and then act the words (examples: *sit, jump, read, open*).

▲ **3.** Learners work in groups. Each learner has a turn to give a simple instruction to the rest of the group. Learners can also mime the instructions and use gestures.

▲ **4.** Teach learners to play a game, such as 'Simon says', in which they have to listen carefully and follow instructions. Explain that you will give instructions. Some instructions begin with 'Simon says' (*Simon says 'Stand up'*) and others will not (*Stand up*). If learners do not hear the words *Simon says*, they must not move or obey the instruction. Play the game with the whole class, giving the instructions yourself until learners are familiar with the game.

▲ **5.** Learners complete activity 1 in the Workbook and match the pictures and the action words.

▲ **6.** Take learners outside and teach them a few instructions relating to games or physical exercises. For example: *Run. Walk. Jump. Skip. Hop*. Let them follow each instruction until you give a new one. You can also use a ball and teach instructions, such as: *Kick the ball. Catch the ball. Sit on the ball.* Demonstrate each action or get learners to volunteer to do the demonstrations.

▲ **7.** Teach learners an alphabet song if you haven't done so already. You could use **Audio 3**. Learners can perform the song with actions.

▲ **8.** Let learners find page 7 (*Our school* picture dictionary) in the Student's Book. They work in pairs and revise the names and beginning letters of objects. (Example: *This is a pen. It begins with 'p'.*) Then they talk about things they can do in the classroom using the pictures as prompts. They can use words rather than sentences to describe an action if necessary. (Example: *This is a book. Read.*)

● **9.** Start a discussion about things we do at school. Mime an action for the class (example: reading a book). Then say: *We read*. Write the word *read* on the board or show learners a prompt card with the word. Teach words such as *read, work, play, sing, paint, draw, write* and *listen*.

● **10.** Learners work in groups and mime things that they do at school. The rest of the learners in the group guess what they are doing.

● **11.** Help learners to make up a song or a chant about school activities. They could clap each syllable as they chant. For example:

We greet. We listen.

Then we work.

We read. We write.

Then we play.

We wash. We drink.

Then we eat.

● **12.** Learners can draw or paint pictures of their favourite school activities. Help them to label the activities. Display the pictures for other learners to look at and read the labels. To develop self-confidence and vocabulary use, let learners try to say a sentence about their picture.

● **13.** Learners work in groups. Introduce prompt cards with simple instructions written on them (examples: *Stand up, Sit down, Skip*). Put the cards face down in a pile and let learners take turns to choose a card. The group reads the card and all learners in the group do the action. Depending on the level of the learners, you may need to help them read the words at first.

● **14.** Learners match instructions to the pictures in activity 2 in the Workbook.

■ **15.** Play **Audio 6** of the story/poem *Time for School*. Let learners look at the pictures that accompany the story as they listen (Student's Book pages 8–9). You can pre-teach some of the vocabulary in the story, but note that is not essential for learners to understand every word. The aim is to look at pictures and understand the gist of the story.

■ **16.** Learners work in pairs. They look at the story *Time for School* and make simple oral sentences about what the children in the pictures do at school. (Examples: *They read. They play.*)

17. The story *Time for School* uses rhyming words. Give learners a few examples of words that rhyme (examples: *school/pool*; *me/see*). Then read the story again, slowly, and ask learners to listen for words that sound the same. They can raise their hands when they hear a word that sounds the same (examples: *come (Mom)*, *day (play)*, *do (too)*).
18. Give learners copies of **PCM 4**. Let them cut out the pictures and rearrange them according to the order of the activities in the story *Time for School*. Then they use the pictures to retell the story using whatever vocabulary they can. Those learners who can already tell the time can refer to the clocks in the pictures to help them sort out the order. Play the **Audio 6** for learners to listen to and to check the order in which they have arranged the pictures.

Wrap-up plenary

Talk about all the things you do at school. Find a story about school days to read aloud to the class.

Quick check

1. Play the game 'Simon says' with the class to check whether they understand the basic classroom instructions you have introduced.
2. Give learners prompt cards with letters of the alphabet. Let them arrange the cards in alphabetical order as they sing an alphabet song.
3. Let learners complete the picture in activity 3 in the Workbook. They draw objects and activities in the classroom and then talk about their pictures.

Assessment

You can complete an oral assessment of the work done in this topic by:

- asking learners to name objects in the classroom
- asking them to describe pictures
- using the prompt cards with letters of the alphabet to check knowledge of sounds (initial sounds) made by phonemes.

Learners can also complete Progress check activities 1, 2 and 3 in the Workbook as a simple assessment. For the first activity, read one of the words in each group and let learners tick the picture that matches the word you read. You could allocate marks for these activities and record these as part of continuous assessment.

Topic 2 All about me

Overview

In this topic the focus is on sharing personal information. Learners will use basic verbs and structures with which to ask and answer questions and share information about themselves. This can be used to help build confidence amongst learners. There are opportunities to integrate activities with health education, civics, art and mathematics.

Units in this topic

Unit A: All about me!

Unit B: My family

Unit C: What I do at home

Teaching focus

- 1Rg1 Recognise, identify, sound and name the letters of the alphabet.
- 1Rg2 Recognise, identify, sound, segment and blend phonemes in individual words.
- 1Rg3 Identify and remember high-frequency sound and letter patterns.
- 1Wa6 Write familiar words to identify people, places and objects.
- 1Uf2 Use common present simple forms [positive, negative, question] to give basic personal information.
- 1Uf5 Use can/can't to describe ability.
- 1Uf6 Use *have got* to describe possession.
- 1Ug1 Use common singular nouns, plural nouns [plural 's'] and proper names to say what things are.
- 1Ug14 Use, with support, a simple picture dictionary.
- 1Ut1 Use the questions *What colour is it? What now?*
- 1Ut3 Use interrogative pronouns *which, what, where* to ask basic questions.
- 1Ut5 Use personal subject and object pronouns to give basic personal information.
- 1Ld3 Understand a limited range of short supported questions which ask for personal information.
- 1Ld4 Understand a limited range of short, basic, supported classroom instructions.
- 1Lg2 Recognise the sounds of phonemes and phoneme blends.
- 1Lg3 Recognise the names of letters of the alphabet.
- 1S1 Make and respond to basic statements related to personal information.
- 1S2 Ask questions in order to find out about a limited range of personal information and classroom routines.
- 1S5 Use words and phrases to describe people and objects.
- 1S7 Take turns when speaking with others in a limited range of short, basic exchanges

Language patterns

Grammar summary for teachers:

- **Regular simple present tense verbs:** Verbs such as *to like* and *to want* are regular verbs that can be used in positive, negative and question forms in all verb tenses. In the third person singular (positive form only) we need to add '-s' to the verb.
- **Irregular simple present tense verbs:** Verbs such as *to be* and *to have* are irregular verbs because they have irregular forms.
- **Verb 'can':** This is a modal, or auxiliary, verb. Modal verbs do not have infinitive forms or *-ing* forms. They also do not have third person singular forms that end in '-s'. The verb does have a past tense form (*could*) and negative forms (*cannot/can't/could not/couldn't*).
- **Personal pronouns:** There are subject pronouns and object pronouns.

Subject pronouns	Object pronouns
I am 6.	I see her/him/them/us.
You are a friend.	
He is a boy.	
She is a girl.	
We are friends.	
They are happy.	

- **Questions:** The auxiliary verb *do* is often used to ask questions and to give short (negative and positive) answers to questions. *Do you have a sister? Yes, I do. No, I don't.*

Unit A All about me!

Resources and materials

- Student's Book p. 10
- Workbook pp. 18–22
- Audio file: Audio 7
- Photocopiable Masters (PCMs) PCM 5; PCM 6
- Prompt cards with key vocabulary words, pronouns, high-frequency words

Key vocabulary

to be (am, is, are), me, my, name, girl, boy, years old

Lead-in ideas

- Ask learners to bring one of their favourite things to class to show the others, if they can. (If not, they could take photos and show those.) Help them to name the articles and to say something about them.
- Teach learners a rhyme or poem with rhyming words, such as *This Is Me* (**Audio 7**). Help learners to change the pronouns and verb *to be* in the rhyme.

Script for the lesson

Introducing vocabulary

Focus on the subject pronouns *I, you, he, she, it, we, they* and the object pronoun *me* as used in simple sentences, questions and answers.

Learners will also need to know words such as *name, age, boy, girl, like*. Numbers can be taught more formally in a later lesson, but ages are introduced in this lesson.

Sounds

Continue to revise initial sounds by referring to the names of learners in the class. Teach a few tongue-twisters (alliteration and rhythm). (Example: *Peter Piper picked a peck of pickled peppers*.)

Help learners to identify phonemes and say the sounds in high-frequency words, including question words and answers.

Introducing structures

Revise the verb *to be* by teaching structures with personal pronouns as subjects. *I am _____. You are _____. He/She/It is _____. We are _____. They are _____.*

Teach simple questions with short answers that learners can use in brief interviews. (Example: *Are you seven years old? Yes, I am. No, I'm not. Do you like* (+ noun) *maths/football/chocolate? Yes, I do. No, I don't.*) If you feel the class is ready, you could also teach: *Where do you live? I live in _____.* Model these interviews with learners who are more fluent and give learners as many opportunities as possible to use the sentences. You do not need to explain the grammar or the irregular verbs.

Previous knowledge

Learners will be able to count in their mother tongue, so focus on number words in English. The symbols/numerals (3, 6, etc.) will help them to make the connections.

Possible areas of difficulty

Learners may confuse the forms of the verb *to be* at first. Correct them when they make a mistake and continue. Depending on their exposure to English, some learners may also struggle to answer questions. Let them start with simple *Yes/No* answers before they move on to *Yes, I do* and *No I don't*.

Activities

Select from these activities depending on the level of challenge needed for different learners, interest levels and what you have time to include. Supplement these with additional activities of your own and/or digital activities from the online resource.

▲ **1.** Teach a simple interview conversation. Demonstrate the interview and then let learners work with different partners to ask and answer the same questions. For example:

Hello. What's your name?

My name is _____.

How old are you?

I am 6/7/8.

Teach the learners to take turns as they ask and answer questions. They should listen to an answer before they ask the next question.

▲ **2.** Teach personal pronouns in sentences such as: *I am the teacher. You are learners. He is a boy. She is 7. It is a ball. We are children. They are happy*. Model each structure, using actions and learners in the class. Then write the personal pronouns on the board and invite learners to make sentences with each pronoun.

▲ **3.** Do some word recognition activities with personal pronouns and other high-frequency words. Write the words on the board and let learners match these with words written on prompt cards, for example. Learners can then complete activities 1 and 2 in the Workbook.

▲ **4.** Learners work in groups. Each learner talks about another learner in the group using structures such as: *This is [name]. He is a boy. He is 7. He likes football*. Learners need to take turns and listen to what each speaker says.

▲ **5.** Read *Our stories* on page 10 of the Student's Book with groups of learners. Discuss the pictures first. For example, let learners identify the boys and girls. Ask them to find the names of the children. Remind them that we write names with capital letters.

Read the stories aloud, one at a time. Talk about 'other names' that we often have (nicknames, or shortened forms of names).

Ask simple questions to check comprehension. (Examples: *What is her name? What does her mother call her? What does her name mean?*)

6. Give each learner a copy of **PCM 5** after they have read *Our stories* in the Student's Book. Read the following sentences, one at a time, to learners and let them tick the appropriate box on their sheet.
   1. *She is a girl.*
   2. *His name is Advik.*
   3. *Her name means 'friend'.*
   4. *His name begins with R.*
   5. *Her friends call her Nix.*
7. Learners complete activity 3 in the Workbook, in which they complete the alphabet in capital letters. They can refer to page 4 in the Student's Book to help them.
8. Learners complete activity 4 in the Workbook. Read this list of names out slowly and let learners listen and complete the names, before they write the names of three friends.

   a) Sue **b)** Anton **c)** Toni **d)** Mary **e)** Fernando **f)** Busi **g)** Haile **h)** Vihaan **i)** Lucy
9. Have a class discussion about first names and family names. Then write some of the family names (surnames) on the board and help other learners to read the names. Let them identify the first letters of the names. Explain to learners that we also write family names with capital letters.
10. Learners read or reread *Our stories* on page 10 of the Student's Book in pairs. You can also make sentence strips with the sentences in the stories and let learners match these strips to the sentences in the Student's Book.
11. Teach another interview conversation to teach the structure *Do you like ______?* and short answers to go with this. Teach vocabulary as needed.

    Demonstrate the interview and then let learners work with different partners to ask and answer the same questions. For example:

    Do you like (maths/school/chocolate)?
    Yes./Yes, I do./No./No, I don't.
12. **Link to mathematics*. Draw the following chart on the whiteboard, or on a poster. Fill in names of some of the subjects and activities that learners do at school, for example:

maths	
English	
writing	
art	
singing	

Read each word on the list and do a survey with the groups of learners to find out which activities they like the most. Tell them that they can each put up their hands twice, so they can only choose two activities. Say a name of an activity and ask learners to put up their hands. Make ticks/tally marks next to each activity. Then count the tally marks aloud with the group to find out which activities are the most popular. This is a good opportunity to reinforce number words.

13. Learners read *Our stories* in the Student's Book again. Then they work in groups and play riddles. They pretend to be characters from *Our stories*. They make up simple riddles about the characters to help the others to guess. (Example: *I am a girl. My name begins with A. My name means 'friend'.*) Work out how learners are to take turns and how to score the game.
14. Learners draw a picture of themselves (activity 5 in the Workbook) and complete a few sentences about themselves using the writing frame in activity 6 and words that they have learnt. If necessary, write a few words on the whiteboard for them to copy.
15. Give each learner a copy of **PCM 6**. Read the questions and let learners underline the appropriate replies. Then let them draw pictures of what they like doing. Make sure that learners have the opportunity to talk about what they have drawn afterwards, so that they practise the language they have learnt. Practise the structure *I like* + verb + *-ing*.
16. Teach the class a few tongue-twisters for fun. These help learners to say beginning sounds clearly and they also help learners get used to the rhythm and intonation of words. The meaning is not important. For example:

    Peter Piper picked a peck of pickled peppers.
    Six silly sisters singing a song.

Wrap-up plenary

Repeat the *This Is Me* rhyme and make it clear that everyone in the class is special. Start to introduce some of the vocabulary that you will be teaching in Units B and C here, along with the structures that learners know. Give learners a chance to participate and teach them appropriate ways in which to do this. They need to take turns during exchanges, and listen to what others have to say. In time they can also begin to ask questions about what others say. Examples: *I am special. I can sing. He is special. He can run. You are special. You can paint. She is special. She can dance.*

Quick check

Make a card game with high-frequency words (examples so far: *am, are, he, she, it, do, you, name, they, this, that*). Make two cards for each word. Add to the cards as you progress. Learners can play matching games with the cards. They can place the cards face down and try and find two cards that match, remembering where the cards are. Alternatively, they can play a game like 'Snap'. They mix up the cards and each take the same number of cards. Then they reveal the cards one at a time. The first person to say 'Snap!' wins the two cards.

Unit B My family

Resources and materials

- Student's Book pp. 11–13
- Workbook pp. 23–27
- Audio files: Audio 8; Audio 9; Audio 10
- Prompt cards with key vocabulary words
- Sentence strips with key sentence structures and sentences from stories in the Student's Book
- Prompt cards with letters of the alphabet (from Topic 1)

Key vocabulary

to have, do, don't, he, she, they, mother, father, sister, brother, baby, grandma, grandpa, aunty, uncle, cousins

Lead-in ideas

Ask learners to bring photographs of their families to school if they can. You can also show learners pictures of a range of different families.

Teach learners to recite a chant about families with actions. For example, play the chant *A Family* (**Audio 8**). You can make finger puppets to go with the chant too.

Teach learners any rhyme or poem that relates to families. For example, play the poem *This Is My Family* (**Audio 9**) and teach the actions.

Script for the lesson

Introducing vocabulary

Use prompt cards to introduce the names of family members. Use whichever names are most familiar or acceptable in your community, but expose learners to other names that are commonly used as well. (Examples: *Mother/Mom/Mum/Mama/Mummy/Mommy, Father/Dad/Daddy/Baba/Pop/Papa, Grandmother/Gran/Grandma/Nonna, Grandfather/Gramps/Grandpa/Grandad, brother, sister, baby, aunty, uncle, cousin, parents*)

Sounds

Continue to revise and teach sounds in the context of the topic. The vocabulary for this topic lends itself to practising blended sounds (such as ***br**other, **gr**andmother*) and 'er' endings (such as *sist**er**, moth**er***).

Let learners identify rhyming words in any poems, rhymes or songs that you introduce, to develop awareness of end sounds and sound patterns.

Introducing structures

Revise the structures *This is* ______ and *That is* ______ from Topic 1.

Revise the subject pronouns *he, she* and *they* in structures such as: *He is my brother. She is my sister. They are my parents.*

Introduce the verb *to have* in simple structures such as *I have a brother*. Then use short conversations or interviews to teach questions that start with *Do*. For example, teach short answers to the questions. (Example: *Do you have a brother? Yes, I do. Do you have a sister? No, I don't.*)

Previous knowledge

Learners will have knowledge of family names. Talk about this with the class and ask them what they call family members. Names such as *Baba* and *Tata* are common and are used when we speak English as well.

Possible areas of difficulty

Learners may have very different family backgrounds, so this is an area that needs to be approached in a sensitive manner.

Some learners may need additional practice with the pronunciation of blended sounds with 'r' in words such as *brother, grandma* as well as with the 'th' sound in words such as *bro**th**er, mo**th**er, fa**th**er*.

Activities

Select from these activities depending on the level of challenge needed for different learners, interest levels and what you have time to include. Supplement these with additional activities of your own and/or digital activities from the online resource.

▲ 1. Use prompt cards to teach (or revise) names of family members. Write the names on the whiteboard and let learners match the names with the names on the prompt cards. Help them to say the 'th' sound in the middle of the words *mo**th**er, fa**th**er* and *bro**th**er*.

▲ 2. Make learners aware of end sounds of names of family members so that they begin to see patterns. Write the words *mother, father, brother, sister, grandmother* and *grandfather* under each other on the board. Ask learners to identify the beginning letters (sounds) of each word. Help them to blend 'br' and 'gr'. If you have any learners in the class who have names starting with these blends (examples: ***Br**endan, **Gr**aham*) draw attention to them. Then look at the endings of all the words (*-er*). Underline the endings and help learners to pronounce each word.

▲ 3. Learners can complete activities 1, 2 and 3 in the Workbook, which focus on sound patterns.

▲ 4. Learners can find words of family members in the word snake in activity 4 in the Workbook. Let them compare their answers with those of other learners afterwards as a means of self-assessment. Learners then complete activity 5.

▲ 5. **Link to social studies*. Let learners find the story *My Family Tree* in the Student's Book (page 11). Tell them on which page the story starts, or write the title on the board and tell them to find the title on the contents page. Then discuss the pictures in the story. Discuss the concept of a family tree.

Read the story with the learners. Help them to use their knowledge of phonemes to decode the words. The words and structures in the story should be familiar by now.

6. Learners read or reread the story *My Family Tree* in the Student's Book in pairs. They ask each other questions. (Example: *Who is this? Is this sister?*)

   Learners complete the family tree diagram in activity 6 in the Workbook after they have read the story.

7. Revise alphabetical order. Remind learners that the words in a dictionary are in alphabetical order. Refer to an appropriate picture dictionary in which words/pictures are arranged in this way. Let learners sing *An Alphabet Song* from Topic 1 again. Give learners some of the prompt cards you made with the letters of the alphabet (Topic 1) and ask them to arrange the words in alphabetical order. Then let them complete activities 7 and 8 in the Workbook to consolidate this work.

8. Talk about families to introduce the structures *I have ______. He/She has ______. Do you have a ______? I have two brothers. Do you have a brother? Yes, I do. No, I don't*. Do this with groups of learners and be sensitive to family circumstances. Some children may not be comfortable talking about families as they may not know their grandparents or fathers, for example. You could also use pictures of families to teach these structures, which is less personal.

9. Introduce questions in the third person with *Does*. (Examples: *Does she have an aunty? Yes, she does*.) Use pictures of families to teach this structure.

10. To extend learner's family vocabulary, teach them a traditional rhyme song like *The Farmer's in the Den*. You can also change the words of the rhyme or leave out some verses. (For example, **Audio 10**.)

11. Learners complete activities 9 and 10 in the Workbook. Let them read Jo's personal story or read it with them. Then let them answer the questions. Check the answers with learners afterwards. Practise the structure *I've/He's got +* family member.

Wrap-up plenary

Talk about families. Ask: *How do we know that people belong to a family?* (They have the same family name. They look the same.) Remind the learners that they need to listen to what others have to say. You could ask them to raise their hands if they want to participate in the discussion.

Quick check

1. Add family names to your collection of prompt cards that learners can use to play games.
2. Write the names of family members in a scrambled order on the whiteboard and invite learners up to come and write the names correctly (example: tersis (sister), thermo (mother), therbro (brother), therfa (father).

Unit C What I do at home

Resources and materials

- Student's Book pp. 14–15
- Workbook pp. 28–35
- Audio file: Audio 11
- Photocopiable Masters (PCMs) PCM 7; PCM 8; PCM 9
- Prompt cards with key vocabulary words
- Sentence strips with key sentence structures and sentences from stories in the Student's Book
- Paint, crayons and paper

Key vocabulary

can, can't, clean, climb, cook, drive, eat, hop, kick, learn, play, read, ride, run, skip, sleep, sweep, swim, walk, wash, work, write

Lead-in ideas

- Ask learners to act some of the things that they do at home. Give them a few examples (such as eating, sleeping). Let the other learners try and say what each learner is acting.
- Teach learners a poem that relates to things that they do every day. Play **Audio 11**. Sing or recite the poem using actions.

Script for the lesson

Introducing vocabulary

Teach learners common verbs that they can use to describe things that they do at home, for example: *wash, eat, sleep, clean, work, play, cook*. Find pictures to illustrate these activities (or use page 14 in the Student's Book). You can also mime these actions and encourage learners to do the same.

Sounds

The story in the Student's Book (*Dad, Gran and the Cat Take a Nap*) provides a context for teaching or revising the short 'a' sound. Learners can also sound out and segment phonemes in short words with this short 'a' sound.

Introducing structures

Use the simple present tense of the verbs that you teach. (Examples: *I **eat** supper. He **plays** in the yard.*)

Teach learners to use the modal verb *can* to describe ability. (Examples: *I can wash my hair. I can't cook supper.*) Learners should also be able to ask and answer simple questions using *can*. (Examples: *Can you drive? No, I can't. Can you ride a bicycle? Yes, I can.*)

Previous knowledge

Learners will know words in their mother tongue. Help them to relate these words to the new English words through pictures. Learners should also know some English pronouns.

Possible areas of difficulty

The letter 'a' has many different sounds in English (examples: *car, all, cat*) and this can be confusing. In this lesson the focus is on the short 'a' sound.

Activities

Select from these activities depending on the level of challenge needed for different learners, interest levels and what you have time to include. Supplement these with additional activities of your own and/or digital activities from the online resource.

▲ **1.** Use *Things we do* on page 14 in the Student's Book to introduce common verbs. Do this over several lessons. Work with groups of learners. Let them look at the pictures and identify the things that they do. Let them name the actions if they can. Then read the verbs under each picture.

Learners can match words and pictures (from *Things we do*, page 14 of the Student's Book) in activity 1 in the Workbook.

▲ **2.** Give learners copies of **PCM 7**. Read a number and then say one of the verbs shown for that number. Repeat the verb and give the beginning sound as well. (Example: *1. sleep. sleep. It begins with 's'.*) Learners tick the box next the picture of someone who is sleeping. Work through from number 1 to number 6. You can call out any verb and reuse this sheet several times to check that learners can identify different words.

▲ **3.** Work with learners in groups. Let learners talk about the things that they do at home. Read the poem *What I Can Do* again and help learners to add a verse to the poem. (It doesn't have to rhyme.)

▲ **4.** Learners look at the pictures in activity 2 in the Workbook which show things that families do at home. They look at the activities and circle the activities they can see. Encourage them to say (or write) the activity: *play, ride, wash, cook*, etc.

▲ **5.** Teach the structures *Can you ______? Yes I can./ No I can't.* using some of the new vocabulary that has been learnt. Then let learners work in pairs to ask and answer questions using these structures. They can look back at the pictures in the Workbook and say what they can/can't do. Walk around and remind the learners to take turns during these exchanges.

▲ **6.** **Link to mathematics*. Draw a chart on the board and write the names of six activities in the chart. You can introduce some new verbs here, but make sure learners understand the words. For example:

ride	
swim	
hop	
climb	
fly	
cook	

Do a survey with groups of learners to find out who can do each activity. Read a word and ask learners to raise their hands. Record the results as tally marks on your chart. Then add up the results and discuss them.

▲ **7.** Teach the short 'a' sound in words (such as *cat, mat, hat*). Use prompt cards. Write the words on the board with the 'a' sounds in a different colour. If you are teaching phonics using the onset and rime method, you can put the rimes (for example '-at', '-an', '-ap') in the different colour. This shows the patterns of the words and it will help learners to decode and then spell the words when they have to write them.

▲ **8.** Read the story *Dad, Gran and the Cat Take a Nap* in the Student's Book. How you do this will depend on the skills of the learners. You may want to read the story with groups of learners, or let learners read the story in pairs or alone. The story has short words, some of which should already be familiar to learners. The story also has many words with the short 'a' sound in it.

Make sentence strips with the sentences from *Dad, Gran and the Cat Take a Nap*. Let learners match the sentences to the sentences in the Student's Book.

Learners can work in groups and act the story for the rest of the class. Let them try and use some simple conversation while they act. (Example: *I want a nap. Oh! It is the cat. Oh! It is Gran.*)

● **9.** Learners work in groups and look at the text *Things we do* on page 14 in the Student's Book again. They name all the actions shown in the pictures. Then they play a game in which one learner mimes an action and the other learners have to say the verb that goes with the action.

10. Give learners copies of **PCM 8**. Let them cut up the pictures and put them in the correct order. They then use the pictures to retell the story of *Dad, Gran and the Cat Take a Nap*.

11. Learners identify words with the short 'a' sound. They can use activity 3 in the Workbook. You can read the words to them and let them listen before they circle the words. Then let learners work alone to complete the words in activity 4, which all have 'a' in them.

12. Learners can work in groups and act the story of *Dad, Gran and the Cat Take a Nap*. Then they can make up their own stories with the same characters. Learners could take turns to narrate the story while the others act the story.

13. **Link to art*. Let learners use any art form to show one of their favourite home activities. They could paint, draw or make a collage. Allow time for each learner to display their work and to say something about it.

14. Read the following text (or something similar) to the class or to groups of learners:

Draw a mat. Draw a cat on the mat. Draw a hat on the cat.

Let them draw a picture as they listen.

When learners have finished the pictures, let them compare their pictures with others in the group. Be clear that this is not a drawing competition, but an exercise to see if you can listen well.

15. Learners complete activity 5 in the Workbook in which they match the words and the pictures based on the verbs on *Things we do* in the Student's Book.

16. Learners read or reread the story *Dad, Gran and the Cat Take a Nap* and then complete activity 6 in the Workbook.

17. Learners complete activities 7 and 8 in the Workbook to practise high-frequency words.

18. Create a Bingo game using the pictures from *Things we do* in the Student's Book and **PCM 9**. Let learners choose six words from the page and write the words on to their Bingo sheets. Give learners six counters each to play the game. Then call out the words. Learners put their counters on words that they recognise on their own sheets. They call out 'Bingo!' when they have covered all the words on their sheets.

19. Give learners prompt cards with some of the high-frequency words they have learnt and some CVC words with 'a' or other vowels. (Examples: *this, is, my, have, can, a, cat, hat, lap, bat, I, hop, Dad*.) Let them make up sentences with these words and say the sentences aloud. Alternatively, write simple sentences on sentence strips. Let learners cut up the sentences into words and use the words to make up sentences again.

Wrap-up plenary

Talk to the class about all the things that they can already do. Then ask them about the things that they still want to learn to do.

Quick check

1. Play another game of 'Bingo' with words from the picture dictionary page and **PCM 9**.
2. Let learners play a game in which one learner acts out something that they enjoy doing and the others have to guess what it is.

Assessment

You can complete an oral assessment of the work done in this topic by:

- asking learners to describe the actions in pictures (use the Student's Book)
- giving learners instructions to do simple actions (hop, run, jump, walk, etc.)
- using the prompt cards with letters of the alphabet to check knowledge of sounds (initial sounds) made by phonemes.

Learners can also complete Progress check activities 1, 2, 3 and 4 in the Workbook as a simple assessment. For activity 1, say one of the words under each picture clearly and let learners tick the relevant boxes. For activity 2, choose one activity in each group (example: *She is sleeping*). Learners tick the appropriate box. You could allocate marks for these activities and record these as part of continuous assessment.

Topic 3 Our colourful world

Overview

This topic allows you to integrate language lessons with other subjects in the curriculum, such as science, art and maths, and to teach the names of colours and how we use colour words and other adjectives to describe things. The concepts are developed using familiar objects and by encouraging learners to draw on their personal experiences and observations of colours in the real world.

Units in this topic

Unit A: Colours

Unit B: Describing things

Unit C: How many?

Teaching focus

- 1Rg2 Recognise, identify, sound, segment and blend phonemes in individual words.
- 1Ug1 Use common singular nouns, plural nouns [plural 's'] and proper names to say what things are.
- 1Ug2 Use numbers 1-10 to count.
- 1Ug3 Use basic adjectives and colours to say what someone/something is or has.
- 1Ug15 Sight read high-frequency words.
- 1Ut1 Use the questions: *What colour is it? What now?*
- 1Ut2 Use determiners *a, the, this, these* to indicate what/where something is.
- 1Ut3 Use interrogative pronouns *which*, *what*, *where* to ask basic questions.
- 1Lg1 Understand very short supported narratives on a limited range of general and curricular topics.
- 1Lg2 Recognise the sounds of phonemes and phoneme blends.
- 1S5 Use words and phrases to describe people and objects.

Language patterns

Grammar summary for teachers:

- **Adjectives:** Adjectives describe nouns. They do not change their form according to gender or singular/plural forms of nouns. They can be used in two different ways:
  *These are **green** hats*. (This adjective is before a noun. This is called attributive use.)
  *The hat is **green***. (The adjective is after a noun and verbs such as *to be, to look, to seem, to taste*. This is called predicative use.)
- **Questions:** *What* is a word that is often used at the beginning of a question, for example: *What is your name? What colour is this?*
- **Verb 'to like':** The verb *to like* can be used in positive, negative and question forms. In the third person singular *he/she/it* (positive form only), we need to add '-s' to the verb.
  *I like red. I like red shoes. He like**s** blue shoes.*
  I don't like blue. I don't like blue shoes. He doesn't like blue shoes.
  Do you like orange? Do you like orange shoes?

Unit A Colours

Resources and materials

- Student's Book pp. 16–19
- Workbook pp. 36–41
- Audio files: Audio 12; Audio 13; Audio 14; Audio 15; Audio 16
- Photocopiable Masters (PCMs) PCM 9; PCM 10; PCM 11
- Two sets (or more) of word cards with the names of colours
- School objects in different colours in a school bag (for example: a blue book, a red pencil, a yellow ruler, a green pen)
- Paper, scissors and crayons for activities
- Paint (blue, green, yellow), paper and paintbrushes
- Coloured pencils
- Pictures of colourful animals for learners to describe. You can draw these pictures yourself, find photographs or pictures of real animals, or colour in the pictures provided in **PCM 11**.
- Colour Bingo cards (See **PCM 9**)

- Pictures of colourful objects, plants and animals from the local environment and any other regions or areas you might be studying
- Traditional or familiar stories that involve colours

Key vocabulary

Colours: red, yellow, blue, green, white, black, pink, purple, orange, grey, brown

colour, coloured, rainbow

Lead-in ideas

- Show the class the bag of objects that you have collected. Ask: *What's in the bag? What colour is the bag?* Take out objects one at a time and ask the same questions. Learners join in as they can. Then play the *What's in the Bag?* song (**Audio 12**). Learners listen and watch as you take out each object in turn. Play the song a few times and encourage learners to sing along. You can use different objects and colours and change the song to fit the objects you have. This game is good for memory training as well as pronouncing the names of colours.
- Label objects in your classroom with the names of different colours. Hold up a word card, say the colour and ask learners to find the object in the classroom with the same colour. You could also label some objects on a table.
- Teach learners any other colour song or rhyme, or let them sing familiar songs/rhymes. Here is an example that can be chanted and acted out (total physical response) or sung in groups with movements:

  Colours chant
  (Sing to the tune of *If you're happy and you know it, clap your hands.*)
  If your clothes have any white, any white [hold up or point to a piece of white clothing]
  If your clothes have any white, any white
  If your clothes have any white
  Stamp your feet with all your might [demonstrate stamping feet]

  All your might.

  Alternative colour chants (make sure you demonstrate the action each time):
  red: *Put your hands above your head.*
  blue: *Pretend you're rowing a canoe.*
  brown: *Jump around just like a clown.*
  black: *Put your hands behind your back.*
  yellow: *Shake your legs like they're jello.*
  green: *Make your face look really mean.*
- Take learners on a walk around the school or a nearby place of interest. Help learners to identify colours in the environment and to appreciate the array of different colours. Ask: *What colour is ______?*

Script for the lesson

Introducing vocabulary

Use the word cards and familiar objects and pictures to introduce or revise the names of colours.

Sounds

Revise and teach sounds in the context of the topic. For example, if you are teaching colours, ask questions like: *This is a colour. It begins with the sound 'yuh'. What is it?* Help learners to identify initial sounds in words so that they can begin to decode the words they see. Note though that some colour words are difficult to decode and will need to be learnt as sight words.

Introducing structures

Make short sentences about objects in different colours, using these structural patterns:

This is a [colour] [object].

What is this? It's a [colour] [object].

I like [colour word]. I don't like [colour word].

Previous knowledge

Some learners may already be familiar with some colour words and will know colour words in their first language. These words can be similar to English words (example: *blue/bleu*) or they may be completely different (example: *blue/azul*). Help learners to pronounce the colour words correctly, especially if the words are similar to words in their first language.

Possible areas of difficulty

Colour words are high-frequency words and some of them are difficult to decode by sounding out as they have difficult spelling patterns. To become familiar with the words and start to recognise them by sight, learners will need to see them many times – in books and on labels, for example.

Some learners may be able to read colour words, but they may not yet be ready to say the words aloud by themselves. Rhymes and songs will help learners to become more confident as they allow them to say words and sentences in groups, rather than alone. Games can also help to build confidence.

Some learners may not be ready to tell or retell stories. Giving these learners picture prompts and encouraging them to say a few words (even if it is not yet a complete sentence) about each picture, will build their confidence, but don't force them if they really are not ready.

Activities

Select from these activities depending on the level of challenge needed for different learners, interest levels and what you have time to include. Supplement these with additional activities of your own and/or digital activities from the online resource.

1. Work with groups. Give learners sets of cards with colour words on them. Let them say the names on the cards and use the cards to label things in the classroom. Encourage them to make simple sentences about the things they label. (Example: *This is a red ball.*)

2. Learners work in pairs. They will each need a set of word cards with colour words. Make two sets of word cards with the names of colours on the cards. Shuffle the cards and let learners play games to match the names on the cards. For example, they can put all the cards face down and take turns to turn two cards over. If the cards match, they can have another turn. The learner with the most pairs wins. This is a good memory game and will help familiarise learners with the words. Learners could also play any other games that you know, such as 'Snap', for example.

3. Work with groups of learners. Put the prompt cards with the colour words on the table. Learners take turns. Say a colour word. A learner picks up the card with the colour word you have said and then finds something in the class that matches the colour on the card.

4. Let learners listen to simple instructions to draw and colour in pictures (**Audio 13**). Give learners a sheet of paper divided into four squares/blocks, numbered 1–4 or use activity 1 in the Workbook. You can play **Audio 13** or compile your own instructions. Make sure that learners listen to each entire instruction before they begin to draw.

5. Learners look at the pictures on page 16 of the Student's Book. The pictures are the same, but the colours used are different. Learners point to the colours and make simple sentences.

6. Revise initial sounds of words with learners using colour words and the objects you have collected. Learners can then work alone and complete activity 2 in the Workbook.

7. Ask learners about the colours that they like. Prompt them to use the structures:

   I like ______. I don't like ______.

8. Tell learners a traditional or familiar story that involves a colour. Use pictures or a puppet as a visual prompt while telling the story. Learners may not understand every word in English, but if they are familiar with the story in their first language, they will soon get the gist of what you are saying. For example, if learners are familiar with the story of *Little Red Riding Hood* in their first language, you could tell the story, in a simple way, in English.

9. Learners find colour words in the puzzle in activity 3 in the Workbook.

10. Learners work in groups and play the 'I spy' game with colours. Teach them to use the structure: *I spy with my little eye, something red. It starts with the sound 'p'. [pencil]*. Work with the whole class first and then, when learners are more confident, let them work in small groups.

11. **Link to art and science*. Give learners paint in the three primary colours (red, blue and yellow). Let them paint any picture that they like. Tell them to mix the colours to make new colours. Then let them describe the pictures they have painted. For example: *This is a yellow and green house*.

12. Give learners copies of **PCM 10**. Look at the pictures and let learners say what they can about each picture. Teach any vocabulary that is not familiar. Learners listen to the story on **Audio 14**. Let them listen a few times. Learners cut up the pictures and put them in order. They can colour in the pictures and use them as prompts to retell the story in pairs or small groups. Pictures provide good prompts for retelling stories, which some learners may find difficult.

13. **Link to mathematics*. Draw the following chart on the whiteboard.

red	
white	
blue	
black	
orange	
pink	
green	
yellow	
purple	
brown	

Do a survey in the class to find out which of these colours learners like most. Ask each learner to choose one colour. Run through the colours and ask learners to put up their hands to show which one they have chosen. Write the totals next to the colours on the chart. Ask questions about the chart. Use the language that learners will be exposed to in their mathematics lessons. For example: *How many learners like white? How many learners like green?*

Next, display a pictogram showing the results for the class. For example:

Colours we like

red	☺☺☺☺☺☺☺
white	☺☺
blue	☺☺☺☺☺
black	☺☺
orange	☺☺☺
pink	☺☺☺☺
green	☺☺☺☺☺
yellow	☺☺
purple	☺☺☺
brown	☺

Key: ☺ = 1 learner

Ask learners questions about the pictogram. For example: *Which colours did learners choose?*

(Read the names.) *What does the smiley face mean? How many learners like yellow? How many learners like green? Which colour do you like best? Which colour did five learners like?* And so on.

14. Use activity 4 in the Workbook and have learners find four different objects in the classroom. They draw pictures of the objects and use tally marks to count them.

15. In their journals, learners draw and write about colours in their environment.

16. Read the poem *My Colouring Book* in the Student's Book. Read the poem once and ask learners what it is about. Then read it again and teach new vocabulary as necessary. Learners can then recite the poem. Help them to pronounce the words correctly and use the correct intonation. Let two learners recite each verse.

    Learners can then complete activities 5 and 6 in the Workbook. They listen to the poem and colour in the picture.

17. Read *Colours around us* in the Student's Book. Help learners to talk about pictures and decode words.

18. Use the story to focus on sounds. Help learners to pronounce the initial sounds 'fl', 'h' and 'k' and the vowel sound 'ow' and to blend these sounds to form the words *flower, house, cow*. Point out that *ou* and *ow* can have the same sound. Read out a list of other familiar words and let learners say which words have the same vowel sound. For example: *blue now how book towel*.

19. Play the song *The Colour Purple* (**Audio 15**). Let learners listen a few times. Then ask some simple comprehension questions. For example: *What colour does she like? What colour are her socks? What colour is her hat? What else is purple?* Learners can then work in pairs or small groups and make up their own songs, using different colours.

20. Let learners complete activity 7 in the Workbook independently. You can either let them choose their own colours and write the names, or you can use this activity to reinforce specific colour vocabulary by showing a flashcard with a colour name on it for each item. Learners then choose the correct colour to colour the item and write the name of the colour. If you display the flashcards, they can refer to them for spelling as needed.

21. Show the class that you can mix two colours together to make another colour. For example, mix red and white and show learners that this makes pink. Let them experiment with powder paints (you could give each group four colours only and let them see how many different colours they can make) and spend some time talking about what they learnt about colours.

22. Discuss the colours used in your community for different purposes. For example, black and white for zebra crossings, flashing blue lights for police vehicles, red paper money for good luck at New Year, and so on.

Wrap-up plenary

Talk with learners about how colours are used in different countries. Ask questions relevant to their own culture and traditions. For example, ask learners: *When do you wear white clothes? What colours do people wear when they get married/celebrate a national holiday?*

Quick check

1. Play 'Colour Bingo' with the class or with groups. Make copies of the Bingo template (**PCM 9**). Give one blank Bingo sheet to each learner. Display the names of all the colour words that you have taught the class. Tell learners to choose six colours. They can colour in the blocks on their Bingo sheets and write the names of the colours too.

   Give each learner six counters (buttons or small stones, for example). Start to call out the colours. As you call each colour, learners look to see if they have the colour on their Bingo sheet. They put a counter on the colour if they do. They call out 'Bingo!' when they have covered all the colours on their Bingo sheets.

2. Teach the learners the *Colour Action Song* (**Audio 16**). Let them sing the song with actions. They can also add their own verses.

Unit B Describing things

Resources

- Student's Book pp. 20–22
- Workbook pp. 42–45
- Audio files: Audio 17; Audio 18
- Photocopiable Masters (PCMs) PCM 11; PCM 12
- Collect objects in different shapes and sizes and textures to teach the following adjectives: *soft, hard, long, round, square, small, big*
- Prompt cards with the names of shapes (include a simple diagram of the shape on each card as well: *square, circle, triangle, rectangle, star, hexagon*)

Key vocabulary

Adjectives: colour words (revision), big, small, fat, thin, round, tall, soft, hard, long

Shapes: circle, square, triangle, rectangle, star, hexagon

Lead-in ideas

- Teach learners any song or rhyme with simple descriptions. *Do You Know That?* is an example that can be chanted and acted out (total physical response) or sung in groups with movements. You can add your own verses to the chant. Use gestures and movements to suggest the adjectives in the chant (**Audio 17**). Show learners pictures of any animals that may not be familiar.

Script for the lesson

Introducing vocabulary

Introduce common adjectives that learners can use to describe people and things. These words can describe what something looks like (*tall, big, small, thin, fat, round, long, square*), sounds like (*loud, soft, noisy*) or feels like (*soft, hard*). The names of colours, shapes and numbers are also useful adjectives. (Numbers are introduced in Unit C.)

Sounds

Provide learners with practise in saying and recognising the short 'a' vowel sound (as in *cat*). Then introduce the short 'o' sound (as in *log*).

Other vowel sounds can also be taught in context if you feel learners are ready to learn more. For example, you can write the word *red* on the board and then ask learners to identify other words that have the same 'e' sound (such as *leg, beg*) or the same rime *-ed* (such as *bed, fed*).

Include songs and poems with rhymes as often as possible in your lessons to help build awareness of sound patterns.

Introducing structures

Teach learners to use adjectives in these two structures: *This is a big book* (before a noun). *The book is big* (after the verb *to be*).

Teach learners to use the determiner *the* to indicate what/where something is. (Example: *Give me the red book, please*.)

Teach the connecting word *and* to use in simple descriptions. (Example: *The cat is brown and white*.)

Previous knowledge

Colour words, short 'a' sound, basic structures.

Possible areas of difficulty

Some learners may put adjectives in the incorrect place in sentences at first. In some languages, adjectives are placed after nouns, for example. If learners do this, simply correct them without trying to explain the grammar at this stage.

Activities

Select from these activities depending on the level of challenge needed for different learners, interest levels and what you have time to include. Supplement these with additional activities of your own and/or digital activities from the online resource.

1. Teach learners the adjectives *big* and *small*. Give learners a set of pictures of colourful animals. You could colour these in, or ask learners to colour in, the pictures on **PCM 11**. Depending on the level of your learners, you could also add spots and simple patterns to the pictures.

   Then make up simple riddles about each picture and let learners work out which picture you are referring to. For example: *It is big and green. It is small and white. It is long and red with pink spots.* This introduces use of the connecting word *and*. Give further examples and explain what the word means, if necessary.

   Then let learners make up their own riddles and work in pairs to do the same thing.

2. Teach learners the adjectives *soft* and *hard*. Show them examples of soft and hard objects. Put hard, soft, big and small objects in a bag. Let learners put their hands in the bag and touch an object. They then describe it and identify it using adjectives and the connecting word *and*. (Example: *It is small and hard. It is a box*.)

3. Choose a few colourful objects or pictures of familiar animals (examples: *a toy, a crayon, a ball, a cat*) and teach learners more about the adjectives that we can use to describe the objects. As you teach, make word spiders on the board and fill in appropriate adjectives.

   Example: Make word spiders as follows:

   ball – round small yellow blue hard

   cat – soft fat brown grey big noisy

   The spider could look like this:

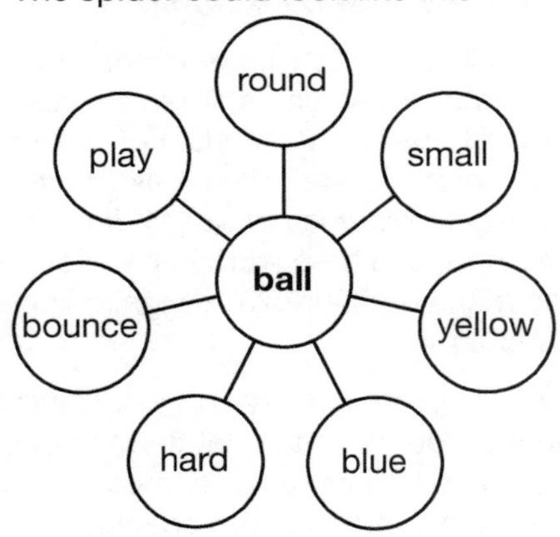

4. Tell learners that they are going to listen to a story about someone who has some visitors. Play the story *Rat-a-tat-tat* (**Audio 18**). Then ask a few questions to see how much learners have understood: *What is "rat-a-tat-tat"? Who comes to play?* Play the story a second time. Then tell learners that they can join in and say *rat-a-tat-tat* as they listen to the story.

5. Learners can colour in the pictures in activity 1 in the Workbook after they have listened to the *story Rat-a-tat-tat*. They use the words in the box to label their pictures in activity 2.

6. Teach the short 'o' sound in words (such as *box, sock, fox, frog, pot*). Use prompt cards. Write the words on the board with the 'o' sounds in a

different colour. If you are teaching phonics using the onset and rime method, you can put the rimes (for example, -ot, -og) in the different colour. Help learners to identify other simple words with the rimes.

Then revise words with short 'a' sounds. Write the words on prompt cards and let learners sort the words into groups or play matching games with the cards.

Learners can then complete activity 3 in the Workbook.

7. Teach or revise the names of the following shapes: *square, circle, triangle, rectangle, star, hexagon*. Use prompt cards. Then take a walk outside with learners and let them find these shapes in the environment around them.

8. Let learners find the story *Bad Bat* in the Student's Book (pages 20–22). Do some pre-reading activities before you read the story to learners. Teach the names of the animals as necessary. The story uses repetition to help learners understand ideas and actions. It also has words with short 'a' and 'o' sounds. The adjectives in the story will also help to expand learners' vocabulary of adjectives that they can use to describe things. The adjectives are words that express feelings (*bad, cross, mad, sad*).

9. Give learners copies of **PCM 12**. Read the sentences next to each picture and then tell learners to tick the sentence that matches the picture. If learners can read the sentences by themselves, let them do this.

10. Learners complete activities 4 and 5 in the Workbook. They identify words with the short vowel sounds 'a' and 'o' and then fill in letters to complete short words with the vowel sounds.

11. Make up some more complex riddles for learners to solve in pairs or groups. (Examples: *It is small and round. It is hard. It is different colours. You can play with it. What is it?*) Learners can make up their own riddles for others to solve.

12. Learners can work in groups and act out the story of *Bad Bat*. Read the story again and help learners to retell the story. Then let them act the story. They can use their own words as well as words from the story. Prompt and help as necessary to help them use appropriate structures and adjectives. Example:

    Bat: *I like the dark. I like to play tricks. Boo!*

    Mouse: *I'm sad. I don't like bat.*

    Owl: *I'm MAD! Bat is BAD!*

13. **Link to art*. Let learners make simple masks of animal characters to use in the plays they have made up. Talk about the shapes of the faces and the colours that they can use to make these masks.

14. *Link to mathematics.* Learners complete activities 6 and 7 in the Workbook, which recaps knowledge of shapes and counting.

15. Learners can match the pictures and the sentences in activity 8 in the Workbook. This assumes that learners are familiar with the story *Bad Bat* in the Student's Book.

16. Work with groups of learners and make simple poems, using any adjective that they know. Use the word spiders that you made earlier as a starting point and add adjectives to the spiders. Help learners to write the poems and display them in the class for additional reading. Learners can also recite their poems for the rest of the class. Example:
    My cat
    cute and soft
    black and white
    noisy and cuddly
    I love my cat.

17. Learners can work in groups and make their own picture dictionary pages, using vocabulary they have learnt. Give each group a different topic, for example: Animals; Colours; Shapes and Sizes; School. Let them choose six to eight words that they know. Help them to write the words correctly. Then they arrange the words in alphabetical order and copy them, in order, on to a sheet of paper. Provide a grid for this, depending on how many words you want learners to include on a page. They draw a picture to match each word, or find a picture and paste it.

18. Learners work in pairs. They each need a pencil, some crayons and a piece of paper. They sit back to back. One learner gives an instruction to draw a simple picture. (Example: *Draw a big bat. The bat is black and blue*.) The other learner has to listen carefully and draw the picture from the oral instruction. Then both learners check what has been done and swap roles.

    This can also be done in groups. Give the instructions yourself.

Wrap-up plenary

Talk about feelings. Ask learners if they sometimes feel sad or cross. Ask them to act how they feel. What do they do when they feel this way?

Quick check

1. Give learners a few more riddles to solve. For example: *I am small and black. I like the dark. I am an animal. What am I?*

2. Learners play a game in which they have to make up words from individual letters. The first group to use all the cards and be able to say each word they have made, wins. Give each group of learners cards with the following letters, for example: a (x3), o (x3), h t (x2), c m b x d g.

Unit C How many?

Resources

- Student's Book p. 23
- Workbook pp. 46–50
- Audio files: Audio 19; Audio 20; Audio 21
- Photocopiable Masters (PCMs) PCM 9; PCM 13; PCM 14
- Collection of objects for learners to count (for example: stones, buttons, pencils, shapes)
- Prompt cards with number words 1–10
- Poster with numbers 1–10
- Prompt cards with shape words
- Ingredients to make fruit or vegetable salad

Key vocabulary

numbers 1–10 (for counting and as adjectives)

How many?

some animal names (bat, owl, fox, mouse), wheel

Lead-in ideas

- Teach the learners number songs (or chants and rhymes) or let them sing familiar songs/rhymes. You can play some examples in **Audio 19**, **Audio 20** and **Audio 21**.

Script for the lesson

Introducing vocabulary

The vocabulary in this unit links up with vocabulary in mathematics. Most number words are sight words, so learners need to see them as often as possible in order to remember them. Make sure the number words are displayed in class.

Sounds

Teach the short 'e' sound in context (in words such as *red, ten, seven*) and revise words with short 'a's and 'o's as they occur.

Teach the end sound 's' in plural nouns.

Introducing structures

Teach learners to ask and answer questions starting with *How many?* For example: *How many ducks are there? There are* ______ ______. The word order in the question and answer is different. You do not need to teach this formally, just provide opportunities to practice the two structures.

Introduce plural forms of nouns (-*s*) as learners count objects.

Previous knowledge

Learners should know some of the numbers from 1–10 from mathematics, but they may not be familiar with number words in English. They may also know the names of shapes in their mother tongue, but not in English.

Possible areas of difficulty

Make sure learners hear and use the final 's' sound in plural words.

Activities

Select from these activities depending on the level of challenge needed for different learners, interest levels and what you have time to include. Supplement these with additional activities of your own and/or digital activities from the online resource.

▲ 1. *****Link to mathematics*. Revise or teach numbers from 1–10. Let learners count real objects. Provide several groups of objects for the learners to count. Ask: *How many* ______ *are there?* Let learners estimate. Then let them count to check their estimates.

▲ 2. Learners match the numbers and number words in activity 1 in the Workbook.

▲ 3. Teach learners to read number words. Use prompt cards with numerals (numbers) and number words and let learners match them. Help them to decode the words as far as possible. They should easily decode ten and six, for example. Some of the other numbers (two, four) are more challenging and these will need to be learnt as sight words.

▲ 4. Play a game with groups of learners. Use a 1–6 spinner (from **PCM 14**) for this. Let each learner spin the spinner twice. Each learner says each number and then adds the two numbers together.
Alternatively, teach learners to toss coins and identify the front and the back of the coin. Then let learners take turns to toss coins. Each learner has five chances. When the learner is finished he or she says how many 'fronts' and how many 'backs' they had in their turn.

▲ 5. Learners use activity 2 in the Workbook to play a game. They will need counters and a 1–6 spinner (from **PCM 14**) for this game. They take turns to spin the spinner, move their counters and follow the instructions in the text.

▲ 6. Give learners copies of **PCM 13**. Learners look at the pictures and tick the picture that you describe. You can choose any picture and the sheet can be reused. (Example: *1. two hens 2. six pens*)

▲ 7. Let learners find the non-fiction text *Wheels* in the Student's Book (page 23). Do some pre-reading activities before you read the text with the learners. Talk about the pictures and ask learners to name other vehicles that have wheels. Ask questions, such as: *Do they all have the same number of wheels? How many wheels do they have? Are the wheels big or small?* The adjectives in this story include number words.

8. Make sentence strips with the sentences in the non-fiction text *Wheels* in the Student's Book. Let learners match the strips to the sentences in the Student's Book. Alternatively, let learners cut up the sentences into single words and use the words to remake sentences. They should read the sentences and words aloud.

9. Teach the short 'e' sound and revise words with the short 'a' and short 'o'. You can introduce words from familiar songs or stories or ask learners to suggest words with the same 'e' sound as *red* (examples: *elephant, egg, bed*). Write the words on the board and put the letter 'e' in a different colour. If they suggest words that sound the same, but are spelt differently (examples: *said, bread*), explain this briefly but do not write the words on the board.

   Then write some simple words on the board (examples: *ten, red, bed, dog, cap, tap*). Let learners use their knowledge of sounds to decode the words. Then remove the vowel letters and let learners complete the words, first orally and then in writing.

10. Teach the plural forms of nouns. Use the objects you have collected. Then learners can each choose a few of one type of object. Make sentences such as: *I have three buttons. He has six stones. She has nine pens.*

    Write the singular words on the board and then add an *-s* after each word. Read the words with the class. Learners can then complete activities 3 and 4 in the Workbook.

11. Do a counting activity outside the classroom. Learners work in pairs. Give each pair two or three things to count. You can do this orally. For example, say: *John and Vijay: Count the cars in the car park. Then count the trees in the garden and the school gates. Mary and Mariam: How many classrooms are there in the school?*

12. Learners make their own number books in pairs or small groups. They choose a subject (examples: *cars, food, school*). Let them take photographs or draw or find pictures to illustrate their books. Each number from 1–10 should have a picture, a number word and a numeral. Help them to put the pages together and bind the books.

13. Learners work in pairs. They sit back to back and give each other instructions to draw simple pictures. For example: *Draw three hens. Draw one house and two trees*. They check that they have understood the instructions and drawn the pictures correctly. Then they swap roles.

14. Teach learners how to make a simple fruit or vegetable salad. Collect suitable ingredients and teach learners the names of the ingredients. Then talk about and count the ingredients you have collected. (Examples: *This is a long cucumber. It is green. We have three carrots and one cucumber. There are two tomatoes and six lettuce leaves.*)

    When the salad is ready, let them talk about the salad and taste it. Prompt them to make sentences such as: *That is a carrot. This is a tomato. I like tomatoes. Tomatoes are red. Carrots are orange*.

15. *****Link to mathematics*. Make up some simple maths problems for learners to solve orally. Use vocabulary and structures that have been introduced. (Example: *The hen has ten eggs. A boy takes six eggs. How many eggs does the hen have left?*)

16. *****Link to mathematics*. When learners have had some practice solving oral maths problems, let them work in small groups and make up their own problems for the rest of the group to solve.

17. Learners work in groups and make up a story about making a fruit salad. The steps could include: first discussing what is in a fruit salad (bananas, oranges, apples, melons), then going to buy the ingredients, and, finally, making the salad. Help learners to use simple structures in their story. They can act what they can't say. (Examples: *We have three apples and one melon. Three bananas and two oranges, please.*)

18. Ask learners to think about when and how they use numbers every day and consider why numbers are useful. (For example: for shopping, for telling the time, and so on.)

Wrap-up plenary

Let learners count in other languages they know, from 1–10. Ask the class to identify numbers that sound similar in other languages. (For example, *six* in French is similar to *six* in English.)

Quick check

1. Give learners blank Bingo sheets (from **PCM 9**) and let them choose numbers to write on the sheets. Play 'Bingo' in the usual way.
2. Sing a familiar counting song with numbers 1–10.
3. Let learners match colours and numerals with words on prompt cards.

Assessment

You can complete an oral assessment of the work done in this topic by:

- asking learners to name or point to colours of objects in the classroom
- asking learners to read aloud the number words of numbers 1–10
- asking learners to describe an object using an adjective (*big, small*, etc.).

Learners can also complete Progress check activities 1, 2 and 3 in the Workbook as a simple assessment. For activity 1, say some of the colour words and let learners tick them as you say them.

You could allocate marks for these activities and record these as part of continuous assessment.

Topic 4 Food

Overview

This topic allows you to integrate language lessons with other subjects in the curriculum, such as science, mathematics and art, in order to reinforce the language being used in those subjects. Learners will learn how to name foods and mealtimes and describe what they like and do not like. The language and structures used are developed using familiar items. Learners are encouraged to draw on their personal experiences of meals and different foods.

Units in this topic

Unit A: Fruit and vegetables

Unit B: Let's eat

Unit C: What I like

Teaching focus

- 1Rg2 Recognise, identify, sound, segment and blend phonemes in individual words.
- 1Wo1 Include a full stop when copying very high-frequency short sentences.
- 1Uf2 Use common present continuous forms [positive, negative, question] to give basic personal information.
- 1Ug1 Use common singular nouns, plural nouns [plural 's'] and proper names to say what things are.
- 1Ug2 Use numbers 1–10 to count.
- 1Ug3 Use basic adjectives and colours to say what someone/something is or has.
- 1Ug10 Use *Would you like* + noun to enquire.
- 1Ug11 Use *let's* + verb.
- 1Ug12 Use *like* + verb + *-ing* to express likes and dislikes.
- 1Ug13 Spell some familiar high-frequency words accurately during guided writing activities.
- 1Ug15 Sight read high-frequency words.
- 1Ut1 Use the questions *What colour is it? What now?*
- 1Ut2 Use determiners *a, the, this*, *these* to indicate what/where something is.
- 1Ut3 Use interrogative pronouns *which, what*, *where* to ask basic questions.
- 1Ut5 Use personal subject and object pronouns to give basic personal information.
- 1Ut6 Use conjunction *and* to link words and phrases.
- 1Ut7 Use *me too* to give short answers.
- 1Ld1 Understand some specific information and detail of short, supported talk on a limited range of general and curricular topics.
- 1Lg1 Understand very short supported narratives on a limited range of general and curricular topics.
- 1Lg2 Recognise the sounds of phonemes and phoneme blends.
- 1S2 Ask questions in order to find out about a limited range of personal information and classroom routines.
- 1S5 Use words and phrases to describe people and objects.
- 1S7 Take turns when speaking with others in a limited range of short, basic exchanges
- 1S8 Express basic likes and dislikes.

Language patterns

Grammar summary for teachers:

- **The present continuous tense:** This tense is used to describe actions that are happening at the present moment.
  The positive form of the verb is formed with the verb *to be* and by adding *-ing* to the main verb (*I am eating. She is eating. They are eating*).
  The negative form uses *not* after the verb *to be* (*She is not eating*).
  We form questions by changing the order of the words (*Is she eating?*) or using a question word (*What is she eating?*).
- **Short answers:** Short answers are answers such as *Yes, I do. No, I don't. Me too*. These are commonly used to answer questions instead of longer, more formal answers.
- **Object pronouns:** These are words such as *me, you, him, her, them* (*Please give **me** the book. I am giving **him** the book.*).
- ***Like* + verb + *-ing* (gerund):** This structure is commonly used to express likes and dislikes (*I like swimming.*).

Unit A Fruit and vegetables

Resources and materials

- Student's Book p. 24
- Workbook pp. 51–55
- Audio files: Audio 22; Audio 23; Audio 24; Audio 25; Audio 26
- Photocopiable Master (PCM) PCM 15
- Prompt cards with names of common fruit and vegetables as well as separate cards with the names of the fruit and vegetables
- Some real fruit and vegetables to describe, taste and use in salads

Key vocabulary

Here is a list of common fruits and vegetables. You can also teach the names of other fruit and vegetables that are common in your country.

Fruit: apple, pear, banana, orange, mango, pineapple, guava, pawpaw, strawberry, fig, peach, plum, apricot, melon, grapes

Vegetables: carrot, potato, onion, chilli, spinach, pumpkin, cucumber, beans, cabbage, broccoli, cauliflower, peas

Lead-in ideas

- Teach learners any chant, rhyme or song about food, mealtimes or eating. **Audio 22** and **Audio 23** are examples that can be chanted and acted out (total physical response) in groups with movements.

Script for the lesson

Introducing vocabulary

Labelled pictures of a wide variety of fruit and vegetables can be used to introduce vocabulary. You can also use real fruit and vegetables to introduce names, if these are available.

(Note: Start by letting learners name foods with which they are familiar (that is, foods that are common in your community and foods that are currently in season). Adapt any of the materials to suit these foods.)

Sounds

Revise initial sounds and the end sound 's' in plural words.

Make learners aware of the blended initial sounds in words such as: ***ch**illi* ('ch'), ***str**awberry* ('str'), ***sp**inach* ('sp'), ***gr**apes, **gr**een* ('gr') and ***cr**unch* ('cr').

Help learners to break words down into syllables (segments).

Introducing structures

Revise the following structures using familiar objects: *This is ______. There are ______. These are ______.*

Teach the following question structures with the context of the topic: *Do you like ___? Would you like ___?* (to make a polite request).

Teach the short answer *Me too* in the context of a conversation.

Previous knowledge

Colour words, *This is ______. There are ______. These are ______.* Familiar nouns. Pronouns.

Learners will know the names of fruits and vegetables in their mother tongue. Some names may be similar to the English names, for example, *mangue/mango*.

Possible areas of difficulty

Learners may use a plural noun with the wrong form of the verb *to be*, for example, *There is two mangoes*. Correct them when they say this and provide additional opportunities to practice the correct structure in simple conversations until learners use this verb correctly. Do not try and explain the grammar at this stage.

Activities

Select from these activities depending on the level of challenge needed for different learners, interest levels and what you have time to include. Supplement these with additional activities of your own and/or digital activities from the online resource.

1. Find out what learners know about fruit and vegetables. Hold up pictures (or real fruit and vegetables) and ask: *What is this?* If learners are not sure, give them a clue, like the initial sound. Then tell them the name and write it on the board. You could also play a game. Put real fruits and vegetables, or pictures, on a table, hold up a prompt card, read the word and let learners take turns to point to the fruit or vegetable you have named.
2. Workbook, activity 1. Learners complete the names of fruits and vegetables by filling in the beginning sounds.
3. *Link to mathematics*. Learners work in pairs and sort pictures of fruit and vegetables in different ways. They can sort by type (fruit or vegetable), colour (green, orange, red, yellow), by size or shape (big, small, long, round) or by preference (I like/I don't like) if they are already familiar with these structures.

   Then ask learners to explain what they have done. Prompt them to make sentences, such as: *There are two groups. These are green fruits and these are orange fruits. These are small and these are big. These are round and these are not round.*

   Put eight or ten of the same fruits (or pieces of fruit) on a table and ask learners how they would share the fruit equally between two or four people.

4. Use real fruit or pictures to teach plural forms of fruits and vegetables. Focus on -*s* forms only and not on other plural forms at this stage. (Examples: *apples, plums, grapes, cucumbers, pumpkins*, not *strawberries*.) Write the singular forms on the board and then add an -*s* to each (in a different colour) to help learners see the spelling pattern. Teach learners to pronounce the -*s* at the ends of the nouns clearly. Help learners to make simple sentences with numbers to describe the fruit or vegetables. For example: *There are six apples. There is one pumpkin*.

5. Workbook, activity 2. Learners write the number words and the plural forms of the nouns.

6. Learners say the following words and clap the number of syllables in each word. Use singular and plural words. Let learners take turns to choose a word and then let everyone clap the syllables. For example:
ba/na/nas
pine/ap/ple
ca/rrots
po/ta/to
straw/be/rry

7. Workbook, activity 3. Learners find the names of fruit and vegetables in a word search puzzle.

8. Give learners copies of **PCM 15**. Learners listen to the recipes (**Audio 24**). As they listen, they tick the names of the ingredients needed for each recipe. Then they listen for a second time and write down how many of each fruit or vegetable is needed.

9. Teach learners the meaning of the expression *Me too*. Play the chant *I like bananas* (**Audio 25**). Select a few learners to demonstrate this. Teach this conversation, using fruits that most people like:

   Teacher: *Do you like bananas?*

   Learner: *Yes, I do.*

   Teacher: *Me too!* [Gesture towards yourself.] (If the learner says: *No, I don't*, repeat the question with another fruit.)

   Learners work in groups and practise this conversation.

10. Learners work in groups. They make picture dictionary pages for fruits and vegetables. Give each person in the group a square piece of paper (about 10 cm X 10 cm). Give each group a clear instruction. Some can draw fruit and others, vegetables. Examples:

    Group 1: Draw fruits that begin with the letters a to l (*apple, apricot, avocado, banana, grape, guava, fig, lemon*).

    Group 2: Draw fruits that begin with the letters m to z (*mango, melon, mandarin, orange, pawpaw, peach, plum, strawberry*).

    Group 3: Draw vegetables that begin with the letters a to l (*carrot, chilli, broccoli, cauliflower, beans, cabbage, beetroot*).

    Group 4: Draw vegetables that begin with the letters m to z (*potato, onion, spinach, pumpkin, squash, peas, maize*).

    Each person draws a picture of one fruit or vegetable and writes the name underneath. The groups need to discuss what they are doing, so that everyone in the group does a different picture. When the pictures are complete, the groups put the pictures in alphabetical order. You can then use the pictures to make a picture dictionary on a wall poster, sticking down all the words in order, with the help of the class.

11. Make simple sentences with familiar words. Include colour and number words. Write the sentences on strips. For example:
    There are two yellow bananas.
    She has a red apple.
    He likes oranges.
    The banana is long and fat.

    Write the same sentences on the board and let learners match the sentences. Then cut each strip into individual words and let learners make up the sentences again.

    Learners can then make sentences with similar words in activity 4 and draw a picture and complete a sentence in activity 5 in the Workbook.

12. Teach the polite question *Would you like ______?* You do this by offering a learner a fruit. *Would you like a banana?* Prompt the learner to reply: *Yes, please/No, thank you*. Then let learners work in pairs or groups to practise this structure. Remind learners to take turns and to listen to the questions carefully.

13. Let learners find the story *What Would You Like?* in the Student's Book. Discuss the pictures first and then read the story with the learners or let them listen to **Audio 26**.

    Then do some word recognition activities. Write high-frequency words on the board (*like, you, a, no*) and ask learners how many times they can see each word in the story.

14. This is a good time to start a spelling programme with the class, if you have not already done so. Learners can copy words into a spelling book and practise writing the words correctly. Give learners a few high-frequency words in context to learn each week and give them opportunities to use the words in writing activities. Start with words such as *I, you, he, she, a, the, and, like, is, are, am*. (See page 7 of this Teacher's Guide for a list of the high-frequency words that learners need to recognise and write.)

15. *Link to science*. Make a salad with seasonal fruit or vegetables. Show learners how you peel and cut the fruit. Then mix the fruit up and let the learners taste the fruit to identify it. Teach them simple adjectives to describe the taste and texture of each fruit (examples: *sweet, sour, juicy, soft, hard, crunchy*). Learners then take turns

to describe pieces of fruit. (Examples: *This is banana. It is white. It is soft and sweet.*)

Learners can then group the fruits according to taste and texture, or according to vegetables that we need to cook or those we can eat raw.

Ask learners about the parts of plants that we eat. For example, a carrot is a root, a tomato is a fruit, spinach is a leaf, and so on.

16. Play a game of riddles with the class. Write the names of five or six fruits on the board. Read three riddles to the class and let them write down the answer, choosing one of the fruits you have written on the board. Examples:

1. *I am round. I am red or green. I am crunchy to eat. What am I?*
2. *I am long and fat. I am green and then I am yellow. I am soft and sweet. What am I?*
3. *I am small and round. I am juicy and sweet. What am I?*

After that, learners can work in groups or pairs and think of their own riddles to ask the rest of the class. They can also complete activity 6 in the Workbook.

17. **Link to mathematics*. Draw a chart like the one below on the whiteboard and fill in names of familiar fruits (and/or vegetables).

apples	
tomatoes	
bananas	
grapes	
carrots	
spinach	
oranges	

Do a survey in the class to find out which of these fruits and/or vegetables learners like most. Write the totals next to the names of the fruit/vegetables on the chart. Ask questions about the chart. Use the language that learners will be exposed to in their mathematics lessons. For example, ask: *How many learners like oranges? How many learners like carrots?*

Next, display a pictogram showing the results of the class survey. For example:

Fruits (and/or vegetables) we like

apples	☺☺☺☺☺
tomatoes	☺☺
bananas	☺☺☺☺☺
grapes	☺☺☺
carrots	☺☺☺
spinach	☺☺☺☺☺☺☺
oranges	☺☺

Key: ☺ = 1 learner

Ask learners questions about the pictogram. For example: *Which fruit did many learners like?* (Read the names.) *What does the smiley face mean? How many learners like carrots? How many learners like spinach? Which fruit did five learners like?* And so on.

18. Learners can keep a record of how many fruits and vegetables they eat each day for one week. They write a list of the fruits and vegetables each day. Then, at the end of the week, they can write a short journal entry about what they ate. Give them a writing frame for this, for example: *This week I ate ______ fruits and ______ vegetables. I ate ______, ______, ______ and ______.*

Ask learners if they know how many fruits and vegetables they should eat every day. Some countries have guidelines about this, for example, five portions of fruit and vegetables per day.

19. **Link to art*. Learners can make models of fruits and vegetables out of any material, for example: papier mâché, clay, dough, wire, wax. As learners work, let them describe the shape and colour of what they are making. When they have completed their models, they can display them in class and provide short oral or written descriptions. Give them a simple writing frame to use for the description. For example: *This is a ______. It is ______ and ______.*

Wrap-up plenary

**Link to science*. Discuss why fruit and vegetables are good to eat. Prompt learners to talk about the taste and texture (*sweet/crunchy*).

Then talk about the health benefits of fruit and vegetables. (Example: *They are healthy. They protect our bodies. They have vitamins.*)

You can also talk about rules for eating fruit. For example, ask: *Would you wash a banana or peel it? Why must we wash fruits and vegetables?*

Quick check

1. Learners can play a matching game with names and pictures of fruits.
2. Give learners sentence strips from the texts that they have read in this unit. Cut up the sentences and let learners use the words to make up the sentences again.
3. Learners can play 'I spy' with pictures of fruit and vegetables.

Unit B Let's eat

Resources and materials

- Student's Book pp. 25–29
- Workbook pp. 56–61
- Audio files: Audio 27; Audio 28; Audio 29; Audio 30
- Photocopiable Masters (PCMs) PCM 9; PCM 16; PCM 17
- Simple menus from restaurants and takeaways
- Prompt cards
- Sentence strips
- Pictures of different types of food
- Menus, empty food containers and advertisements
- Ingredients to make a salad, sandwich or pancake, if available

Key vocabulary

to eat, to drink, meal, breakfast, lunch, supper, tea, dinner, snack, cereal, toast, egg, yoghurt, sandwich, pizza, bread, biscuits, milk, water, pasta, curry, sausage, chocolate, salad, cheese

Lead-in ideas

- Use menus (which you could also make) and/or advertisements to teach vocabulary and talk about what learners like to eat.
- Teach any rhymes, chants or songs related to the topic. *Pat-a-Cake* (**Audio 27**) and *Put the Kettle on* (**Audio 28**) are two good examples.

Script for the lesson

Introducing vocabulary

Teach the names of familiar foods and beverages using pictures or empty food containers.

Teach the names of different mealtimes: *breakfast, lunch, tea, supper/dinner, snack*. If learners are learning about times in mathematics, link these mealtimes to times, such as *six o'clock, eight o'clock*. You can also introduce times of day such as *morning, afternoon* and *evening*.

Sounds

Revise short vowel sounds ('a', 'e' and 'o') and introduce new sounds ('u' and 'i') in context in words such as *carrot, apple, cabbage, orange, chilli, fig, pizza, milk, yum, fun, yuk,* which are used in this topic. You can introduce or revise other words as well, such as *pig, big, sun, Mom*.

Teach the end sound 'ng' which is used at the end of verbs in the present continuous tense.

Introducing structures

Introduce the present continuous tense (example: *I am eating. She isn't eating.*) in Listening and Speaking activities. Introduce positive and negative forms. You can introduce question forms in the next unit. This tense is very common, but it is more difficult to read and write, so leave that for later.

Previous knowledge

Learners will know the names of foods and mealtimes in their mother tongue. Take time to compare these names with English names.

Possible areas of difficulty

Some learners may be allergic to certain foods (peanuts, seafood, milk) or their diets may be restricted for other reasons beyond their control. Be sensitive when discussing healthy diets and mealtimes.

Activities

Select from these activities depending on the level of challenge needed for different learners, interest levels and what you have time to include. Supplement these with additional activities of your own and/or digital activities from the online resource.

▲ **1.** Teach the names of familiar foods and beverages. See the suggested list of words in the key vocabulary list. Include any other words that are familiar in your country.

▲ **2.** Revise and teach short vowel sounds, using words from the songs, rhymes and texts in this topic. Use short words. For example:
   - Write words on the board, without vowels. Say the words and let learners suggest which letters are missing.
   - Learners can put words in groups according to the vowel sounds. Prepare prompt cards with suitable words.
   - Make up sentences in which short vowel sounds are repeated (CVC words) Read each sentence to learners and ask them which vowel sound they can hear the most. Then write the sentences on the board and let learners identify the common vowel sounds. (Examples: *This pot is hot. This pot is not hot. Yum! Yum! I like buns. Ben has ten red hens. That's a fat black cat.*)

▲ **3.** Learners can complete activities 1 and 2 in the Workbook. They complete and build familiar CVC words.

4. Give learners some spelling words and help them to learn the words. Short CVC words from this topic would be suitable. Let learners practise the spelling words in different ways. For example:
   - Jumble the letters and let them rearrange the letters to form the words.
   - Learners write each word once, then cover the word and try to write it without looking.
   - Learners can practice in pairs. One learner says a word and the other learner writes it. They check if the word is correct.

5. **Link to mathematics*. Teach the words *breakfast, lunch, supper, snack, dinner* and relate these to the times (hours) learnt in mathematics (seven o'clock, six o'clock, and so on).

   Then write the words on the board in a mixed order and let learners put the meals in the order in which we eat them.

   Learners can then complete activities 3 and 4 in the Workbook in which they relate times to different meals.

6. Let learners find the story *What's for Breakfast?* in the Student's Book. Discuss the pictures first and introduce the words *ant, ants* and *breakfast*. Then let learners read the story in pairs or let them listen to the Audio (**Audio 29**). The illustrations will help them to understand the story. Ask some simple questions afterwards to check comprehension. For example, ask: *What do the ants like? What don't they like?*

   Learners can then work in groups to act the story. They can change the questions and the foods too, for example: *What's for lunch, Mom? Pizza. We like pizza.*

7. Learners complete activity 5 in the Workbook, which is based on the story *What's for Breakfast?* Learners should read the story again first.

8. Give learners copies of **PCM 16**. Read the following text and let learners tick the correct pictures on the sheet. Do one section at a time.
   1. *What does Benji have for breakfast? Tick the pictures.*
      Benji has a big breakfast every morning. First he has some fruit. He has an apple and a mango. He also has an egg.
   2. *What does Linda have for lunch? Tick the pictures.*
      Linda has lunch at one o'clock. She has a salad. She also has some water.
   3. *What does Tim have for tea? Tick the pictures.*
      Tim has tea in the afternoon. He has a sandwich and some milk.

9. Learners can draw pictures to answer the questions in activity 6 in the Workbook. Once they have completed the drawings, it is important to let learners describe their pictures orally in groups. Learners should take turns when they do this. Each learner in the group should have a chance to describe his or her picture.

10. Teach the present continuous tense. Use actions to support the meaning of what you are saying. Use common verbs associated with classroom or other daily routines. (Examples: *I'm eating/drinking/reading/writing/drawing/listening/jumping/playing*.) Then act each verb and ask learners: *What am I doing?* Prompt them to reply: *You are ______ing.*

    Learners can then work in groups and take turns to act. As they act, they say: *What am I doing?* The others in the group have to guess and make sentences with the structure: *You are ______ing.* They could also use *He/She is ______ing.*

    As learners work, help them to pronounce the 'ng' sound at the ends of the verbs.

11. Learners can complete activity 7 in the Workbook. They say what the people are doing in each picture and then they circle the correct word under each picture. They should look at the beginning sounds of the words if they are not sure of the words. Then ask them to make oral sentences about each picture. (Examples: *She is eating. She is eating a sandwich. He is drawing. He is drawing a picture.*)

12. Introduce negative forms of the present continuous tense. Use any pictures you have collected, or pictures from the Student's Book, for example, of a girl drinking some water. Ask: *What is she doing?* Let learners answer (*She is drinking water.*). Then ask: *Is she eating?* Let learners answer (*No.*). Then say: *No, she isn't eating.* Repeat this with several pictures.

    Then let learners work in pairs and practise asking and answering questions in the same way.

13. Learners complete activity 8 in the Workbook. Learners are given the names of the four ingredients to make pancakes. They are asked to draw them and write the name of each ingredient under the picture.

14. Let learners find the story *Fox and Stork* in the Student's Book (pages 28–29). Teach the names of the animals and find out what the learners know about each animal. Let learners try and describe the animals using any adjectives they know (example: *The fox is brown. The stork is tall.*) and to describe what kinds of food these animals eat in real life. (Example: *A stork eats fish. A fox eats chickens, mice, rabbits and other small animals.*) Read the story or let them listen to **Audio 30** and explain what *dine* and *trick* mean.

15. Give each learner a copy of **PCM 17**. Learners cut up the pictures and put them in the correct order. They use the pictures to tell the story of *Fox and Stork*. Ask them what trick Fox plays on Stork, and what trick Stork plays on Fox.

16. Choose a simple recipe of something that learners could eat for lunch. (Examples: *a sandwich, a pancake, a fruit salad*.) If it is possible to actually make the recipe together, collect the ingredients and make it, or if not possible, you can mime.

Write a list of the ingredients on the board, and read the list with the class, for example:

We need:
flour
milk
eggs
sugar

Either make the recipe, or pretend to, miming the actions. Give very simple descriptions as you work and ask learners to say what you are doing. For example:

Teacher: *I am mixing the eggs and the sugar. What am I doing?*

Response: *You are mixing the eggs and the sugar*.

Then continue in the same way with these descriptions:
I am putting milk in the bowl.
I am putting flour in the bowl.
I am frying the pancakes.
I am tossing the pancakes. [If you can do this!]
We are eating the pancakes.

Wrap-up plenary

Talk about healthy meals again. Ask learners to suggest healthy snacks and healthy meals for breakfast, lunch and supper. Let learners suggest some of their favourite meals.

Quick check

1. Play 'Bingo' with short, familiar words. Write a list of names of common foods and CVC words on the board (examples: *hen, egg, yuk, fig, hot, pot, milk, pizza, mango, apple, tea*). Let each learner copy nine words on to their blank Bingo sheet (**PCM 9**). Then play 'Bingo' in the usual way.
2. Learners can play a game in which one learner acts and the other learners have to guess what he or she is doing. (Example: *What am I doing? You are skipping*.)

Unit C What I like

Resources and materials

- Student's Book pp. 30–31
- Workbook pp. 62–66
- Audio files: Audio 31; Audio 32
- Photocopiable Master (PCM) PCM 18
- Sentence strips
- Pictures of different types of food
- Menus, empty food containers and advertisements

Key vocabulary

names of familiar foods

verbs describing common routine actions (eat, drink, sleep, play, and so on)

Lead-in ideas

- Teach any poem chants or songs related to the topic. **Audio 31** *Do You Like Them?* and **Audio 32** *What I Like* are two good examples.

Script for the lesson

Introducing vocabulary

Teach the names of familiar foods and beverages using pictures or empty food containers.

Revise and introduce a range of common verbs that learners can use to describe everyday actions and routines.

Sounds

Revise short vowel sounds and beginning blends as they occur in activities (Examples: 'ch' in *chocolate*, 'sn' in *snack*, 'sl' in *sleep*, 'dr' in *drink*, 'pl' in *play*).

Introducing structures

Introduce the structure *I like* + verb that ends in *-ing*. (*I like eating.*) You can also let learners add nouns to the structures. (*I like eating chocolate.*) Use pictures and/or actions to do this.

Use verbs that are already familiar to learners.

Teach question forms of the present continuous tense in which the order of the words is reversed (*Is she eating?*). Learners can then give positive or negative answers.

Previous knowledge

Learners should know some common verbs and subject pronouns by this stage.

Possible areas of difficulty

Learners may say *I like eat chocolate* instead of *I like chocolate* or *I like eating chocolate*. Correct them and provide practice until they can use the verb *like* correctly.

Activities

Select from these activities depending on the level of challenge needed for different learners, interest levels and what you have time to include. Supplement these with additional activities of your own and/or digital activities from the online resource.

1. Let learners find the text *What do you like?* in the Student's Book (pages 30–31). Most of the structures and vocabulary in this text have already been introduced. Spend some time discussing and revising the vocabulary. Learners can also ask each other questions about the pictures, to practise asking questions. (Examples: *Is he eating? What is this? Do you like porridge? Do you eat noodles?*)

   Depending on the level of learners, let them work in pairs to read the text, or read the text with groups of learners.

2. Learners complete activities 1 and 2 in the Workbook, which is based on the text *What do you like?*

3. Learners work in pairs and interview each other about likes and dislikes, using the different question forms they have learnt. Each learner should ask five or six questions. For example, they could ask:

   Do you like chocolate? Do you like spinach? Do you like eggs?

   Do you like reading? Do you like playing? Do you like drinking water?

4. Give learner copies of **PCM 18** or use suitable menus that you have collected. Learners work in groups and discuss the menu. They ask each other questions about what they like and dislike. For example, they could ask: *Do you like pizza? Yes, I do. No, I don't. What do you like? I don't like bread. I like rice.*

5. Teach learners to use the conjunction *and*. Use pictures of food as well as real items if you can. Put a selection of foods in front of a group of learners and ask them what they like. Tell them that they need to choose two things. They make a sentence to describe their choice. (Example: *I like cereal and eggs*.) Write the sentence on the board and help learners to read the sentence. Then let learners write sentences about what they like, using the word *and*. They should learn to spell the word *and*.

6. Play a game with learners, to practise using the word *and*. Learners have to think of two things that they like. Each thing (which can be a noun or a verb/gerund) must begin with the same letter. For example:

   I like swimming and surfing.

   I like tea and toast.

   I like chips and chocolate.

   I like football and fishing.

   Work out a scoring system. So, for example, if a learner gives two correct words and uses *and*, they get one point and another chance. If they get an answer wrong, they get another chance, but no points.

   Ask learners to think about which foods and drinks go together well. For example, tea and toast go together, but a mango and a cup of coffee or glass of milk may not taste so good if you have them at the same time.

7. Learners work in groups and role-play a simple scene in a restaurant or supermarket. A small group (friends or family) go into the restaurant/supermarket and talk about what they like and don't like to eat. Then someone assists them and they order some food. The conversation could go like this:

   Friend 1: *I like fish.*

   Friend 2: *I don't like fish. I like chicken.*

   Friend 3: *Me too.*

   Waiter: *Would you like chicken? Would you like water?*

   Friend 1: *No, thanks. I like orange juice.*

   Friend 2: *Me too.*

   Friend 3: *I like milkshake.*

   Waiter: *Would you like a chocolate milkshake?*

   Friend 3: *Yes, please!*

   Help learners to take turns during these exchanges. Explain that they cannot all talk at the same time or the waiter will not know what they want to order.

8. Write some words on the board and let learners suggest how to rearrange the words to make sentences. Teach them that the first word of a sentence begins with a capital letter. They should look for the word with a capital letter to start. When the sentence is complete, teach learners to put a full stop at the end of the sentence. Examples:

   biscuits She likes and tea = She likes biscuits and tea.

   don't like I milk cereal and = I don't like milk and cereal.

9. Learners complete activities 3 and 4 in the Workbook. They do some word recognition activities and then they write simple sentences using the given words.

10. *Link to mathematics*. Learners look at the graph in activity 5 in the Workbook and answer the questions. If you think learners need assistance with this, discuss the graph orally first to help them interpret it. Then let them complete the answers in writing.

11. Learners listen to the main ideas in a short story. Read this story and then ask the questions.

Story: *The ice-cream*

Susan and her mother go the shop. Mom wants a pear and milk. Susan wants an ice-cream. She likes ice-cream.

"Would you like a pear?" asks Mom.

"No, thanks. Can I have an ice-cream, please?" asks Susan.

"No," says Mom.

"I like ice-cream," says Susan.

"Me too," says Mom. "But fruit is healthy!"

Questions:

What does Mom want?

What does Susan want?

Does Mom like ice-cream?

Does Mom buy ice-cream?

12. Learners can make up their own stories about food in a shop or restaurant, using the structures and vocabulary they have learnt. They can perform their stories for the rest of the class.

13. Teach learners to play the *Yes/No* game in groups. One learner thinks of something they like to eat. The other learners ask questions. The first learner may only answer *'Yes'* or *'No'*. For example:

Learner 1: *I am thinking about a food that I like.*

Learner 2: *Is it chocolate?*

Learner 1: *No.*

Learner 2: *Does it begin with 'p'?*

Learner 1: *Yes.*

Learner 2: *Is it pasta?*

Learner 1: *Yes. Now it's your turn.*

Wrap-up plenary

Sing the *Do You Like Them?* rap song again, adding verses. Encourage individual learners to add their own words.

Quick check

Learners work in pairs. They ask each other a few questions and report back to the class with three sentences about what their partner likes and dislikes. (Example: *Viyay likes curry. He doesn't like milk. He likes swimming*.)

Assessment

You can complete an oral assessment of the work done in this topic by:

- asking learners to name or point to real fruits and vegetables or pictures of them
- asking learners to describe a fruit or vegetable using an adjective (*long, sweet, juicy*, etc.)
- showing learners a time on a clock and ask them which meal they eat at that time.

Learners can also complete Progress check activities 1, 2, 3 and 4 in the Workbook as a simple assessment. You could allocate marks for these activities and record these as part of continuous assessment.

Topic 5 Let's have fun

Overview

In this topic the focus is on the language of playing games and sports and sharing information on general and curricular topics. This can be used to help build confidence amongst learners. There are opportunities to integrate activities with health education, physical education, art, mathematics and moral education.

Units in this topic

Unit A: Fun and games

Unit B: Sports

Unit C: I am bored

Teaching focus

- 1Rg2 Recognise, identify, sound, segment and blend phonemes in individual words.
- 1Wo1 Include a full stop when copying very high-frequency short sentences.
- 1Uf1 Use imperative forms of common verbs for basic commands and instructions.
- 1Uf3 Use common present continuous forms [positive, negative, question] to talk about what is happening now.
- 1Uf4 Use *have got* + noun to describe and ask about possessions.
- 1Uf5 Use *can/can't* to describe ability.
- 1Uf6 Use *have got* to describe possession.
- 1Ug1 Use common singular nouns, plural nouns [plural 's'] and proper names to say what things are.
- 1Ug2 Use numbers 1-10 to count.
- 1Ug3 Use basic adjectives and colours to say what someone/something is or has.
- 1Ug6 Use basic prepositions of location and position to describe *at, in, near, next to, on* to describe where people and things are.
- 1Ug7 Use prepositions of time: *on, in* to talk about days and time.
- 1Ug8 Use *with* to indicate accompaniment.
- 1Ug9 Use *for* to indicate recipient.
- 1Ug10 Use *Would you like* + noun to enquire.
- 1Ug11 Use *let's* + verb.
- 1Ug12 Use *like* + verb + *-ing* to express likes and dislikes.
- 1Ug13 Spell some familiar high-frequency words accurately during guided writing activities.
- 1Ug14 Use, with support, a simple picture dictionary.
- 1Ug15 Sight read high-frequency words.
- 1Ut1 Use the questions: *What colour is it? What now?*
- 1Ut2 Use determiners *a, the, this*, *these* to indicate what/where something is.
- 1Ut3 Use interrogative pronouns *which*, *what*, *where* to ask basic questions.
- 1Ut5 Use personal subject and object pronouns to give basic personal information.
- 1Ld1 Understand some specific information and detail of short, supported talk on a limited range of general and curricular topics.
- 1Ld2 Use contextual clues to predict content in short, supported talk on a limited range of general and curricular topics.
- 1Lg1 Understand very short supported narratives on a limited range of general and curricular topics.
- 1Lg2 Recognise the sounds of phonemes and phoneme blends.
- 1S2 Ask questions in order to find out about a limited range of personal information and classroom routines.

Language patterns

Grammar summary for teachers:

- **Prepositions:** Prepositions are used in many ways, for example, to describe locations (places) direction, position, time, and accompaniment. The use of prepositions is very often idiomatic. Learners will need to remember when to use each preposition, so they will require a lot of practice and exposure.
- ***Let's* + verb:** This structure is commonly used to make suggestions. *Let's* is a contraction of *Let us*. (Example: *Let's play a game*.)

A Fun and games

Resources and materials

- Student's Book pp. 32–33
- Workbook pp. 67–71
- Audio file: Audio 33
- Photocopiable Masters (PCMs) PCM 14; PCM 19; PCM 20; PCM 21
- Prompt cards with prepositions: at, on, in, near, next to
- A spinner (from PCM 14) and counters to play board game
- Additional board games or computer games for learners to play
- Paper or other materials to make a frog

Key vocabulary

Prepositions: in, on, under, next to, near, with, for

names of games and basic equipment (bike, board, counters, hopscotch, skipping, snakes and ladders, spinner, computer and phone games)

Lead-in ideas

- Play a familiar game with learners. (Example: 'Simon says')
- Play a game in which someone hides something in the class. Everyone else closes their eyes. Then say: *Where's the ______?* Learners suggest where the object is hidden.
- Play a game in which one learner is blindfolded and the other learners give instructions about where to go or where to find something. Monitor this carefully so that no learner gets hurt.
- Revise basic instructions and vocabulary. Give learners oral instructions to draw a simple picture. Use this to practise short vowel sounds. Use familiar words. For example, say:

  Draw a picture of a mat. The mat is a square. Colour the mat in pink and red.

  Draw six eggs. One egg is red, two eggs are yellow and three eggs are pink.

Script for the lesson

Introducing vocabulary

Teach the names of common/familiar games that learners in your class play. (Examples: *hide and seek, hopscotch, skipping, snakes and ladders, computer and phone games*)

Sounds

Revise the short vowel sounds in prepositions such as: *at, in, on, next, with, under, up, off* and *for*. Learners need to be able to hear the difference and sound the words clearly.

Revise beginning sounds in context, for example, 'b' (bike), 'k' (counters), 'd' (down).

Introducing structures

Allow plenty of time for learning and practising prepositions in all the units in this topic. Focus on the prepositions listed in the curriculum framework (*at, in, near, next to, on, with, for*), but introduce a few other common prepositions for extension as well. (See the texts in the Student's Book.)

Introduce the structure *Let's* + verb to make suggestions. The full form *Let us* is very formal, so teach the contracted form. Use familiar verbs (*play, work, eat*).

The structure *Play with* (*me/him/her/them*) will help learners to use object pronouns as well as the preposition *with* (to mean accompaniment).

Learners will use and be exposed to the present continuous tense again in this topic. Learners should practise asking and answering questions, using this tense. (Example: *What is he/she doing? He/She is ______ing. What are they doing? They are ______ing.*)

Learners can practise giving and obeying basic commands, rules and instructions when playing games.

Previous knowledge

Learners will need to know some common verbs, pronouns and nouns.

Possible areas of difficulty

Prepositions are often used idiomatically and differently in different languages, so it is not helpful to translate them. Learners need to hear them often and be encouraged to use them in sentences.

Activities

Select from these activities depending on the level of challenge needed for different learners, interest levels and what you have time to include. Supplement these with additional activities of your own and/or digital activities from the online resource.

▲ **1.** Teach basic prepositions of location and position: *at, on, in, near, next to*. To do this, position objects in places in the classroom and make sentences to describe where each object is. (Example: *This book is on the table. This book is next to the bag.*) Use the prompt cards. Read the words on the cards with learners. Then place the cards with the relevant objects and let learners make sentences like the examples you used.

Place learners in certain positions (examples: *near the door, next to the window, on the grass*). Make sentences to describe each position. (Example: *Pierre is near the door.*) Let the other learners find the matching prompt cards with prepositions.

Then hold up the prompt cards one at a time and let learners go to a position to show that they understand what it means. You could take learners outside to do this.

2. Learners play a game in groups. One learner hides an object while the others close their eyes. Then they have to guess where the object is.

3. Learners complete activity 1 in the Workbook. Read the sentences and let learners tick the sentence that matches each picture.

4. Let learners find the story *Let's Play Hide and Seek* in the Student's Book. Discuss the pictures and let learners predict what the story is about. Help them to name the hiding places in the pictures. Ask the questions in the talk bubble and check that they understand the concept.

   Read the story or let learners read in pairs or alone, depending on their reading level. Then read the story again and discuss each picture. Ask: *Where is Ben?* and let learners reply.

   Learners can then complete activities 2 and 3 in the Workbook.

5. Play the conversation *Play with me* (**Audio 33**) to the learners. Repeat the sentences and questions. Then let learners work in groups of four or more and role-play a similar conversation.

6. Let learners get into small groups. Give each group a copy of **PCM 19**, which is a snakes and ladders game. Each group will also need a 1–6 spinner (**PCM 14**), and counters. Explain to learners how it works. Give simple instructions and then let them play the game in groups. Say the following instructions:

   Spin the spinner. Go up the ladders. Go down the snakes. Take turns.

7. Let learners find the story *My Bike Ride* in the Student's Book (page 33). Discuss the pictures and let learners predict what the story is about.

   Read the story, or let learners read in pairs or alone, depending on their reading level. Then read the story again and discuss each picture. Ask: *What is she doing? Where is she going?*

   Learners can mime the story afterwards to show that they understand the prepositions in the story.

8. Teach learners about full stops at the ends of sentences and capital letters to start sentences. Then let learners practise finding sentences both in the story *My Bike Ride* and any other familiar story.

   Learners can then complete activity 4 in the Workbook.

9. Practise the present continuous tense. Choose any story or pictures that you have available. Learners can work in pairs and ask each other questions about the pictures. (Example: *What are they doing?*)

10. Learners write a journal entry. They can draw and write about a game that they enjoy playing. Help them with vocabulary and give them sentences to copy if necessary.

11. Learners complete activities 5 and 6 in the Workbook. Learners read the high-frequency words in the box. Then they circle the words in the sentences. After that they make their own simple sentences with the words.

12. Give each learner a copy of **PCM 20**. Read one of the prepositions in each row and let learners circle the preposition you have read in colour. Then read another preposition in each row and let learners circle this preposition in a different colour.

    For activity 2, read lists of familiar words with the same short vowel sound and let learners identify the sound. Include prepositions in each group of words, for example:

    a) *at cat mat hat*

    b) *on pot dog sock*

    c) *in pin it this dish*

    d) *next bed leg hen*

    e) *up bus mud dust*

13. Learners work in groups and make up a story about a hide and seek game. They act the story for the rest of the class. They should use familiar question structures and prepositions in their drama.

14. Learners work in pairs and give each other instructions to draw pictures. The instructions should include prepositions and sentences in the present continuous tense. (Example: *Draw a bike. The bike is going up the hill. Draw a girl on the bike.*)

15. Learners complete the game in activity 7 in the Workbook. Then they play the game.

    They should number all the boxes in sequence.

    Then they draw pictures and/or write simple sentences and instructions for the players.

    They circle the instruction in red to show that the player must go back one block. They circle the box in another colour to show that the player must go forward one block. For example:

    The car is in the mud. (Circle in red.)

    It is hot. (Circle in green.)

16. **Link to art*. Make a jumping frog with the class. You could teach them how to make an origami frog by folding a square of paper (**PCM 21**). The frogs could also be made of wire or clay or papier-mâché (but these will not be able to jump). When the frogs are complete, let learners use them to practise prepositions. Learners put the frogs in certain places and then make sentences. (Example: *The frog is under the table. The frog is near the book*.)

17. Learners can write their own simple stories about doing an activity that they enjoy, like the *My Bike Ride* story. They can make up short four to six page books with their stories. You could provide writing frames for this. For example:

This is my ______.

I am ______.

I am going ______.

I am ______ ______.

18. Learners play any board game or appropriate computer game. Encourage them to talk as they play and practise basic commands and instructions.

Wrap-up plenary

Learners can talk about their favourite games. Some learners may also know traditional games that they can teach to the rest of the class (example: *board games, card games, clapping games*).

Quick check

1. Play 'Simon says' with learners. Give instructions that include prepositions. For example, say: *Put your hands on your head. Put your hands in your pockets. Put your hands under the tables. Put your hands up in the air.*
2. Let learners take turn to act while the other learners try to guess what they are doing.

Unit B Sports

Resources and materials

- Student's Book pp. 34–35
- Workbook pp. 72–76
- Audio file: Audio 34
- Photocopiables Masters (PCMs) PCM 9; PCM 22
- Picture dictionaries
- Balloons, paper and glue to make papier-mâché balls
- Paper to make booklets
- Pictures about sports stars and events
- Some sports equipment (ball, hockey stick, tennis racquet, net)

Key vocabulary

Names of common sports: athletics (track), basketball, cricket, cycling, football (soccer), hockey, judo, netball, rugby, sailing, swimming, table tennis, tennis, volleyball, wrestling

Sports equipment: ball, goal, shoes, bike, stick, whistle, racquet (also spelt as 'racket'), padding, helmet, gloves, posts

Lead-in ideas

- Collect some photographs about sports events that you think will interest the class. Show the photographs and find out what the class know about them. Prompt them to make statements such as: *That's [name of team/player]. She is playing [name of sport].* Help with vocabulary as needed.
- Take the class outside and let them play a game with a ball. Talk about the game and what the players have to do. Introduce words such as *catch, kick, throw, hit, score* as you speak.
- Learners can sing a familiar, appropriate song to support a sports team.

Script for the lesson

Introducing vocabulary

Use a picture dictionary, or the picture dictionary-style page in the Student's Book (page 34) to introduce vocabulary. Teach the names of sports that you think will interest learners the most. Learners should also be able to name basic equipment used in sports.

Sounds

Revise and teach sounds within the context of this theme. For example: the long 'a' sound in *ball* (*all, tall, mall, fall*) and the 'ay' sound in *play* (*day, say, may*).

Introducing structures

Allow plenty of time for learning and practising prepositions in this unit. Learners can also practise using demonstrative pronouns *this/that/these*. Learners can also practise giving and obeying basic commands and instructions when playing games.

Revise the structures *I like* + verb ending in *-ing* to express likes and dislikes and *I can* ______ */I can't* ______ to talk about ability.

Teach the structure *have got* to describe and ask about possession. Teach the question form *Have you got* ______*?* You can also teach the short answers *Yes, I have./No, I haven't.*

Previous knowledge

The structures *I can/I can't, I like* ______*ing*, basic instructions, some prepositions and demonstrative pronouns.

Possible areas of difficulty

Some vocabulary and abbreviations are used in certain ways in a sports context, but the words may have different meanings in everyday life. (Examples: *ref* (referee/reference), *forward/lock* (position in football/rugby and preposition or verb), *time* (meaning time is up or a specific time.) Explain these as necessary during your lessons.

Activities

Select from these activities depending on the level of challenge needed for different learners, interest levels and what you have time to include. Supplement these with additional activities of your own and/or digital activities from the online resource.

1. Use the *Sports* picture dictionary page on page 34 in the Student's Book to introduce the names of sports. Read the names and then ask questions such as: *Which sport is your favourite? What do you need to play each sport? Who plays this sport? Where do you play?*

2. Learners can work in groups to mime sports activities. Other learners can guess what they are miming. Work out a system of scoring and teach vocabulary as necessary.

3. Learners can match words and pictures about sports in activity 1 in the Workbook.

4. Revise and practise the structures *I can* ______/*I can't* ______ using the names of sports activities that you have introduced. Teach learners when to use the verb *play* in the structure. (Examples: *I can/can't play tennis/volleyball/hockey/basketball/football*. But: *I can/can't swim/cycle/ride a bike*.)

   Learners could then work in pairs or small groups. Each learner draws up a list of six sports. They can copy six sports from the picture dictionary page in the Student's Book. Then they use their lists to interview each other about sports on their lists. They ask questions such as: *Can you swim? Can you play table tennis?* The learner being interviewed should reply: *Yes, I can./No, I can't.* Learners tick the names of the sports as they ask the question.

   You could also help them to compile a record sheet (data collection sheet). They can then tick the relevant column and add up the totals afterwards, for example.

Sports	Can	Can't
Football	✓	
Tennis		✓
Volleyball		✓
Swimming	✓	
Hockey		✓
Cycling	✓	
	3	3

5. Work with groups of learners. Read them a short text using familiar words and vocabulary that has been introduced. Read the text twice and then ask questions. Learners give oral answers. Here are some examples of what you could do.

   Text A

   Li and May are playing tennis. They have tennis racquets and three yellow tennis balls. They like tennis. Can you play tennis?

   Questions:

   What are they playing?

   What do they use to play?

   How many balls do they have?

   What colour are the balls.

   Can you play tennis?

   Text B

   Linda and Luke like swimming. They go to the swimming pool at the gym club. They wear swimming costumes and caps. They have a lot of fun.

   Questions:

   What do Linda and Luke like?

   Where do they go?

   What do they wear?

   Can you swim?

6. Revise the demonstrative pronouns *this/that/these*. You could use real sports equipment to do this. (Examples: *This is a hockey stick. These are balls. This ball is for football and this ball is for tennis.*)

   Ask learners to think about different balls and what we use them for. For example: *Which balls do we kick? Which do we hit?* If you have pictures or real balls available, let learners sort the balls or pictures and make sentences such as: *We kick these balls. We hit this ball.*

7. Learners find the text *Let's play football* in the Student's Book (page 35). To prepare learners for reading, ask: *What do you need to play football?* Let them try and identify things in the pictures in the story. Read the story with learners, or let them read alone or in pairs, depending on their level.

8. Learners complete activity 2 in the Workbook, which is based on the text *Let's Play Football*. They label and complete the picture.

9. Teach the structure *have got*, which shows possession. You could use real sports equipment and classroom objects. Teach the question forms as well as short answers. Let learners work in pairs to practise these structures using a short conversation, for example:

   A: *Have you got a ball?*

   B: *Yes, I have.*

   A: *Let's play football then.*

   B: *Okay!*

10. Learners complete activities 3 and 4 in the Workbook which provides practise in recognising high-frequency words, using prepositions and using full stops and capital letters.

11. Learners make up a short story about going to play a sport, using the structures and vocabulary they have learnt. They can work in small groups.

12. Learners play a chain game in groups. The first learner makes a statement and asks a question. The next learner in the chain has five seconds to give an answer. If he or she gives a correct answer, he/she turns to the next learner and makes a statement with a question. For example:

A: *I have got a ball. What can we play?*

B: *Football. I have got a ball. What can we play?*

C: *Tennis. I have got a ball. What can we play?*

D: *Volleyball. I have got a stick. What can we play?*

E: *Hockey.*

And so on. If a learner gives a wrong answer, the next learner in the chain gets a chance to answer. Learners can change the piece of equipment.

13. Read learners a short report about a sport. They listen and then answer questions in order to describe the main ideas of the text. Read the text twice and then ask questions. Learners give oral answers. Here is an example of what you could do.

Text A

Mara likes playing volleyball. She has got a ball. She plays with her friends. There are two teams. They play volleyball on the beach. They hit the ball over a net.

Questions:

What does Mara like playing?

How many teams are there?

Where do they play?

14. Learners complete the sentences in activity 5 in the Workbook, using high-frequency words and prepositions. Learners then complete activity 6, which asks them to draw a picture of a sport they like and write a sentence about it.

Ask learners how many players there are in different teams. For example, in a football team, in a hockey team, in a volleyball team.

15. **Link to mathematics*. Learners look at the graph in activity 7 in the Workbook and answer the questions. You may want to discuss this with learners orally before they complete the questions.

16. **Link to art*. Give groups of learners copies of **PCM 22**. This shows how to make a ball out of papier-mâché. Read the instructions with the class first, then have learners make a papier-mâché ball in their groups.

17. Choose some high-frequency words and let learners practise them for spelling. Learners can work in pairs to practise the words. Here are some words that you could use: *can, like, play, have got, this, that, these, is, are, what*. You can choose words from the list on page 7 of this Teacher's Guide.

18. Learners can make up simple poems/songs about the sports they like, using words and structures that they know. Play the poem *Let's Play!* as a model (**Audio 34**).

19. Learners work in pairs or small groups on a project. They compile a booklet about sports or about their favourite sports. Use the sentences from the text *Let's Play Football* as a model. You can write these sentences up on the board as a frame:

This is ______.

These are ______.

This is ______.

He is ______./She is ______.

Let's play ______.

Learners can take photographs, draw pictures or cut out pictures from magazines to illustrate the sports. When the books are complete, they can be displayed for other learners to read.

20. Learners can write an entry in their journals about a sport that they enjoy or watch. You could give them a writing frame, or let them write freely. Do not worry about spelling or punctuation if you do this. It is more important that the learner can read back to you what he or she has written.

Wrap-up plenary

Talk about current sports events again and encourage learners to join in, using the new vocabulary and structures they have learnt.

Talk about how to be fair when playing games and taking part in sport. You can do this in your mother tongue if necessary first and then sum up with a few English sentences which learners can easily remember. (Example: *Don't cheat. Wait for your turn. Be fair.*)

Quick check

1. Use pictures to check that learners can name different sports. You could also let learners make Bingo sheets (use **PCM 9**) with the names of sports.
2. Let learners play a telephone game to check listening skills. Learners work in groups. Give the first learner a sentence from the unit on a piece of paper (or whisper it to the learner). For example: *I like cycling but I don't like tennis*. The learner repeats what he or she hears to the next learner in the chain until all learners have had a chance. The last learner says the sentence aloud and the first learner says the original message aloud.

Unit C I am bored

Resources and materials

- Student's Book p. 36
- Workbook pp. 77–81
- Audio files: Audio 35; Audio 36
- Photocopiable Master (PCM) PCM 23
- Prompt cards with adjectives: bored, busy, happy, excited
- Analogue clocks for teaching times
- Pictures of activities that learners would enjoy
- Prompt cards and school timetable with days of the week.

Key vocabulary

bored, happy, sad, busy, excited

morning, afternoon, evening, night, midday, o'clock

in, at, on

Monday, Tuesday, Wednesday, Thursday, Friday, Saturday, Sunday

Lead-in ideas

- Read any suitable poem or story that you have about what people do when they are bored.
- Sing a familiar song to introduce times of the day. For example, *This Is the Way* (**Audio 35**). You could add verses such as: *This is the way we eat our lunch … in the hot afternoon.*

Script for the lesson

Introducing vocabulary

Teach phrases that describe times of the day, for example: *in the afternoon, in the morning, at night, at midday*.

Teach further adjectives that learners can use within the context of this topic. Adjectives that describe feelings and activities are useful (examples: *happy, bored, excited, busy*). If learners are familiar with emoticons you can use these to introduce English words for feelings. You can also act or use exaggerated facial expressions to convey the meanings of adjectives.

Sounds

Help learners to recognise and pronounce different end sounds, for example, the sound 'ee' in adjectives such as *busy, happy* and the end sounds 'd' and 'id' in adjectives such as *bored* and *excited*.

Introducing structures

Revise the structures *I like* + verb ending in *-ing* to express likes and dislikes.

Teach the prepositions of time: *at, in* and *on* in phrases such as *at six o'clock at night, in the afternoon, on Monday*.

Learners can also revise the prepositions *with* (accompaniment) and *for* (recipient).

Previous knowledge

Numbers 1–12 (for telling the time).

Possible areas of difficulty

Prepositions are difficult to teach as so many are used idiomatically, so do not expect learners to get these correct immediately.

End sounds are also more difficult to hear and distinguish. You should exaggerate end sounds until you feel learners have grasped these.

Activities

Select from these activities depending on the level of challenge needed for different learners, interest levels and what you have time to include. Supplement these with additional activities of your own and/or digital activities from the online resource.

▲ 1. Teach the adjectives *bored, busy, excited, happy*. You can act how you feel or use pictures to help learners understand. Then use the prompt cards. Read the words with the learners. Then tell learners to act when you show each card.

▲ 2. Learners work in groups and play a chain game. Each learner in turn gives a suggestion to answer a question, and then asks the next learner the same question. For example:

   A: *I am bored. What can I do?*

   B: *You can play a game. I am bored. What can I do?*

   C: *You can help me! I am bored. What can I do?*

   D: *You can play with me. I am bored. What can I do?*

   E: *You can do your work.*

   And so on.

▲ 3. Learners find the text *I Am Bored* in the Student's Book. To prepare learners for reading, ask questions to prompt them to predict what the story is about, such as: *What do you think this story is about? How does the boy feel? Why?* Read the story with the learners, or let them listen to the Audio (**Audio 36**). Alternatively, let them read alone or in pairs, depending on their level.

▲ 4. Learners complete activity 1 in the Workbook, which is based on the text *I Am Bored*. They complete the speech bubbles.

5. Let learners practise writing some high-frequency words. Choose five or six words. (See the list on page 7.) Write two columns of words on the board, one in which the words are spelt correctly and the other in which the words are jumbled. Invite learners to come up and match the words. For example:

atth	with
thwi	can
nac	that
evha	have
elik	and
dna	like

6. **Link to mathematics*. Use a clock to revise basic times such as *ten o'clock, six o'clock*, and so on. Then relate these times to times of the day: *in the morning, in the afternoon, in the evening, at night*. Ask learners what they do at these different times.

   (Note: Before you do this, check that learners have already done this in mathematics. If not, wait until they have done so.)

7. Learners complete activity 2 in the Workbook. They identify the time of day in each picture, draw the hands on the clock and circle the word that matches the picture.

8. Practise end sounds. Tell learners you will read three words. Two of the words have the same sound at the end. They listen and identify the sound. Use words with final 'ing' and 'ee' sounds. Here are some groups of words you could read:

   busy happy bored

   play sunny funny

   skipping hopping jump

   playing swimming bicycle

   Write the words on the board afterwards and highlight the end sounds in some way, so that learners can see the words as well.

9. Revise object pronouns. Use real objects and demonstrate as you make sentences such as: *Give me the ball. Give him/her the ball. Show me the pictures.*

10. Give learners copies of **PCM 23**. Say the times and let learners draw the faces on the clocks (examples: *five o'clock, eight o'clock, one o'clock*). When learners have completed the clocks, let them take turns to point to their clocks and say the times.

    (Note: Before you do this, check that learners have already done this in mathematics. If not, wait until they have done so.)

11. Find an interesting picture about some activity that learners might enjoy. Then make up a simple story about the picture. Give your story a name and tell learners that you are going to tell them a story. Ask learners to predict what the story is about. Prompt them with questions such as: *Who is that? Where are they? What are they doing?* Then read your story to the learners.

12. Practise some more end sounds. This time focus on words that end with the sounds 'd', 'id' and 'k'. Read the words in groups and ask learners which words have the same end sound. For example:

    Words ending in the sound 'd': *bored whiteboard field cupboard bed*

    Words ending in the sound 'id': *excited interested*

    Words ending in 'k': *clock duck bike*

13. Teach or revise the names of days of the week. Use prompt cards and your school timetable. Get learners to put the days in order.

14. Learners complete activities 3 and 4 in the Workbook by choosing the correct preposition for each sentence. Then they find the names of the days of the week in a puzzle and put the names in the correct order. Note that the list does not contain the names of all of the days of the week.

15. Have a discussion with groups of learners. Let them take turns to discuss what they do when they are bored. Let the focus be on listening to others and on everyone participating. Accept all reasonable suggestions from learners.

16. Help learners compile an ideal timetable. Draw a template like the one below on the board. Let learners tell you where to write each day of the week. Then discuss what they could do on each day. Write the words under the names of the days.

Monday						

17. Read learners a story from one of the reading books that you have in class. Then ask them questions to see if they can understand the main ideas of the story. Let them answer the questions orally.

Wrap-up plenary

Choose a game and get the class to explain the rules to someone who hasn't played it before. Let learners choose a sport and say what they know about it, for example, teams, what kind of equipment, rules. This could also be turned into a guessing game in which one learner describes a sport or game and the other learners have to guess what it is.

Quick check

1. Learners act some of the adjectives that they have learnt and let other learners guess how they are feeling.
2. Play a game. One learner says a time. One of the learners in the group responds with a suggestion about what they can do. Example: *It's four o'clock. Let's play volleyball.*

Assessment

You can complete an oral assessment of the work done in this topic by:

- showing learners pictures of different games and sports and let them say the names
- asking learners to make two oral sentences about a favourite game or sport.

Learners can also complete Progress check activities 1, 2 and 3 in the Workbook as a simple assessment.

For activity 1 read sentences that match only one of the pictures in the Workbook. For example: *He is riding his bike down a hill* (which matches b).

You could allocate marks for these activities and record these as part of continuous assessment.

Topic 6 Out and about

Overview

This topic allows you to introduce basic vocabulary and knowledge of English phonemes while assessing the prior knowledge of learners in your class. There are opportunities to integrate language lessons with other subjects in the curriculum, such as art, drama, mathematics and science. Vocabulary and concepts are developed by encouraging learners to express themselves using whatever knowledge they already have. Learners are encouraged to participate enthusiastically in activities to develop confidence.

Units in this topic

Unit A: What can I wear?

Unit B: At the weekend

Unit C: How I feel

Teaching focus

- 1Rg2 Recognise, identify, sound, segment and blend phonemes in individual words.
- 1Rg15 Sight read high-frequency words.
- 1Wo1 Include a full stop when copying very high-frequency short sentences.
- 1Uf1 Use imperative forms of common verbs for basic commands and instructions.
- 1Uf3 Use common present continuous forms [positive, negative, question] to talk about what is happening now.
- 1Uf4 Use *have got* + noun to describe and ask about possessions.
- 1Uf5 Use *can/can't* to describe ability.
- 1Uf6 Use *have got* to describe possession.
- 1Ug3 Use basic adjectives and colours to say what someone/something is or has.
- 1Ug5 Use basic adverbs of place, *here*, *there* to say where things are.
- 1Ug6 Use basic prepositions of location and position to describe *at, in, near, next to, on* to describe where people and things are.
- 1Ug7 Use prepositions of time: *on, in* to talk about days and time.
- 1Ug8 Use *with* to indicate accompaniment.
- 1Ug9 Use *for* to indicate recipient.
- 1Ug10 Use *Would you like* + noun to enquire.
- 1Ug11 Use *let's* + verb.
- 1Ug12 Use *like* + verb + *-ing* to express likes and dislikes.
- 1Ug13 Spell some familiar high-frequency words accurately during guided writing activities.
- 1Ug14 Use, with support, a simple picture dictionary.
- 1Ut1 Use the questions *What colour is it? What now?*
- 1Ut2 Use determiners *a, the, this*, *these* to indicate what/where something is.
- 1Ut5 Use personal subject and object pronouns to give basic personal information.
- 1Ut6 Use interrogative pronouns *which*, *what*, *where* to ask basic questions.
- 1Ld1 Understand some specific information and detail of short, supported talk on a limited range of general and curricular topics.
- 1Ld2 Use contextual clues to predict content in short, supported talk on a limited range of general and curricular topics.
- 1Lg1 Understand very short supported narratives on a limited range of general and curricular topics.
- 1Lg2 Recognise the sounds of phonemes and phoneme blends.
- 1S7 Take turns when speaking with others in a limited range of short, basic exchanges.

Language patterns

Grammar summary for teachers:

- **Adverbs of place:** Words such as *here* and *there* are adverbs, which describe where things are. The adverbs can be used in positive and negative sentences and in questions. The adverbs are usually placed at the end of sentences or after verbs. For example:

  The jeans are here.
  You put your glasses there.
  His shoes aren't here. Maybe they are there?
  Are my clothes here/there?

Unit A What can I wear?

Resources and materials

- Student's Book pp. 37–38
- Workbook pp. 82–87
- Audio files: Audio 37; Audio 38; Audio 39
- Photocopiable Masters (PCMs) PCM 24; PCM 25; PCM 26
- Real clothes to describe, if available
- Pictures of people wearing different clothes
- Prompt cards with the names of items of clothing

Key vocabulary

Clothing nouns: dress, skirt, jeans, sock, shoes, sandals, hat, jacket, jumper, coat, scarf, gloves, trousers, shirt, glasses, sunglasses

Verbs: wear, put on, get dressed

Adverbs: here, there

Lead-in ideas

Teach learners a chant relating to getting dressed. You can add verses too. *Put on Your Shirt* (**Audio 37**) is an example. Cultural sensitivity is needed for this topic to ensure no offence is caused by having children miming 'getting undressed'. (Use **Audio 37** if you are confident that it won't be culturally inappropriate. Alternatively modify it using different clothing items such as shoes, hat, coat.)

- Play a game with the class. Bring a bag of clothes to class. Learners take turns to pick an item out of the bag and try and name it. This could be a baseline assessment to check prior knowledge.
- Collect pictures of people wearing different clothes in different colours. Make a poster with the pictures or show them on an electronic device. Ask questions such as: *Who is wearing red/blue/yellow? Who is wearing a dress/sock/shoes?*

Script for the lesson

Introducing vocabulary

Teach or revise the names of clothing items that are familiar to learners first. Then teach additional clothing vocabulary. You can use the picture dictionary on page 37 of the Student's Book to revise and teach the names of clothes, or use real clothes and pictures you have collected. As appropriate, you can include words for items of clothing which reflect the local area/culture.

You should also teach verbs and expressions associated with clothing such as: *What are you wearing? Please get dressed. Put on your hat. Take off your jacket.*

Sounds

Use the names of clothing items to teach or revise initial sounds such as 'sh', 'sk', 'sc', 'bl,' 'cl', 'gl' and 'tr'. Help learners to recognise the sounds of these phonemes and blended phonemes.

Learners should be able to start decoding these words by focusing on the beginning sounds and vowel sounds, but do not expect them to be able to spell the longer words yet without support.

Introducing structures

Continue to revise the present continuous tense and let learners form and use the tense as often as possible when describing actions or pictures.

Teach or revise the preposition *for* to indicate a recipient (*This is for you*).

Some verb phrases are commonly used when talking about clothing. Examples include phrasal verbs and collocations such as *get dressed, dress up, put on, take off*. Teach learners how to understand and use the phrases. You do not need to explain the grammar.

Teach adverbs of place (*here, there*) to describe where things are. Teach these words in context. You could, for example, put clothes in various places and describe where they are.

Previous knowledge

Present continuous tense, colours.

Possible areas of difficulty

Phrasal verbs, such as *dress up, take off* and *put on* are tricky because words are used together to make a phrase with an idiomatic meaning. Do not teach too many of these yet – just a few that relate to the context. Learners do not need to know that these phrases are called phrasal verbs, or that they are idiomatic.

Activities

Select from these activities depending on the level of challenge needed for different learners, interest levels and what you have time to include. Supplement these with additional activities of your own and/or digital activities from the online resource.

▲ **1.** Let learners find *Clothes* in the Student's Book (page 37). Ask learners to find items of clothing. Tell them the name and ask them what the beginning letter is. Remind them that the words are arranged in alphabetical order on the dictionary page to help us find words more easily. Alternatively, make prompt cards with the names of the clothes. Hold up one card at a time, say the name and let learners find the relevant picture in their books. If culturally appropriate include some words for locally worn clothes.

▲ **2.** Learners match the names and the pictures of clothing in activity 1 in the Workbook.

▲ **3.** Teach the adverbs of place *here* and *there*. Use real objects and places in the classroom. (*The door is there. My bag is here.*) You can combine this with simple instructions for revision. (*Put the books there. Come here.*)

4. On the board, write five words that begin with double consonants. You can select from the names of clothing items (examples: *glasses, gloves, shirt, shorts, skirt, scarf, blouse*). Read the words with the learners. Ask them to say the initial (blended) sound of each word. Then read a list of other words that begin with the same blends. Ask learners to identify the initial sound and match it with a word you have written on the board. Write the suggested words on the board if they are correct. You could end up with a table like this, depending on the vocabulary of the learners:

glasses	gl-	gloves, glad, globe
shirt	sh-	shorts, ship, sheep, shop
scarf	sc-	skirt, scared, scan, skip
blouse	bl-	blue, blood, block, blow
dress	dr-	drop, drip, drain

(Note: *sk* and *sc* can sound the same, but the *sc-* in *science*, for example, is different.)

5. Learners complete the crossword puzzle in activity 2 in the Workbook. If they are not familiar with crossword puzzles, do this puzzle together to show them how it works.

6. Give each learner a copy of **PCM 24**. Give learners time to look at the picture carefully. They could also colour it in. Then let them listen to a short story about the picture, *Where Are My Jeans?* (**Audio 38**)

Learners listen for the main ideas in the story. After the story here are some questions you could ask to check listening comprehension:

Where is Sandi going?

Which clothes does she want?

Where are her jeans?

Where is her scarf?

Who helps Sandi?

What does Sandi wear to the party?

(Note: This activity also revises prepositions of place. You may want to revise them first.)

7. Let learners find the rhyme *Here Are Grandma's Glasses* in the Student's Book (page 38). Let learners look at the illustrations and say what they think the rhyme is about. Then read the rhyme aloud a few times, with actions. Teach the rhyme to the learners and let them use actions when they recite it.

8. Teach or revise the preposition *for* to indicate recipient (*This is for you*). Let learners listen to a short conversation first, *Is that for me?* (**Audio 39**) Then let them role-play the conversation in groups of three.

9. Learners work in groups. They take turns to mime putting on items of clothing such as a scarf, socks, shoes, a coat, etc. The others in the group have to guess which items they are putting on. Prompt them to make sentences such as: *What am I doing? You are putting on a shirt. You are putting on shoes. That's right. I am putting on a shirt. No, I'm not putting on a shirt.* This will help them to practise the present continuous tense, pronouns and clothing vocabulary.

10. **Link to mathematics*. Give learners copies of **PCM 25**. Then give them oral instructions to colour in the pictures. For example, say:

Colour the dress green and yellow.

The T-shirt has a yellow circle on it.

The jersey is brown.

The socks have stripes in three colours. [Explain what a stripe is if necessary.]

The hat is blue.

The scarf is pink, blue, yellow and white. It has a pattern. [Explain what a pattern is if necessary.]

11. Learners complete activities 3 and 4 in the Workbook. Let learners listen again to the story *Where Are My Jeans?* (**Audio 38**) before they do this. Then they draw clothes on the washing line as instructed.

12. Do further revision on initial blends such as 'sh', 'sk', 'sc', 'bl', 'cl', 'gl' and 'tr', using words in context as far as possible. Learners complete the words in activities 5 and 6 in the Workbook.

13. Read or reread the poem *Here Are Grandma's Glasses* in the Student's Book. Let learners identify the rhyming words in the poem. Explain what this means if the learners are not sure. After they have done this orally, let them complete activity 7 in the Workbook. Read the rhymes with the learners. They are all taken from rhymes, poems or songs that have been introduced earlier in the course.

14. Teach learners to play a chain game, which practises vocabulary and develops memory skills. The first learner makes a sentence or two short sentences. The next learner repeats the sentence and adds a noun. The game goes on until the learners cannot remember the whole sentence. The game could go like this:

Learner 1: *Go to the cupboard. Put on a dress.*

Learner 2: *Go to the cupboard. Put on a dress and a jumper.*

Learner 3: *Go to the cupboard. Put on a dress, a jumper and a coat.*

Learner 4: *Go to the cupboard. Put on a dress, a jumper, a coat and a scarf.*

Learner 5: *Go to the cupboard. Put on a dress, a jumper, a coat, a scarf and shoes.*

And so on.

15. **Link to drama and art*. Teach learners the expression to dress up. Then let them make up a story in which they dress up for a special occasion, like a themed birthday party or a school play, for example. The learners discuss what they will wear and then pretend to dress up. If you have access to costumes, let learners use real clothes to dress up. They could also make simple masks for this.

16. Learners work in small groups or pairs and compile a dictionary page of their favourite clothes. Let them choose about eight items. They need to name the items, draw them and put them in alphabetical order on a sheet of paper. These can then be displayed for others to read.

17. Learners can make up another verse for the rhyme *Here Are Grandma's Glasses* (Student's Book page 38). Write this frame on the board and help them to find words to use in the gaps.

    Here are ______ ______

    And here is ______ ______

    And here's the way ______ ______ ______ ______

    And ______ ______ ______ ______ ______.

18. Learners complete activities 8 and 9 in the Workbook. They complete the sentences with high-frequency words.

19. Learners can write a journal entry about their favourite clothes. They can draw pictures too. Perhaps they can write about clothes that they wear on special occasions. Let them write freely or let them tell you what they want to say. Then write a few simple sentences for them to copy into their journals.

Wrap-up plenary

Talk about traditional clothes that learners may wear for special occasions. Ask them to bring photographs if they can and to describe the clothes. Encourage learners to accept that people dress in different ways.

Talk about looking after clothes. Ask learners what they do to take care of their clothes. Discuss why we should take care of clothes. You can do this in a mother tongue and then summarise a few key ideas in English for the learners to remember. (Example: *Wash and iron our clothes. Don't tear them. Clothes are expensive.*)

Quick check

1. Learners can match words and items of clothing or pictures.
2. Learners can work in groups of six and play a listening game. Give each learner **PCM 26**, a sheet of paper that is divided into six numbered blocks. Learners take turns to describe an item of clothing for other learners to draw. For example: *Find block number 3. Draw a pair of socks. The socks are blue and black.*

Unit B At the weekend

Resources and materials

- Student's Book pp. 39–41
- Workbook pp. 88–91
- Audio file: Audio 40
- Photocopiable Master (PCM) PCM 27
- A few balls
- Sentence strips for the story *Super Ben*
- Prompt cards with names of days of the week

Key vocabulary

names of days of the week, weekend

activities that learners do at the weekend (go to visit family, play, sleep, clean, and so on)

Lead-in ideas

- Teach learners a rhyme or song about days of the week. *Days of the Week* (**Audio 40**) is an example.

Script for the lesson

Introducing vocabulary

Revise the names of days of the week. These are words that learners should begin to recognise and use. They should also begin to spell the words correctly, as sight words.

Introduce the word *weekend* (using the names of days that form the weekend in your community) and the phrases *at/on the weekend, at/on weekends, on Saturdays* and *on Sundays*. As the learners are not focusing on future forms, use the present simple tense and plural forms of the nouns to talk about regular actions. (Example: *We go to visit family on Sundays*.)

Sounds

Provide practice in recognising and using long vowel sounds (such as 'ee' and 'ay') in context. (Examples: *ay*: names of days of the week; *ee*: words such as *week, weekend, feel, tree, knee, me, feed*)

Help learners to pronounce and recognise the sound made by the letters *wh* in the question words that they will practise in this unit (*what, where, which*).

Introducing structures

Introduce and practise the question words *where, what, which* to help learners to discuss what they do at weekends.

Learners can practise using the present simple for habitual actions. (Example: *We play golf on Saturdays*.) Introduce verbs that relate to the real experiences of the learners in your class. They can also practise using prepositions of time and location, which have already been introduced.

Previous knowledge

Present simple tense, preposition of time and location.

Activities

Select from these activities depending on the level of challenge needed for different learners, interest levels and what you have time to include. Supplement these with additional activities of your own and/or digital activities from the online resource.

▲ **1.** **Link to physical education*. Take the learners outside and ask them what they can do with a ball. Ask questions such as: *Can you throw the ball? Can you bounce it? Can you catch it? Can you kick it? Can you spin it?* Invite some learners to demonstrate. Then give the whole group or class some instructions relating to catching, throwing, kicking, bouncing and spinning balls.

▲ **2.** Read the poem *The Bouncy Ball*.

Hold the ball, spin the ball,
Kick it at the wall.
Throw it up and catch it,
It's a bouncy ball!
Pick it up and walk around,
Bounce it on the ground,
Listen to the noise,
As it makes a bouncing sound!

Read the poem again and let learners mime the actions as you read. Explain *spin* and *bounce*. The learners listen to the poem and then join in with the words as you read it a few more times.

Then read the poem again and let learners identify the rhyming words (*wall/ball, ground/around/sound*).

Let learners name all the things they can do with balls (throw, catch, bounce, kick, hit, sit on, throw (or pass), spin).

▲ **3.** Learners complete activities 1, 2 and 3 in the Workbook. They identify the high-frequency words in the poem. Then they find the words that rhyme.

▲ **4.** Let learners find the story *Super Ben* in the Student's Book on pages 39–41. Let them look at the pictures and predict what the story is about, using the vocabulary that they already know. Ask learners if they go to a park on the weekend. Talk about how we dream about things that we want to do. Talk about superheroes and let learners tell you about the one they like best. Give some examples of your own and then let learners give some examples. (Examples: *I want to be Batman. I dream about flying. I dream about driving a big car.*) Don't worry too much about structures at this stage, but help with vocabulary as necessary.

Read the story or let learners read the story in pairs. You may want to pre-teach words such as *puddles* and *splash*. Encourage learners to look for context clues in the pictures.

▲ **5.** Learners who are struggling to read will benefit from using the sentence strips you have prepared for the story *Super Ben*. They match the sentences to the sentences in the story. Then cut up the strips and let learners build up the sentences again.

Learners can also use the sentence strips as prompts. Put them face down on a table and let each learner take a strip. (Make sure there are enough for the whole group.) Each learner takes the strip, reads it silently and then acts the sentence.

▲ **6.** Build awareness of words with long 'ee' sounds. Write some familiar words on the board, some with the 'ee' sound and some without (examples: *weekend, Sunday, feel, bee, tree, read, need, dream, me, draw, puddle, feed*). Then read each word aloud and ask learners to raise their hands when they hear the long 'ee' sound (as in the word *week*).

▲ **7.** Revise the names of the days of the week. Let learners sing a song or a rhyme that they know. Write the names of the days underneath each other on the board. Write the final letters *-ay* in a different colour. Ask learners what they notice. Let them say the words. Then ask if they know any other words with the same sounds (examples: *may, play*).

▲ **8.** Learners can complete activities 4 and 5 in the Workbook which provide practise in recognising phonemes.

▲ **9.** Introduce a discussion about what people do at weekends. Teach the word *weekend*. As you discuss this, use the question words *where, what* and *which*. Ask questions such as: *What do you do? Where do you go? Which places do you visit?* Prompt learners to reply using structures such as *I go to the shop at the weekend/on Saturdays.* Help learners to take turns during this discussion and encourage them to engage with other learners to extend the discussion. For example if one learner asks: *What do you do?* the answer could be: *We go out on a boat.* Another learner could then say: *Do you go fishing? Do you go on the river?*

● **10.** Learners work in pairs and interview their partner about weekends. They can take turns to ask questions using the question words *which, what, where.* Prompt them to extend their questions by asking questions based on the replies that they get to questions. Help learners to pronounce and recognise the sound made by the letters *wh* too. Examples:

What do you do on Saturdays?

I go to the shop with my Dad.

Which shops do you go to?

We go to the supermarket.

Where do you go on Sundays?

I go to my grandma.

Do you have lunch there?

Yes, we do.

Which TV programmes do you watch?

I watch [name of programme].

What's your favourite programme?

It's [name of programme].

Afterwards some of the pairs can report back to the class. They make sentences such as: *Mariam goes to her grandma on Sundays.*

11. Learners can work in groups and play a chain game. The first learner asks: *What do you do on Saturdays/ Sundays?* The second learner replies and then asks the third learner a question, and so on.

12. Learners work in pairs. They read and learn the poem *The Ball Song* in the Workbook. Let them perform the poem with actions in class.

13. Let learners find the story *Super Ben* in the Student's Book on pages 39–41. Let them look at the pictures and predict what the story is about. Let learners read or reread the story in pairs and then answer the comprehension questions in activities 6, 7 and 8 in the Workbook.

14. **Link to mathematics*. Learners work in groups and conduct a survey about what other learners in the class do at weekends. Some of the groups could survey what learners do on Saturdays and others could survey what learners do on Sundays. Alternatively, use the names of days that form the weekend in your community. Each group should ask ten people what they do. Give them sheets on which to write their questions and collect their answers. Then ask each group to report back to the class. You could give learners copies of **PCM 27** to record their questions and answers.

15. Show the learners how to make a very simple, short acrostic poem. Do this together on the board. You could choose a name or a familiar noun or verb as a starting point. Then get learners to suggest words to complete the poem. The words should have something to do with the letters that begin the poem. Here are some examples.

walk
eat
enjoy
kick

sun
happy
orange
run
talk
splash

16. Learners can complete activities 9 and 10 in the Workbook. You can do the activities orally with the class first before asking them to write sentences.

17. Learners can work in groups and tell others in the group what they do at weekends. They can then use this to write a story about a weekend. They can use the story *Super Ben* as a model, or you can give them a writing frame. For example:

On ______, ______ goes to ______ with ______.

He/She ______.

Then he/she ______.

Encourage learners to draft and then revise their stories. They can display them in the class for others to read.

Wrap-up plenary

Talk about what makes a good weekend. Encourage learners to suggest things they can do to relax, be healthy and help others.

Quick check

1. Write the names of the days of the week in a jumble. Let learners work out which name is which and then identify the days that are weekend days.
2. Learners can work in groups and play a telephone game. The first learner makes a sentence about something he or she does at the weekend. The learner whispers this to the next learner, who in turn whispers the sentence to the following learner. The last learner and the first learner say out loud what they said and heard.

Unit C How I feel

Resources and materials

- Student's Book pp. 42–43
- Workbook pp. 92–98
- Audio files: Audio 41; Audio 42
- Photocopiable Master (PCM) PCM 28
- Collect pictures, stories and other media texts about the weather
- Draw some of the symbols used in weather forecasts on a poster

Key vocabulary

feel, feelings (happy, sad, unhappy, bored, excited, lonely, cross, grumpy), friends, secret

Weather: rainy, windy, sunny, hot, cold, cloudy, stormy

Lead-in ideas

Learners can sing any familiar songs about the weather or about feelings.

The *Rainbow Song* and *I Hear Thunder* (**Audio 41** and **42**) are good examples.

The well-known *If you're happy and you know it* song is also a good song to teach learners for expressing feelings, and you can add extra verses as appropriate. Good versions of this song exist on the internet, and the words are provided below. Learners can do actions as they sing along.

If you're happy and you know it, stamp your feet.
If you're happy and you know it, stamp your feet.
If you're happy and you know it, and you really want to show it, stamp your feet.

Examples of extra verses:
If you're happy and you know it, *clap your hands*.
If you're angry and you know it, *blink your eyes*.
If you're sad and you know it, *nod your head*.
If you're sad and you know it, *turn around*.
If you're sad and you know it, *hug a friend*.

Script for the lesson

Introducing vocabulary

Revise adjectives that describe feelings and introduce a few new words as well, to allow learners to start talking about their feelings around friendships.

Revise or teach adjectives to describe the weather (*rainy, sunny, cloudy, windy, hot, cold, warm*). You can link the weather to feelings about the weather (*happy, cross, grumpy*).

Sounds

Continue to revise long vowel sounds 'ee' and 'ay/ai' dipthongs in context. Words from the texts in this unit that have these sounds include: *feel, tree, rain, again*.

You can also revise the end sound 'ee' in words such as *rainy, cloudy, sunny, windy, happy*.

Introducing structures

No new structures are introduced in this unit, but learners will practise using adjectives in short sentences. They can also practise using the present continuous tense in question, positive and negative forms.

Previous knowledge

Learners will have some understanding of simple questions and adjectives. They will also know something about the weather in their mother tongue.

Activities

Select from these activities depending on the level of challenge needed for different learners, interest levels and what you have time to include. Supplement these with additional activities of your own and/or digital activities from the online resource.

1. Start a simple discussion in class about the weather, if it's culturally appropriate to do so. (You may decide not to do this if children haven't experienced a mix of different kinds of weather.) Ask: *Do you like rain? How do you feel when it rains? Are you afraid of thunder and lightning? Why do we need rain?* Use any language for this initial discussion, but identify key words in English and write them on the board as you speak.

   Then teach the rhyming song *I Hear Thunder* (**Audio 42**).

2. Talk about the weather that day. (Examples: *I'm happy today. It's sunny and hot. I'm feeling cold today. Are you cold or are you hot? Is it rainy or cloudy?*) Read learners a simple weather report to introduce words that describe the weather. If you have pictures, let learners describe the weather in each picture.

3. Write the words *rainy, cloudy, sunny, windy, happy* on the board under each other. Write the last letter (*-y*) in a different colour. Say each word aloud and ask the learners what they notice. Ask if they know any other words that end with the same sound. Write appropriate words on the board (examples: *party, busy, noisy, lucky, friendly*).

   Learners could learn some of these words as spelling words. Alternatively, give learners words from the list of high-frequency words on page 7 of this Teacher's Guide to practise for spelling.

   Show the learners symbols that are used to describe the weather in weather reports and forecasts. Ask them to suggest what each symbol stands for.

4. Learners complete activities 1 and 2 in the Workbook.

5. Learners find the story (which takes the form of a rhyming poem) *Bob's Secret Hideaway* in the Student's Book. Let them look at the pictures and predict what the story is about. Explain the following words: *hideaway, moonlight, noise*. Then read the story aloud.

   Story: *Bob's Secret Hideaway*
   Bob had a secret hideaway
   That only he would know.
   He crept up there alone at night,
   to watch the moonlight glow.
   Then Bob invited all his friends,
   but all they brought was noise.
   So Bob decided not to share
   his treehouse or his toys.
   Now Bob was left alone again
   in his treehouse feeling sad.
   He found his secret was no fun
   without the friends he had.
   He heard a knock upon the door,
   and opened it a crack.
   He peeped outside and happily saw,
   that his friends had all come back.

   Ask a few questions to see if learners have understood the gist of the story. They do not need to understand every word of the story.

   (Note: The verbs in this story are in the simple past tense (which is very natural and common in stories). You do not need to teach this tense at this stage, just expose the learners to it.)

6. Read or play the story *Bob's Secret Hideaway* in the Student's Book. Talk about how Bob feels and how the friends feel. Refer to the pictures and introduce words such as *happy, unhappy, sad, cross, lonely, excited*.

   Learners could act the story about Bob's hideaway in small groups. They should pay attention to how Bob and the other friends feel.

7. Revise the long vowel sound 'ee' using words from the story *Bob's Secret Hideaway*. Write the

following words on the board: *treehouse, peep, feeling*. Read the words aloud and ask learners to say which parts of each word sound the same. Circle the letters in each word. Then discuss other words that have the same sound (examples: *see, read, be, bee, green, bean*).

8. Use the pictures you have collected, or use the pictures in the Workbook. Talk about the pictures using the present continuous tense. Then let learners practise in pairs, using the following conversation as a model:

Learner 1: *Is it raining?/Is the sun shining?/Is the wind blowing?*

Learner 2: *Yes, it is./No. it isn't./The sun is shining.*

9. Revise or teach *ai* and its sound 'ay' in context. Words from the texts in this unit that have these sounds include *rain* and *again*. Other words that may be familiar include *paint, snail, pail, nail, sail*. Learners can then complete activities 3, 4 and 5 in the Workbook.

10. Give each learner a copy of **PCM 28**. Reread the story *Bob's Secret Hideaway*. Let learners cut out the pictures on the PCM and put them in the correct order. They can use arrows to link the pictures and show the order.

Working in pairs, they tell the story to each other in their own words, using the pictures as prompts.

11. **Link to science*. Learners can make a weather chart for the week. Give them a template like the one below. They record the weather on the chart each day, along with a smiley or sad face to indicate how this makes them feel. Then, at the end of the week, they report back on the weather. They will need to use the simple past tense of the verb *to be* for this activity. Don't teach the tense – just give them examples of what they can say. (Example: *It was sunny on Monday, Tuesday and Thursday. It was cloudy on Wednesday and Friday. It was a happy week.*)

Weather chart

Monday	Tuesday	Wednesday	Thursday	Friday	Saturday	Sunday

12. Learners draw pictures and make simple sentences in activities 6 and 7 in the Workbook.

13. Learners can work in groups and make up a story about friends and how friends feel. You can read them another story about friendship if you have one, or spend a little time discussing what friendship means. Learners need to think about an incident in which someone made a friend happy or sad and use this as the basis for their story. They can mime the story and use words where they can.

14. Reread the story *Bob's Secret Hideaway*. Help learners to identify the words that rhyme in the story. Read a sentence and tell them which word is the target word. Then read another sentence and ask them to put their hands up when they hear the same sound.

They then complete activities 8 and 9 in the Workbook.

Ask learners if they feel like hiding away sometimes. Why? Does it make them feel better?

15. Learners can imagine that they are Bob. They write a journal entry about their hideaway. You could give them a writing frame, for example:

My hideaway

I have a hideaway. It is ______.

I go there ______.

My friends ______.

16. Give learners oral instructions to draw a picture. Use vocabulary and structures that have been introduced this year. Read the instructions slowly and repeat them a few times. For example, say:

Draw a house. The house is brown and white.

Draw a treehouse next to the house. The tree is brown and green. The treehouse is blue.

It is sunny. Draw the sun. Colour it yellow.

There are two white ducks under the tree.

17. Learners can work in pairs and play the game in activity 10 in the Workbook.

Wrap-up plenary

Talk about the importance of having friends and how friends make us feel. What do friends do to make us happy? What do friends do to make us cross or unhappy?

Quick check

1. Use prompt cards with adjectives. Hold up an adjective, say the word and let learners act what the words mean.
2. Write adjectives on the board. Call out an adjective, and let learners either come and identify the adjective on the board, or copy it into their exercise books.

Assessment

You can complete an oral assessment of the work done in this topic by:

- showing the learners picture of different clothes and let them say the names
- asking learners to make two oral sentences about favourite clothes.

Learners can also complete Progress check activities 1, 2 and 3 in the Workbook as a simple assessment.

You could allocate marks for these activities and record these as part of continuous assessment.

Topic 7 Our world

Overview

In this topic the focus is on the language which we use to describe the world in which we live – our homes, and the plants and animals with which we share our environment. There are opportunities to integrate activities with art, science and mathematics in this topic.

Units in this topic

Unit A: Homes
Unit B: Plants and animals
Unit C: Living in our world

Teaching focus

- 1Rg2 Recognise, identify, sound, segment and blend phonemes in individual words.
- 1Wo1 Include a full stop when copying very high-frequency short sentences.
- 1Uf2 Use common present simple forms [positive, negative, question] to give basic personal information.
- 1Ug1 Use common singular nouns, plural nouns [plural 's'] and proper names to say what things are.
- 1Ug3 Use basic adjectives and colours to say what someone/something is or has.
- 1Ug5 Use basic adverbs of place *here*, *there* to say where things are.
- 1Ug6 Use basic prepositions of location and position to describe *at, in, near, next to, on* to describe where people and things are.
- 1Ug7 Use prepositions of time: *on, in* to talk about days and time.
- 1Ug8 Use *with* to indicate accompaniment.
- 1Ug9 Use *for* to indicate recipient.
- 1Ug13 Spell some familiar high-frequency words accurately during guided writing activities.
- 1Ug14 Use, with support, a simple picture dictionary.
- 1Ug15 Sight read high-frequency words.
- 1Ut1 Use the questions *What colour is it? What now?*
- 1Ut3 Use interrogative pronouns *which, what*, *where* to ask basic questions.
- 1Ld1 Understand some specific information and detail of short, supported talk on a limited range of general and curricular topics.
- 1Ld2 Use contextual clues to predict content in short, supported talk on a limited range of general and curricular topics.
- 1Lg1 Understand very short supported narratives on a limited range of general and curricular topics.
- 1Lg2 Recognise the sounds of phonemes and phoneme blends.
- 1S2 Ask questions in order to find out about a limited range of personal information and classroom routines.

Language patterns

Grammar summary for teachers:

- There are no new structures to be taught in this topic. Instead, structures that have already be introduced will be revised and practised.

Unit A Homes

Resources and materials

- Student's Book pp. 44–45
- Workbook pp. 99–106
- Audio files: Audio 43; Audio 44
- Photocopiable Master (PCM) PCM 9
- Additional pictures of homes, including animal homes
- Prompt cards with the names of parts of houses, furniture
- Sentence strips with words from the texts in the Student's Book

Key vocabulary

Names of parts of a home: bathroom, bedroom, dining room, door, floor, garage, garden, gate, kitchen, living room, roof, window

Furniture: bath, bed, bin, carpet, chair, computer, couch/sofa, cupboard, curtain, dishes, fork, fridge, kettle, knife, light, pot, shower, sink, stove, table, tap, toilet

Names of animal homes: kennel, pen, barn, hole, nest, stable

Lead-in ideas

Read or tell the learners a traditional story or rhyme about houses. For example, *There Was a Crooked Man* (**Audio 43**). Explain if necessary that this is a fun rhyme and is not realistic.

(Note: rhymes can use tenses and words with which the learners are not yet familiar. This doesn t matter with rhymes, as even first language English children do not fully understand all the rhymes that they recite. The rhymes allow learners to become accustomed to the intonation and rhythm of a new language.)

Script for the lesson

Introducing vocabulary

Teach the names of different parts of homes and common furniture in homes as well as the names of the most common animal homes. You could use the picture dictionary on page 44 in the Student's Book or any other pictures or appropriate dictionaries you have available.

Teach the words that are used in your country. For example, some people say *sofa*, others say *couch*, others say *lounge chair*. You can also teach the names of the most common animal names. See the suggested lists above.

Sounds

Revise sounds in the context of the unit. You could for example revise the sound 'sh' in *shower, ship, dish*, the long 'oo' sounds in room, *broom, bedroom* and also in *door, floor*, or short vowel sounds in words such as *ship, sink, dish, bin, tap, sad, bed, tent*.

Introducing structures

The structures used in this unit have already been introduced. Revise any structures that your learners find particularly difficult.

Previous knowledge

Present simple tense, adjectives, pronouns.

Possible areas of difficulty

Some learners may live in different levels of housing or different types of homes. It is important that children should not feel bad if they live in a house that is very different from those of other children in the class.

Activities

Select from these activities depending on the level of challenge needed for different learners, interest levels and what you have time to include. Supplement these with additional activities of your own and/or digital activities from the online resource.

▲ 1. Teach the names of the main parts of houses and common household furniture. Use the page *Houses* in the Student's Book (page 44) or any other pictures, videos or dictionaries that you have available. You can let learners match words and pictures if you make prompt cards with the words you are going to teach.

▲ 2. Learners can label the pictures in activities 1 and 2 in the Workbook. They should use the page *Houses* in the Student's Book to find the words they need to label the pictures. This will help them to learn to use this page, which is like a dictionary page, as a reference source.

▲ 3. Learners find the text *Homes* in the Student's Book (page 45). Ask them to read the title and to predict what the story is about. You may want to pre-teach some of the vocabulary (*float, quiet, noisy, high*) or you can read the text with learners and let them try and work out what the words mean, using context clues from the pictures.

   Let learners use sentence strips to match with the sentences in the text. Cut up the strips into individual words or phrases and let learners make up the sentences again.

▲ 4. Learners find the following high-frequency words in the text and practise writing the words for spelling: *we, in, are, some, have, on*. Let them work in pairs to test each other.

▲ 5. Show the learners some pictures of familiar animal homes: kennels, pens, barns or nests, for example. You could even take learners to see some of these homes if there are any near your school. Teach the vocabulary. Ask learners why animals also need homes and what they make their homes out of. Then let learners work in pairs. Each pair makes a page for a booklet/table presentation on animal homes. They draw or find a picture and write a short sentence or two to describe it. (Example: *This is a nest. A [name of bird] lives in this nest.*) Assist learners to write simple sentences to describe what they have drawn or sourced.

▲ 6. Learners complete activities 3 and 4 in the Workbook, which revise adjectives (*big, small, noisy, quiet*).

▲ 7. Read learners the story *A New Home* or play **Audio 44**. Read the title and ask learners to predict what the story is about. Be sensitive to learners in the class who may have had similar experiences to the boy in the story. Discuss what happens to the boy and how he feels. Ask a few questions to check comprehension, such as:
   Why do the family have a new home?
   How do they get to their new home?
   Why is Sam sad?
   What does Sam like in his new home?
   Who is his new friend?
   What do they like playing?

   Learners can then complete activity 5 in the Workbook.

8. Teach or revise sounds in the context of the unit. Write some words with short vowel sounds on the board. Ask learners to read the words and say which words have the same vowel sound (examples: *boat/home; live/big; bed/tent; grandparents/sad*). Then ask them to think of other words with the same sounds.

9. Learners can complete activity 6 in the Workbook. They put words in alphabetical order and find words in a word search puzzle (activity 7).

10. Learners play a *Yes/No* game. Give learners prompt cards with the names of animal homes. Each learner reads the given card but doesn't show it to the rest of the group. The learner answers questions about the home and may only answer *Yes* or *No*. For example:

Is it big? No.

Does the word begin with 'n'? Yes.

Is it 'nest'? Yes.

11. Learners read or reread the story *Homes* in the Student's Book. Then they use words from the story to complete the sentences in activity 8 in the Workbook and then draw a picture of their own home or another home, in activity 9.

12. Let learners complete activity 10 in the Workbook, practising shapes.

13. Teach the learners about the sounds made by the letters *oo*. Write the words: *floor, door, room, broom* on the board. Read each word. Ask learners which words sound the same. Then write a short rhyme on the board and let learners decide which words to use to make the sentences rhyme. Example:

This is the floor

And this is the ______.

Take the broom

And sweep the ______.

14. Let learners listen to the story *A New Home* (**Audio 44**) again. Then let them complete activities 11, 12 and 13 in the Workbook. They copy the sentences from the story in the correct order. Then they tell the story to a partner.

15. Learners draw simple plans of their own homes. They label the pictures and then use the pictures to talk about their homes.

16. Learners write a simple story about moving to a new house. Discuss this with learners first and help them to plan their stories. You can draw simple word spiders on the board and add words as you discuss ideas.

For example:

Ask:

Where do you live? Where did you move?

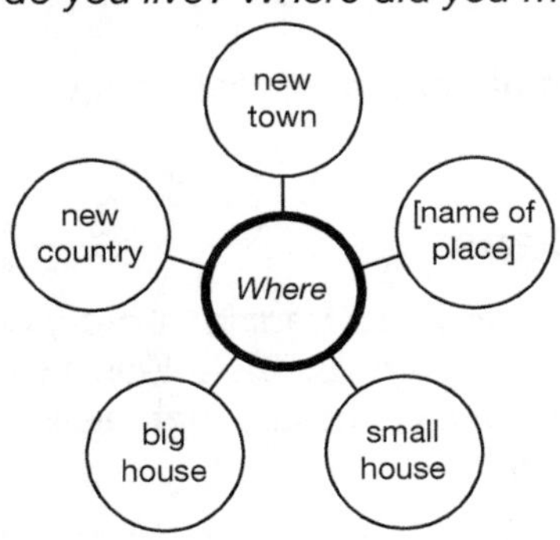

Ask:

How did you move?

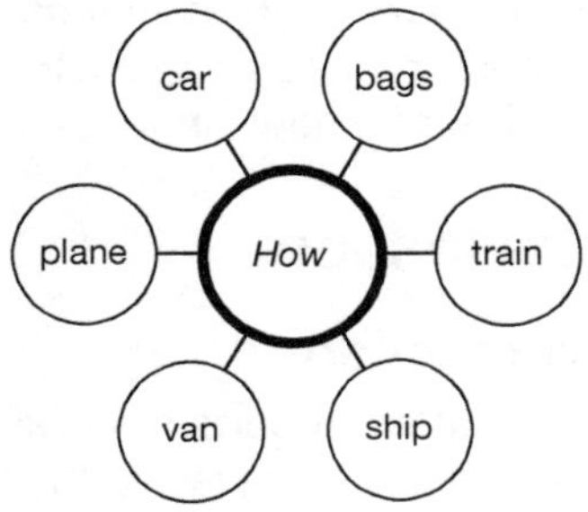

Ask:

What did you feel?

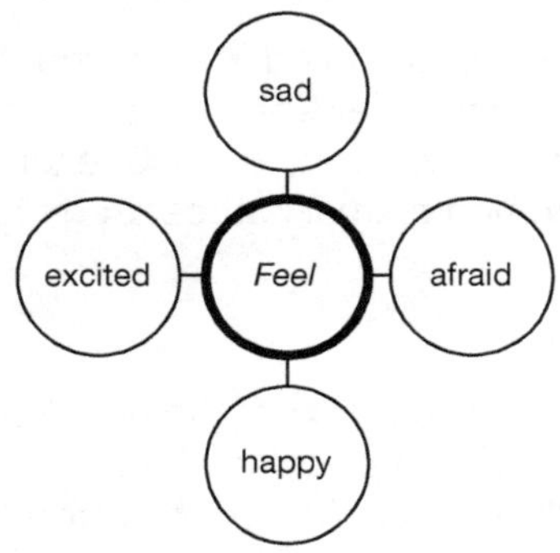

17. Read learners a short item of news about people who have moved from one place to another. The news should be a short item and quite simple. You can write it yourself. Read the news twice and then ask learners some questions to see if they have understood the main ideas (not the details) of the story.

18. Give learners an opportunity to write about their homes in their journals. They can write what they like (or don't like) about their homes. They can also mention the people who live in their homes. Encourage them to use adjectives to describe their homes too – colours, sizes – and to mention different rooms. Provide a simple writing frame if you want a structured piece of writing. For example:

I live in a ______ house. The house has ______ rooms. There is a ______ and ______. I live in the house with ______.

Wrap-up plenary

Talk about why people have to move from their homes. Who helps them? Why do they move? How do they feel? What do they take with them? Prompt learners to use some of the vocabulary they have learnt in this unit to talk about this issue.

Quick check

1. Give learners blank Bingo sheets (**PCM 9**). Let them choose 12 words from the picture dictionary-style page in the Student's Book (page 44) and write them on the sheets. Then play 'Bingo' in the usual way.
2. Learners work in pairs and describe rooms in a house. The partner has to guess which room they are describing. For example: *It is small. It has a bed and a cupboard.* (bedroom)

Unit B Plants and animals

Resources and materials

- Student's Book p. 46
- Workbook pp. 107–111
- Audio files: Audio 45; Audio 46; Audio 47; Audio 48
- Photocopiable Master (PCM) PCM 29
- Stories, pictures, videos about plants and animals
- Real seeds, seedlings and other plants

Key vocabulary

plants, roots, leaves, stem, seeds, flowers

Animals: domestic animals (cat, dog, goat, hen, duck, cow, horse, donkey, rabbit)

Lead-in ideas

- Tell any traditional story about animals or plants or play a video of such a story. For example, *The Little Red Hen* (**Audio 45**). If you tell a story, use gestures to help learners understand what you are saying.
- Sing a song about animals, for example, *Old MacDonald Had a Farm*. You can find good versions of this on the internet.

Script for the lesson

Introducing vocabulary

Teach or revise the names of the different parts of plants (*root, leaf, stem, flower, seed, trunk*). Link this with science lessons. Revise and teach the names of common domestic animals that are culturally appropriate. (Select from: *cat, dog, pig, goat, duck, sheep, hen, horse, donkey, rabbit.*) Introduce some wild animals in stories as well.

Sounds

Revise sounds in context. The short 'e' sound and the long 'ee' sound occur in the vocabulary of this unit (*red, hen, egg, stem; sheep, seed, leaf, wheat*). You could also do further activities around the long 'oo' sound (*root, moo, too*).

Introducing structures

No new structures are introduced in this unit, but learners will have the opportunity to revise structures such as *Me too*, the conjunction *and*, and the present simple tense within the context of stories and other texts.

Previous knowledge

Present simple tense.

Activities

Select from these activities depending on the level of challenge needed for different learners, interest levels and what you have time to include. Supplement these with additional activities of your own and/or digital activities from the online resource.

1. Learners find the story *Jack and the Beanstalk* in their Student's Books. The pictures tell the story but there are no words. Let learners look at the pictures and say what they think the story is about. They may recognise the story. Teach the word *giant*. Tell the story or play **Audio 46**. The story is told in the simple past tense on the Audio.

   Give learners copies of **PCM 29**. Learners cut out the pictures and put them in order. They use the pictures as prompts to retell the story.
2. **Link to science.* Refer back to the story of *Jack and the Beanstalk*. Teach learners some key words about seeds and plants while doing a practical activity (*plant, seed, grow, sun, water soil*). Show the learners some real seeds, bean seeds, for example. Ask learners what the seeds need to grow (*sun, water, soil*). Let learners plant some seeds in small containers. Find a sunny spot in the class for the seeds to grow. Learners water and observe the seeds. When they start to grow, teach the words *roots, stems* and *leaves*. Learners draw pictures of what they see and label their pictures.
3. Learners draw and label a picture of a plant in activity 1 and then complete activity 2 in the Workbook.

4. Teach or revise sounds in the context of the unit. Write some words with short 'e' and long 'ee' vowel sounds on the board. Ask learners to read the words and say which words have the same vowel sound (examples: *red, hen, egg, stem; sheep, seed, leaf, wheat, feed*). Then ask them to think of other words with the same sounds. After that, erase the vowels from the words and ask learners to complete the words.
5. Read or tell the story *The Very Big Carrot* (**Audio 47**). As a pre-reading activity, find out what learners know about carrots. Ask questions such as: *Where do they grow? What part do we eat? What colour and shape are they?* Learners can then complete activity 3 in the Workbook.
6. Revise and teach the names of common domestic animals. Play a game to find out what the learners know already. Write the first letter of a name on the board. Say: *I am thinking of an animal. The name begins with ['g'/'p'/'sh', etc.]. This animal is [small/big/brown/pink]. What is it?* Let learners guess and then write the name of the animal. Learners can play the same game in groups.
7. Tell the learners a story about a domestic animal. You can make up a story or tell a real story. You can also read any appropriate story about an animal that you think the learners will enjoy. There is a wide range of stories available on this topic. Then let learners try and share their own stories about domestic animals.
8. Spelling. Learners can learn the names of common animals for spelling. They should already be familiar with the short CVC names, so add a few more difficult words as sight words, for example: *hen, dog, cat, pig, goat, sheep, horse, rabbit*.
9. Learners listen to the story of *Jack and the Beanstalk*. Read the story or play **Audio 46**. Talk about the story, and any similar kinds of fairy stories they may know. Ask them to complete activities 4 and 5 in the Workbook.
10. In pairs, learners practise writing and reading more high-frequency words. Choose another set of words from the list on page 7 of this Teacher's Guide or choose words that the learners find difficult.
11. Learners draw pictures of animals and write short sentences to describe their pictures. Give them a writing frame for this activity. For example: *This is a [name] ______. It is a [size] ______ animal. It is [colour] ______ and ______.*
12. Tell or play the story *The Little Red Hen* again (**Audio 45**). Learners can work in groups and act the story. Encourage them to use conversation from the story while they act. This will provide practice in using the present simple tense, in forming and pronouncing questions and in using the structure *Me too*.
13. Learners listen to the story *The Very Big Carrot* again and then complete activities 6 and 7 in the Workbook.
14. Learners listen to a text about the life cycle of a bean plant (**Audio 48**). Let learners look at the diagram in activity 8 in the Workbook while they listen. Ask a few questions to see if learners have understood the main ideas of the text. Learners then complete activity 9 in the Workbook.
15. Read an animal story to the learners (examples: *The Hare and the Tortoise, The Lion and the Mouse, The Fox and the Stork*). You can read a familiar story or a new story. Let learners listen a few times. Then ask them questions to identify the main ideas in the story, such as: *Who are the characters in the story? What happens first? What happens after that?*
16. Learners can make a poster about animals or a picture dictionary page. The names can be put in alphabetical order with labels.

Wrap-up plenary

Talk about why animals and plants are important. Prompt learners to think about food supplies and how animals (including people) need plants to live. Then talk about why we need animals to live (*for food, to help us work*, etc.).

Quick check

1. Learners can play a chain game with the names of animals. For example:

   Learner 1: *I am at the farm. I can see a brown goat.*

   Learner 2: *I am at the farm. I can see a brown goat and two horses.*

   Learner 2: *I am at the farm. I can see a brown goat, two horses and a big cow.*

   And so on.

   Encourage learners to include colours, numbers and other adjectives in their sentences.
2. Take learners outside and let them identify the leaves, stems, flowers and roots on plants.

Unit C Living in our world

Resources and materials

- Student's Book pp. 47–49
- Workbook pp. 112–119
- Audio file: Audio 49
- Pictures and videos of natural resources

Key vocabulary

mountain, hill, river, seas, desert, jungle, North Pole, South Pole

branch, trunk, bark

Animals: fox, rabbit, mole, worm, woodpecker, owl, crow, bat, squirrel, wasp, beetle, ant, butterfly, caterpillar

Lead-in ideas

- Take the learners outside and identify a few different trees for them to look at. Help them to describe the trees using any words they know. They could also draw pictures of the trees and then label the parts of the trees after they have read the text *The Oak Tree*.
- Teach the learners any rhyme or song about a natural resource such as the sea, a river, a stream, or a mountain. *Row Your Boat* (**Audio 49**) is a good example. You can find good examples of the song version of this rhyme on the internet.

Script for the lesson

Introducing vocabulary

Learners will increase their use of adjectives to describe the weather and nature (*dry, wet, hot, cold, icy*). They will also learn more nouns relating to the natural environment (*mountains, poles, desert, jungle, fox, rabbit, mole, worm, woodpecker, owl, crow, bat, squirrel, wasp, beetle, ant, butterfly, caterpillar*).

Sounds

Teach and revise sounds within the context of the unit. The long sound 'ee' (*these, tree, leaves, beetle*) and various long 'o' sounds (*those, oak, mole, crow*) occur in the texts suggested for this unit. There are also beginning blends that could be taught/revised in words, such as *branch, tree, trunk, crow, squirrel*.

Introducing structures

There are no new structures in this unit but learners will have the opportunity to practise using familiar verbs in the present simple tense, as well as adjectives and demonstrative adjectives.

Previous knowledge

Present simple tense, demonstrative adjectives and adjectives.

Activities

Select from these activities depending on the level of challenge needed for different learners, interest levels and what you have time to include. Supplement these with additional activities of your own and/or digital activities from the online resource.

▲ 1. Learners find the text *The Oak Tree* in the Student's Book (pages 47–48). Remind learners about your discussion about why plants are important. Talk about why trees are important. Let learners look at the pictures and suggest why trees are important.

Read the text with the learners. There is quite a lot of new vocabulary in this story, which you can introduce slowly. The language structures in the main text, however, should be familiar.

▲ 2. Learners complete activities 1 and 2 in the Workbook. Read the story *The Oak Tree* to them again before they do this, or let them work in pairs to read the story.

▲ 3. **Link to science*. Read a simple non-fiction text about trees to the learners and then ask some questions to test listening comprehension. Use familiar vocabulary and structures. Write the name of the tree on the board and find a picture of the tree as well if you can. If possible select a type of tree which is locally appropriate to the learners and is recognisable to them. For example:

The pine tree
The pine tree is a big tree. It has lots of big roots and a tall trunk. It has long branches and thin leaves. Woodpeckers, other birds, and squirrels live in pine trees.

Ask comprehension questions, such as:

What is the name of this tree?

Is the tree tall or short?

What shape are the leaves?

Which animals live in the tree?

▲ 4. Spelling. Choose further high-frequency words from the list on page 7 of this Teacher's Guide. Alternatively, give learners a list of high-frequency words to find in the story *The Oak Tree* (examples: *this, these, lives, who, of*). Let learners practise and learn their spelling words in the usual way.

▲ 5. Talk about the weather and revise words such as *hot* and *cold*. Learners find the text *Our World* in the Student's Book. Take time to look at the photographs and find out what the learners know about the places shown in the photographs, as learners' experiences may vary. Read the text with learners and teach the new vocabulary. Help them to decode as many words as possible.

Make sentence strips with the text and let learners use these to match the text. Cut the strips out into individual words so that learners can build up the sentences again.

6. Practise high-frequency words. Write the words *can, be, is, at, in, the, and* on the board and let learners find them in the text *Our World*.

7. Learners complete activities 3 and 4 in the Workbook.

8. **Link to art*. Let learners paint or draw a picture showing a desert, a jungle, a mountain or a very cold place. Let them use colours and textures to show that they understand what the temperature is like in these places. Once the pictures are complete, let learners describe their pictures orally or write a sentence about the picture.

9. Learners read or reread the text *The Oak Tree* in the Student's Book. Then they complete activity 5 in the Workbook, matching vocabulary and pictures.

10. Learners read or reread the text *Our World* in the Student's Book. They extract all the adjectives from the text and make a list (*cold, icy*, etc.). These words can be learnt as spelling words. Learners can also use them to play a game in pairs or groups. One learner thinks of a place and describes it and the other learner guesses the answer. For example:

    I'm thinking of a place that is cold and icy!

    The North or South Pole!

11. Read a simple non-fiction text about a place in the world to learners and then ask some questions to test listening comprehension. Use familiar vocabulary and structures. For example:

    The jungle

    The jungle is a hot and wet place. People can live in the jungle. There are small plants and big plants in the jungle. There are lots of animals too.

    Ask comprehension questions, such as:

    Is it hot or cold in the jungle?

    What grows in the jungle?

    Who lives in the jungle?

12. Learners draw and describe a place they have learnt about. They can do this in activities 6 and 7 in the Workbook.

13. Learners read or reread the text *The Oak Tree* in the Student's Book. They work in pairs and ask and answer questions about the text. Prompt them to ask different types of questions. For example:

    What are these? [point to picture]

    Who lives in the branches?

    What is this?

    Where do the ants live?

    Do bats live in the trunk?

14. Learners complete activities 8 and 9 in the Workbook. They use high-frequency words to complete the story and then identify rhyming words.

15. Draw a substitution table on the board and let learners make as many sentences as they can with the words from each column. Use familiar words and structures. For example:

There	is	branches.
The tree	are	a trunk.
Animals	has	leaves.
	live	in the tree.

16. **Link to social science/geography*. Learners read or reread the text *Our World* in the Student's Book. Let them look at activity 10 in the Workbook, which has a map of the world showing where the places mentioned in the story are located. Explain that this is a map and check if they know where they live on the map (continent and/or country). Write the names of the continents on the board and let learners copy these into their Workbooks.

Wrap-up plenary

Continue your discussion about the importance of plants and animals and how we need to take care of these resources.

Quick check

1. Play a game of hangman or something similar, to revise new vocabulary learnt in this lesson.
2. Alternatively, write words in a word snake on the board, without space between the words and let learners come up and circle words that they recognise.

Assessment

You can complete an oral assessment of the work done in this topic by:

- showing the learners picture of different types of furniture and ask them to name the furniture
- asking learners to make two oral sentences about a house.

Learners can also complete Progress check activities 1, 2 and 3 in the Workbook as a simple assessment. You will need to read out the words in activity 1.

You could allocate marks for these activities and record these as part of continuous assessment.

Topic 8 Healthy bodies

Overview

There are opportunities to integrate language lessons with other subjects in the curriculum, such as health education and science. Vocabulary and concepts are developed by encouraging learners to express themselves using whatever knowledge they already have. Learners are encouraged to participate enthusiastically in activities to develop confidence in talking about matters that affect their health.

Units in this topic

Unit A: My body

Unit B: Healthy and sick

Unit C: Oh no! I am sick!

Teaching focus

- 1Rg2 Recognise, identify, sound, segment and blend phonemes in individual words.
- 1Wo1 Include a full stop when copying very high-frequency short sentences.
- 1Uf1 Use imperative forms of common verbs for basic commands and instructions.
- 1Uf2 Use common present simple forms [positive, negative, question] to give basic personal information.
- 1Uf3 Use common present continuous forms [positive, negative, question] to talk about what is happening now.
- 1Ug5 Use basic adverbs of place *here*, *there* to say where things are.
- 1Ug6 Use basic prepositions of location and position to describe *at, in, near, next to, on* to describe where people and things are.
- 1Ug7 Use prepositions of time: *on, in* to talk about days and time.
- 1Ug8 Use *with* to indicate accompaniment.
- 1Ug9 Use *for* to indicate recipient.
- 1Ug13 Spell some familiar high-frequency words accurately during guided writing activities.
- 1Ug15 Sight read high-frequency words.
- 1Ug16 Recognise that some sounds have more than one spelling.
- 1Ut1 Use the questions: *What colour is it? What now?*
- 1Ut3 Use interrogative pronouns *which*, *what*, *where* to ask basic questions.
- 1Ld1 Understand some specific information and detail of short, supported talk on a limited range of general and curricular topics.
- 1Ld2 Use contextual clues to predict content in short, supported talk on a limited range of general and curricular topics.
- 1Lg1 Understand very short supported narratives on a limited range of general and curricular topics.
- 1Lg2 Recognise the sounds of phonemes and phoneme blends.
- 1S2 Ask questions in order to find out about a limited range of personal information and classroom routines.

Language patterns

Grammar summary for teachers:

- There are no new structures to be taught in this topic. Instead, structures that have already be introduced will be revised and practised.

A My body

Resources and materials

- Student's Book pp. 50–53
- Workbook pp. 120–127
- Audio file: Audio 50
- Photocopiable Master (PCM) PCM 30
- Poster of a body with the main parts of the body labelled (these could be on detachable prompt cards)

Key vocabulary

Parts of the body: head, shoulders, chest, neck, arms, legs, hands, feet, back, bottom, tummy, nose, eyes, mouth, ears, skin, bones

Lead-in ideas

- Sing familiar songs about the body with the class. *Head and Shoulders* (**Audio 50**) is a good example.
- Play a game like 'Simon says' to assess if the learners can understand the names of the parts of the body. Give instructions such as: *Put your hands on your head. Touch your toes. Bend your knees.*
- Let learners work in groups of three to do this fun activity. Fold a piece of paper into three sections and explain that each learner is going to draw a part of the body, but without seeing what the other learners have drawn on other section of the folded paper. The first learner draws a head on the first top section. The next learner draws a body with arms on the middle section. The third learner draws legs and feet on the third section. Learners must not look at what the other learners have drawn until the three parts are complete. Then they open up the paper to see what they have drawn.

Script for the lesson

Introducing vocabulary

Teach or revise the names of the different parts of the body. Link this to science lessons.

Sounds

Revise sounds in context. The long 'ee' sound occurs in the vocabulary of this unit (*knee, see, feel*). You can also introduce the idea that some sounds have more than one spelling ('ee' for example, in words such as *read, seed, bead*). You could also do further activities around the 'sh', 'sk', 'cl', 'sl' sounds (*shoulder, shake, skip, sleep, clap*) and learners can practise the final 'ng' sound when they read the text *Hands*.

Introducing structures

No new structures are introduced in this unit, but learners will have the opportunity to revise structures such as adjectives and pronouns, the present simple tense and the present continuous tense within the context of stories and other texts.

Previous knowledge

Learners may already know the names of some parts of the body in English or in their mother tongue.

Possible areas of difficulty

For some learners it may be inappropriate to touch certain parts of the body in public, so be sensitive about pointing to parts of the body.

Activities

Select from these activities depending on the level of challenge needed for different learners, interest levels and what you have time to include. Supplement these with additional activities of your own and/or digital activities from the online resource.

▲ **1.** Revise or teach the names of parts of the body, using a poster and prompt cards. Let learners point to the different parts of their own bodies. They can also work in pairs and give each other instructions. For example:

Point to your neck.

Touch your legs.

Show me your shoulders.

▲ **2.** Learners label the picture in activity 1 in the Workbook.

▲ **3.** Give learners each a copy of **PCM 30**. They cut along the lines drawn over the body (not the body itself). They name each part and then paste the body together again on a sheet of paper. Afterwards they can label the picture.

Choose some of the shorter words and give them to the learners for spelling (example: *hand, leg, arm, head, foot, neck*).

Learners can then complete activity 2 in the Workbook.

▲ **4.** Let learners find the text *Bones* in the Student's Book (page 50). Read the title and explain what bones are. Find out if anyone in the class has ever broken a bone in their body. Read the text with learners, helping them to decode and recognise sight words.

▲ **5.** Learners work in pairs and look at *Bones* again. Then they make sentences about themselves. To do this they change the pronouns and possessive adjectives in the text. They also have to change the form of the verb *have*, as follows:

***I have** bones in **my** body./**He has** bones in **his** body./**She has** bones in **her** body.*

***I have** bones in **my** head./**He has** bones in **his** head./**She has** bones in **her** head.*

And so on.

Learners can then complete activities 3 and 4 in the Workbook.

▲ **6.** Let learners find the text *Hands* in the Student's Book (page 51). Read the title and ask learners what the text is about. Read the text with the learners, helping them to decode and recognise sight words.

Then make a list with the learners with verbs describing all the things we can do with our hands. Use the words from the text in the Student's Book and add more words. For example:

We use hands for *painting, pressing, printing, squeezing, building, climbing, eating, working, writing, counting, holding, cleaning, washing, cutting, sticking.*

Then use this list to revise the final 'ng' sound in the words.

Learners can then complete activities 5 and 6 in the Workbook.

▲ **7.** **Link to mathematics*. Let learners find the text *How many?* in the Student's Book (page 52). Read the text with the learners, helping them to decode and recognise sight words. Let them work out the answers to the questions.

8. *Link to science*. Teach or revise the names of the five senses, relating these to relevant parts of the body. Write the following sentences on the board and let learners help you to complete them orally:

I smell with my ______.

I see with my ______.

I hear with my ______.

I taste with my ______.

I feel with my ______.

Learners can then complete activities 7 and 8 in the Workbook.

9. Learners find the chant *Just Like Me* in the Student's Book (page 53). Read the chant to the learners, including actions as you speak. Then teach the chant, letting learners repeat after you and join in as they can.

10. Make learners aware that some sounds have more than one spelling. Use words with which the learners are familiar. Start with words that have the long 'ee' sound, but that are spelt *ee* or *ea*, for example: *read, seed, knee, feel, see, sea, clean, eat*. Write the words on the board or on prompt cards. Let learners sort the words into two groups, according to the spelling. They should read the words aloud as they do this. Give them some of the words to learn for spelling.

11. Learners read or reread the text *Bones* in the Student's Book. Then they complete activity 9 in the Workbook.

12. Learners read or reread the text *Hands* in the Student's Book. They make sentences about the things they can do with their hands. (Example: *I paint with my hands. I climb with my hands.*) Learners can then complete activity 10 in the Workbook.

13. *Link to art*. Learners make hand paintings. There are many ways to do this. Learners can apply paint to their hands and press their hands down on paper to create a picture or a pattern. Prompt the learners to talk about what they are doing as they work, to encourage fluency. (Examples: *I am making a picture. These are birds. I am making blue birds.*)

14. Learners learn or recite the chant *Just Like Me* in the Student's Book. Let them add their own verses to the chant, using the same structure and rhythm. (Example: *Stamp your feet, just like me. Say hello, just like me.*)

15. Talk about what we do with our senses. Talk about one sense at a time. Discuss which part of the body we use and what we actually do. Make a table on the board with the learners. For example:

Sense	Part of the body	What we sense
taste	tongue	food, drinks, sweets, medicine
touch	skin	animals, other people, tables, clothes
sight	eyes	everything around us, colours, people, places
sound	ears	noises (water, cars, animals, people)
smell	nose	food, fire, perfume

Learners can then complete activity 11 in the Workbook.

16. Learners read or reread the texts *Bones* and *Hands* in the Student's Book. Then they work in pairs and make a poster or a short booklet about a part of their body. They draw pictures and write simple sentences to describe their pictures. Walk around and assist as necessary. For example: *These are my hands. I have two hands with ten fingers. I paint and work with my hands.*

17. Let learners write a poem about their bodies or about their senses. Write a poem together on the whiteboard first. Put a writing frame on the board and complete it as you talk. For example:

I use my hands

for ______

for ______

for ______

I use my hands all the time!

I hear with my ______

And I ______ with my ______

I ______ with my ______

And I ______ with my ______.

Then let learners write their own poems using the same writing frame in activity 12 in the Workbook.

Wrap-up plenary

Talk about people who do not have all their limbs or their senses. Discuss questions, such as: *How does it feel to have only one leg? What can/can't you do? How does it feel if you can't see?* Be sensitive and affirming to learners in the class who have disabilities. For example: *Maria can't see very well but she can feel well. She has a very good sense of touch.*

Quick check

1. Play a game like 'Simon says' or sing the chant *Just Like Me* to revise the names of parts of the body.
2. Play 'I spy' to revise initial sounds and revise parts of the body. Learners could look at a picture or poster while playing this game.

Unit B Healthy and sick

Resources and materials

- Student's Book p. 54
- Workbook pp. 128–132
- Audio files: Audio 51; Audio 52
- Photocopiable Masters (PCMs) PCM 31; PCM 32
- Water, soap, basin for practical hand washing activity
- Pictures of healthy foods (from Topic 4)

Key vocabulary

put, wet, rub, count, dry, rinse, wash

toothbrush, toothpaste, soap, towel, water

Lead-in ideas

- Learners can sing songs about doing things that keep them healthy. Here is an example, which was introduced earlier (in Topic 1, Unit C). You can easily add verses to this song by changing the actions. For example:
  This is way we wash our hands, wash our hands, wash our hands.
  This is the way we wash our hands, early in the morning.

Script for the lesson

Introducing vocabulary

Introduce more verbs that the learners can use for giving instructions (examples: *put, wet, rub, count, dry, rinse, wash*).

Introduce nouns that describe common items needed for personal hygiene (examples: *toothbrush, toothpaste, soap, towel, water*).

Sounds

Revise sounds in context. You could also do further activities around the phonemes 'h' and 'sh', for example.

Introducing structures

No new structures are introduced in this unit, but learners will have the opportunity to revise structures such as adjectives and pronouns and the imperative for instructions.

Previous knowledge

Imperatives.

Possible areas of difficulty

The pronunciation of the letter *h* can be difficult, depending on the other languages that the learners speak.

Activities

Select from these activities depending on the level of challenge needed for different learners, interest levels and what you have time to include. Supplement these with additional activities of your own and/or digital activities from the online resource.

1. Use pictures or videos that you used in Topic 4 which show healthy foods. Let learners name the foods in the pictures and suggest which foods they should try and eat every day. Talk about water as well and introduce some simple comparisons. Ask questions such as: *What is better/healthier: water or a bottle of soft drink, cake or fruit?*

   Then talk about other things we can do to be healthy. Prompt the learners to suggest the following and introduce vocabulary as necessary: *exercise, sleep, work, wash, play, visit the clinic/doctor*.

2. **Link to science*. Ask the learners to tell you how they wash their hands. Then ask why washing hands is important. Find out what they know about germs from their science lessons.

   Then let them find the text *How to wash your hands* in the Student's Book (page 54). Ask: *What do you need to wash your hands?* Let learners find the information. Then read each sentence with them, helping them to decode words using their knowledge of phonemes as well as context clues.

   Demonstrate the correct way of washing hands, repeating sentences from the text you have read to make sure that learners understand all the vocabulary.

3. Read the text *How to wash your hands* again and then give learners copies of **PCM 31**. Learners cut out the pictures and put them in the correct order. They then give instructions to a partner about how to wash hands correctly, using the pictures as prompts.

   Learners can also complete activity 1 in the Workbook.

4. Teach or revise initial and end phonemes and blends in context. Let learners identify the 'sh' in words such as *wash, brush, push*. Learners may know other words as well, such as *wish, fish, dish*. Then ask them to identify words that begin with *sh* (*shoe, shirt, ship*). Write the words on the board and highlight the *sh* clearly so that learners begin to see the spelling patterns.

   It may also be useful to practise identifying and pronouncing words with *h* (*hair, hands, help*).

5. Write some sentences on the board, split across two columns. Let learners make sentences by joining words in the two columns. Do this orally. For example:

Wet	soap on your hands.
Put	the soap.
Rub	to 20!
Count	on a clean cloth.

Wet	soap on your hands.
Rinse off	your hands.
Dry your hands	your hands together.

Learners can then complete activities 2 and 3 in the Workbook.

6. Give learners copies of **PCM 32**. Learners choose the activities that are healthy from the pictures. They can colour in the pictures and cut them out. They can then make a poster of healthy activities with the pictures they have chosen. Help them to give their poster a title and to label the activities on the poster using the words in the box.

7. Make up a short series of instructions about how to clean teeth, or read out *How to clean your teeth* or play **Audio 51**. Let learners listen to this text twice. Teach the words *toothbrush* and *toothpaste* first, if necessary. Then ask questions. Afterwards let learners work in pairs. They can mime how to clean teeth and they can give each other instructions.

8. Learners complete activity 4 in the Workbook. They sort out the instructions and write them in the correct order. If they have not yet listened to the instructions about how to brush teeth, play **Audio 51** or read the instructions now.

9. Learners work in groups and give each other instructions about how to do something (examples: *wash and comb or brush hair, have a shower, wash hands, wash face, clean teeth*). The other learners act out the instructions. Remind the learners to take turns and to listen carefully.

10. Spelling. Write some high-frequency words from the instructions on the board and let learners find these in the text in the Student's Book (examples: *on, you're, the, put, hand*). Then let them practise the words for spelling.

11. Learners make instructional sentences with the verbs they have read in the text in the Student's Book (*put, wet, rub, count, dry, rinse, wash*). Here are some examples of sentences they could make orally:

    Put the book on the table.

    Wash your feet.

    Wet the soil in the pot.

    Rub your hands together.

    Dry your hair.

    You can write the sentences on the board or on sentence strips. Then give sentences or strips to the learners and let them read the instructions and act what the instructions say.

    Learners can then complete activity 5 in the Workbook.

12. Start a discussion with the learners about healthy bodies and what they can do to stay healthy. Explain that we need to do certain things to keep our bodies healthy. Play **Audio 52** or read the text *Rules for keeping healthy* to the class.

    Ask the class: *What other things can you do to stay healthy?* Accept suggestions and list them on the whiteboard. Ask learners to draw pictures of two healthy things they do every day. Once they have done this, ask them to talk about their pictures.

13. **Link to mathematics*. Do a survey to find out how many glasses of water each learner drinks every day. Learners can work in big groups. Give them a table like this to complete:

    How many glasses of water do you drink?

1 glasses	2 glasses	3 glasses	4 glasses	5 glasses	6 glasses	7 glasses	8 glasses
Total:	Total:	Total:	Total:	Total:	Total:	Total:	Total:

Let each group report back. They should make sentences such as:

Two people in the group drink three glasses of water every day.

Three people drink five glasses of water.

One person drinks no water.

Learners can then complete activities 6, 7 and 8 in the Workbook. Here they record how many glasses of water they drink each day over a period of a week. Then they write sentences about it.

Wrap-up plenary

Make a list of all the things that we can do to stay healthy and discuss other ideas that you have not yet covered.

Quick check

1. Learners sing the song *This Is the Way*, with different actions.
2. Learners can act healthy activities while others describe what they are doing.

Unit C Oh no! I am sick!

Resources and materials

- Student's Book pp. 55–57
- Workbook pp. 133–139
- Audio files: Audio 53; Audio 54; Audio 55; Audio 56
- Prompt cards with new vocabulary

Key vocabulary

headache, tummy ache, sore, fever, well, sick, cold, flu, hospital, clinic, nurse, doctor, vet, medicine, tissue, cough, sneeze

Lead-in ideas

- Teach learners a simple chant to describe sicknesses. New words can easily be substituted in this chant. *What's the matter?* (**Audio 53**) is a good example.

Script for the lesson

Introducing vocabulary

Introduce simple nouns and verbs that the learners can use to describe how they feel when they are not well (examples: *headache, tummy ache, cold, sore, fever, well, sick, flu, cough, sneeze*). Then introduce other relevant nouns, such as *hospital, clinic, nurse, doctor, vet, medicine*.

Sounds

Revise sounds in context. You could introduce the idea that words are not always spelt in the same way (examples: *bed/head, cough/off*). Sometimes there are also different ways of spelling words that sound the same (examples: *too/two, there/their*).

Introducing structures

No new structures are introduced in this unit but learners will have the opportunity to revise structures, such as the present simple tense (negative, positive and questions). For example: *I feel sick. I don't feel well. Do you have a headache?* They will also practise questions with *Do* and *Does* and learn new adjectives.

Previous knowledge

Present simple tense, adjectives, prepositions. Learners will also know about some symptoms and treatments for illnesses in their mother tongue.

Possible areas of difficulty

It is difficult for young learners to describe symptoms when they are ill. Illnesses may be dealt with in different ways at home, so be careful about recommending treatments. Focus on developing a basic vocabulary in English that will allow learners to describe symptoms to an adult.

Activities

Select from these activities depending on the level of challenge needed for different learners, interest levels and what you have time to include. Supplement these with additional activities of your own and/or digital activities from the online resource.

▲ **1.** Introduce vocabulary in the discussion. Talk about common ailments like colds, tummy/stomach aches and headaches. Talk about how we feel when we have a headache (tired, sore head), tummy ache (sore tummy, cramps) and a cold (headache, runny nose, coughing, sneezing).

▲ **2.** Teach learners a simple conversation about being sick. Play or read **Audio 54**. Ask a few questions to test comprehension. Then teach the conversation and let learners practise it in pairs. Pay attention to the intonation in the questions and the pronunciation of words such as *headache* and *fever*. When learners know the conversation, let them substitute other ailments and symptoms.

▲ **3.** Learners can act/mime different ailments and symptoms in groups. The other learners in the group have to guess what is wrong with them.

▲ **4.** Learners complete activity 1 in the Workbook.

▲ **5.** Learners find the story *In the Hospital* in the Student's Book. Discuss the pictures and title in the usual way. Introduce the following vocabulary in the discussion: *hospital, sick, accident, visit, sore*. Read the story with the learners, or listen to **Audio 55**.

Discuss what happened to Raj in the story. Elicit that he broke his leg.

Find out if any of the learners in the class have broken an arm or a leg. Ask them to describe how they felt. Ask questions such as: *What happened? Was it very sore? Did you have an X-ray? Did you wear a cast? Did you walk? Did you go to hospital?*

▲ **6.** Revise initial phonemes. Read out a list of words and let learners write down the first letter of each word. You could also ask learners to identify words with the same beginning sounds. Here are some words you could use: *hospital, headache, clinic, cold, cough, sneeze, sniff, sick, doctor, leg, fever*.

▲ **7.** Make two sets of prompt cards with the same new vocabulary words. Let learners use the cards to play a game in which they match the words on the cards in some way. Learners can play matching games with the cards. They can place the cards face down and try and find two cards that match, remembering where the cards are. Alternatively, they can play a game like 'Snap'. They mix up the cards and each take the same number of cards. Then they reveal the cards one at a time. The first person to say 'Snap!' wins the two cards.

8. Learners complete activities 2 and 3 in the Workbook to revise the present simple tense (questions) with short answers. You can do this orally with learners first. Complete the conversation with them orally first too. They need to use high-frequency words to complete the conversation.

9. Learners read or reread the story *In the Hospital* in the Student's Book (**Audio 55**). Then they complete activities 4 and 5 in the Workbook, using high-frequency words.

10. Learners find the story *Sam the Big, Bad Cat* in the Student's Book (page 56–57). Discuss the pictures and title, eliciting words they know and helping them predict what is going to happen. Make sure learners understand what a vet is. Read the story to the learners (or listen to **Audio 56**). Ask them simple questions as you read to test comprehension.

11. Revise prepositions of location and let learners listen again to the story *Sam the Big, Bad Cat* (**Audio 56**). They complete activity 6 in the Workbook.

12. Give the learners instructions to draw a picture. Use prepositions and familiar words. For example, say: *Draw a cat under a table. The cat is black and white. The table is brown. Draw three black pots on the table.*

13. Learners work in pairs and act the story of *Sam the Big, Bad Cat*. They should use conversation from the story and add their own words. For example:

    Sam: [groans and looks miserable]

    Tom: *Let's go to the vet.*

    Sam: *MiaaouWWWW!*

    Tom: *I see you. You are under the table.*

14. Learners listen again to the story *Sam, the big bad cat* in the Student's Book (**Audio 56**). They complete activity 7 in the Workbook.

15. Revise sounds in context. You could introduce the idea that words are not always spelt in the same way (example: *bed/head, cough/off*). As you read the words, write them on the board.

    Sometimes there are also different ways of spelling words that sound the same, for example: *too/two, there/their, hear/here*. As you read the words, write them on the board.

    Then write a few sentences on the board and ask learners to choose the correct words. For example:

    a) *I have too/two cats.*

    b) *There/Their is a cat in the cupboard.*

    c) *Hear/Here is my cat.*

16. **Link to science/health education*. Have a discussion about what you do when you are sick. How can you stop germs from spreading to other people? Prompt learners with these ideas:

    Go to bed.

    Cover your nose and mouth.

    Use a tissue.

    Wash your hands.

    Learners can make simple posters with the main ideas.

    Ask them how they feel when they have a cold.

Wrap-up plenary

Discuss what the children should do if they are feeling ill. They should ask an adult for help and never take any medicines by themselves.

You could also have a simple discussion about medicines (both traditional and modern) when they get colds and tummy aches.

Quick check

1. Use prompt cards to revise new vocabulary taught in this unit.
2. Let learners reread the texts in the Student's Book and ask each other questions.

Assessment

You can complete an oral assessment of the work done in this topic by:

- showing learners picture of different parts of the body and let them name the parts
- asking learners to make two oral sentences about how they feel when they are ill.

Learners can also complete Progress check activities 1, 2 and 3 in the Workbook as a simple assessment.

For activity 1, learners need to listen and number the picture in the Workbook according to your instructions. For example:

Number the drawing like this:

The head is number 1.

The neck is number 2.

The arm is number 3.

The leg is number 4.

The foot is number 5.

The hand is number 6.

The shoulders are number 7.

The tummy is number 8.

You could allocate marks for these activities and record these as part of continuous assessment.

Topic 9 Holidays and travel

Overview

In this last unit learners revise and practise what they have learnt during the year as they engage in activities to develop their fluency and confidence. There are opportunities to integrate language lessons with other subjects in the curriculum, such as social sciences, art and mathematics. Learners are encouraged to think about road safety when they learn about types of transportation and they are also encouraged to share and talk about their own cultural heritage.

Units in this topic

Unit A: My town

Unit B: A day out

Unit C: Holidays

Teaching focus

- 1Rg2 Recognise, identify, sound, segment and blend phonemes in individual words.
- 1Wo1 Include a full stop when copying very high-frequency short sentences.
- 1Uf2 Use common present simple forms [positive, negative, question] to give basic personal information.
- 1Ug1 Use common singular nouns, plural nouns [plural 's'] and proper names to say what things are.
- 1Ug3 Use basic adjectives and colours to say what someone/something is or has.
- 1Ug5 Use basic adverbs of place *here*, *there* to say where things are.
- 1Ug6 Use basic prepositions of location and position to describe *at, in, near, next to, on* to describe where people and things are.
- 1Ug7 Use prepositions of time: *on, in* to talk about days and time.
- 1Ug8 Use *with* to indicate accompaniment.
- 1Ug9 Use *for* to indicate recipient.
- 1Ug10 Use *Would you like* + noun to enquire.
- 1Ug11 Use *let's* + verb.
- 1Ug12 Use *like* + verb + *-ing* to express likes and dislikes.
- 1Ug13 Spell some familiar high-frequency words accurately during guided writing activities.
- 1Ug15 Sight read high-frequency words.
- 1Ug16 Recognise that some sounds have more than one spelling.
- 1Ut1 Use the questions: *What colour is it? What now?*
- 1Ut3 Use interrogative pronouns *which, what, where* to ask basic questions.
- 1Ld1 Understand some specific information and detail of short, supported talk on a limited range of general and curricular topics.
- 1Ld2 Use contextual clues to predict content in short, supported talk on a limited range of general and curricular topics.
- 1Lg1 Understand very short supported narratives on a limited range of general and curricular topics.
- 1Lg2 Recognise the sounds of phonemes and phoneme blends.

Language patterns

Grammar summary for teachers:

- There are no new structures to be taught in this topic. Instead, structures that have already been introduced will be revised and practised.

Unit A My town

Resources and materials

- Student's Book pp. 58–60
- Workbook pp. 140–144
- Audio files: Audio 57; Audio 58; Audio 59
- Photocopiable Masters (PCMs) PCM 9; PCM 33
- Pictures of key places in your own community
- Prompt cards with the names of places
- A very simple street map (3-D view)

- A collage of places you think the learners would like to visit in your country or community. Examples could include: a game park, a dam, a famous monument, an amusement park.

Key vocabulary

clinic, bank, police station, park, hospital, dentist, hairdresser, supermarket, library, school, shop, stadium, pool, bus station, mountain, hill, lake, river, sea

Lead-in ideas

- Take the learners on a trip around your town or community if possible and point out the key places (park, library, bank, stadium, and so on). Learners can draw pictures of a place that interests them. Help them to label their pictures. You can also talk about different types of transport as you do this, to prepare learners for the next unit.
- Sing any familiar song. For example, you could adapt the song *The Wheels on the Bus* to sing about what you do in places around the town. For example:

  (library) *This is the place where we read some books, read some books, read some books.*

  (sports centre) *This is the place where we play football, play football, play football.*

  (dentist) *This is the place where they check our teeth, check our teeth, check our teeth.*
- Teach a new song, *Getting Around,* or play **Audio 57**.

Script for the lesson

Introducing vocabulary

Introduce and revise vocabulary that will allow learners to describe important places in their own and other communities (examples: *clinic, bank, police station, park, hospital, dentist, hairdresser, supermarket, library, school, shop, bus station, stadium, pool, mountain, lake, river, hill*).

Sounds

Revise phonemes that learners find difficult. The texts in this unit allow for practise of final 'ng' (*fishing, playing*) and beginning sound 'w' (*waterfall, wood, walk, went*), for example. You can also continue to make learners aware of sounds that have different spellings (*ee/ea, ai/ay*).

Introducing structures

Revise and practise familiar structures introduced this year as the learners start to speak and write with more confidence.

Previous knowledge

Subject pronouns, present simple tense, structure *I like* + noun and *-ing* form.

Possible areas of difficulty

Some learners in the class may have travelled to many places and other may not have. Be sensitive to this during discussions about visiting places.

Activities

Select from these activities depending on the level of challenge needed for different learners, interest levels and what you have time to include. Supplement these with additional activities of your own and/or digital activities from the online resource.

1. Introduce and revise the names of places in a town. Use pictures you have collected or page 58 in the Student's Book, *My town*. Learners can match the words on the prompt cards to the words on the page.

   Let them work in pairs and talk about going to different places in *My town*. They say: *I'm going to* ______ and then they trace the path they would take with a finger.
2. Learners label the places in the town in activity 1 in the Workbook.
3. Revise prepositions of location with the learners. Do some total physical response activities. Give learners instructions with prepositions and let them act out the instructions. For example, say: *Put your heads on the desks. Put your hands under the desks.*
4. Then let learners talk about places that they like or dislike in the place where they live, using familiar structures. (Examples: *I like the swimming pool. I don't like going to the dentist.*)
5. **Link to cultural or heritage studies*. Show learners the pictures you have collected or the collage you have made of places people like to visit in your country. Discuss in as much detail as possible. Help the learners to name and describe the places using the structures and vocabulary that they know. Write new words on the whiteboard or on prompt cards so that the learners become familiar with them. (Example: *This is a game park. There are animals in the park. They are playing on the field. This is an amusement park. The children are having fun! This a statue of a famous person. He/She is a hero.*)

   Ask learners a few questions about the places that they mention. Why do people go there? Are they important places? Why?
6. Learners complete activities 2 and 3 in the Workbook. They draw a picture of a place that they like to visit. If learners are not sure of vocabulary, write words on cards and let them copy the words into the simple writing frame that is given in the Workbook.
7. Let learners find the text *A Day Out* in the Student's Book (pages 59–60). Note that this text introduces a high-frequency word (*went*) which is the past tense of the verb *go*. By this stage in the year learners will have heard some stories in the past tense but you do not have to teach the tense yet. It is enough for learners to recognise and use went as a high-frequency word. Let learners look at the pictures and say what the story is about.

Teach the word *bear* if this is unfamiliar. Read the story as they try to follow along.

You can use this story to revise words that begin with *w: wood walk, waterfall, went*.

8. Read the story *A Day Out* again. Let learners follow the route on the map in activity 4 in the Workbook. They can then trace the route in colour and complete the names of the places.

9. Tell the learners a simple story about a trip to town, you could use *Joy and Her Aunt Go to Town* (**Audio 58**). Give each learner a copy of **PCM 33**. Learners listen and number the pictures according to the order in which the person in the story visits the places in the town. Read the story twice and then check how learners have numbered their pictures.

You can reuse this PCM to tell different stories for revision or assessment later on.

10. Learners look at the story *A Day Out* again and then complete activities 5 and 6 in the Workbook, matching pictures and new vocabulary as well as completing simple sentences.

11. Look at the list of high-frequency words on page 7 of this Teacher's Guide again. Select words that learners haven't learnt for spelling yet, or words that they find difficult. Give learners a list of words to learn for spelling.

To test that the learners know how to use and spell these words in the context of simple sentences, write a few sentences on the board. Each sentence should have one or two words missing (high-frequency words, the spelling words you have given the learners). Learners copy the sentences. Then they listen as you read each full sentence. They fill in the missing words in the sentences. Here are some examples. The words you could leave out are given in brackets.

(My) brother (is) (with) (me).

(We) (went) (up) (the) hill (and) (over) (the) bridge.

(I) (like) bears (and) monkeys.

(You) (and) (I) (are) good friends.

(They) (are) going (to) (the) mountain.

12. **Link to art*. Learners can draw or paint a picture of a place that they like to visit. Display the pictures in the class and allow time for the learners to talk about their pictures to help them develop confidence. They should name the place they have drawn or painted and describe it – the colours, where it is, who goes there, how big/small/pretty it is.

13. Learners write in their journals. They write about a place they like to visit. Let them write freely using any words or structures that they know. Make sure the learners have an opportunity to read to you what they have written. This will help you to assess their progress and it will also build confidence.

14. Learners imagine that they go on a day trip. They go to a few places during the day. Talk about this first. As you talk draw a simple map of the places on the whiteboard and label the map. Then let learners try and draw a simple map in activity 7 in the Workbook. They should label their pictures and use them to talk about places they went to.

15. Make learners aware of more sounds which have more than one spelling. Here are some familiar groups of words that you could use:

long 'ee' sound: *see sea bee be me eat*

'ay' sound: *rain pain main day say play*

Write the words on the board or on prompt cards. Let learners sort the words into groups, according to the spelling. They should read the words aloud as they do this. Give them some of the words to learn for spelling.

16. Make up another story about someone who goes for a walk. Tell the story *Sanjay Goes to the Museum* (or play **Audio 59**) and then ask questions to see if learners understood the main ideas, such as:

Where does Sanjay go?

Who goes with Sanjay?

What do they see?

What does Sanjay like?

Then where do they go?

What do they do?

Ask learners if they enjoy going to a museum. Why do we have museums?

Wrap-up plenary

Talk about places of cultural heritage in a bit more detail. Help learners to identify and describe others places in the country that are culturally important.

Quick check

Give learners copies of **PCM 9**. Let learners make up Bingo sheets with the names of places. Write these names on the board for the learners to choose from: *clinic, bank, police station, park, hospital, dentist, hairdresser, supermarket, library, school, shop, stadium, pool, bus station, mountain, hill, lake, river, sea, museum.* Play 'Bingo' in the usual way.

Unit B A Day Out

Resources and materials

- Student's Book p. 61
- Workbook pp. 145–150
- Audio files: Audio 60; Audio 61
- Photocopiable Master (PCM) PCM 34
- Pictures of different methods of transport (boat, ship, train, car, scooter, rickshaw, plane, bicycle, helicopter, train, bus, taxi, and so on)
- Pictures of a few common road signs and markings (stop, pedestrian crossing, green traffic light)
- Prompt cards with the names of different types of transport that you will be teaching
- Paper and crayons/paints to paint or draw
- Paper to make a folded (origami) boat

Key vocabulary

boat, ship, train, car, scooter, rickshaw, plane, bicycle (bike), helicopter, train, bus, taxi

Lead-in ideas

- Take the class outside if you can. Tell them to close their eyes and listen carefully. What sounds do they hear? Can they hear cars? buses? trains? animals? Let them describe everything they hear. Then ask them to open their eyes and name all the things they can see that people use for getting around or for moving things around.
- Teach or sing a song about a means of transport. For example, you could teach *The Wheels on the Bus Go Round and Round*. There are some good versions of this on the internet.

Script for the lesson

Introducing vocabulary

Teach or revise names of all common means of transport. Pay particular attention to types of transport that learners in your class use. Ask learners what they call these types of transport and help them to make the links to the English words by using pictures or videos.

Sounds

Revise phonemes that learners find difficult.

Introducing structures

Revise and practise familiar structures introduced this year as the learners start to speak and write with more confidence. There are opportunities to revise and extend the learners' knowledge of common adjectives as well as singular and plural forms in this unit.

Previous knowledge Learners will know words that describe types of transportation in their mother tongue. Some of these words may also be commonly used by people when they are speaking English.

Activities

Select from these activities depending on the level of challenge needed for different learners, interest levels and what you have time to include. Supplement these with additional activities of your own and/or digital activities from the online resource.

1. Use the pictures you have collected and the prompt cards to teach the names of different types of transport. Help learners to read the names on the cards by sounding out some of the phonemes they recognise in the names. Some words will be easy to sound out. Longer words such as *helicopter* can be read more easily if they are broken down into syllables: *he/li/cop/ter*.
2. Let learners play a game. Display a selection of pictures of types of transport. Then place the matching prompt cards on a table, face down. Learners take turns to choose a card, turn it over and read it and then match it to a picture.
3. Learners complete activity 1 in the Workbook, matching the pictures and the words.
4. Ask learners to think about how many wheels each different type of transport has. They can group the pictures you have collected according to the number of wheels. Then they make sentences. For example: These have got two wheels. They have got four wheels.
5. Revise common adjectives such as *big/small*, numbers and colour words, relating these to the pictures you have collected. Let learners make sentences such as: *This bus is big. The yellow taxi is small. The blue bus has six wheels*.

   Learners complete activities 2, 3 and 4 in the Workbook. They follow the instructions to colour in and draw pictures.
6. Revise singular and plural forms of nouns. Write the following on the board in a table or chart. Then ask the learners to suggest what we say when we have more than one. Write the plural words on the chart as you speak.

One	More than one
train	trains
car	
taxi	
plane	
scooter	
bike	

   You could also teach the plural of *bus* (*buses*) as it is quite common.

   Learners can make sentences with the plural words too. (*There are three trains at the station. There are two cars under the tree.*)
7. Learners complete activities 5 and 6 in the Workbook to revise plural forms.

8. **8.** *Link to art*. Learners can make posters about types of transport. They can collect pictures and paste them together to make a collage or they can paint and draw their own pictures. Alternatively let learners use soft wire to make small cars or boats or bicycles.

9. *Link to civics*. Ask the learners to show you how to cross a road safely. Discuss this. Take the class outside and use chalk to draw an imaginary road on the ground. Make sure they know what is safe and what is not safe. Teach vocabulary as necessary as you do this.

10. Teach the rhyme *Stop! Look! Listen!* about road safety (or play **Audio 60**). Let learners act as they recite the rhyme.

Discuss this question with the class: *What else can you do to be safe on the street?* Talk about safe places to cross roads at traffic lights and pedestrian crossings. Talk about holding hands with an adult or friends as well.

11. Let learners find the story *At the Bus Station* in the Student's Book (page 61). Let them read the title and then look at the pictures and discuss them. Let them predict what they think the story is about. Encourage them to read in pairs, if you feel they are able to do this. Then read the story to them (or play **Audio 61**).

12. Learners read the story *At the Bus Station* again in pairs. Then they complete activity 7 in the Workbook.

13. Talk about road safety again. Let learners sing any road safety song that they know (for example, *Stop! Look! Listen!* **Audio 60**). Help learners make up their own poems about road safety. Brainstorm some words to use and write these on a word spider. Learners can use the words from the word spider to make a poem.

14. Revise any sounds that you feel need additional practice. Help learners to pronounce the short and long vowel sounds in the words correctly (examples: *boat/float/coat, ship/trip/pip, train/plane/pain*).

15. Give learners a list of high-frequency words and let them find the words in the story *At the Bus Station*. Then let them complete activities 8 and 9 in the Workbook.

16. Give learners copies of **PCM 34**. Read the instructions with them and help them to make a simple boat by folding a piece of paper.

17. Ask learners how they get to school. Let them make short sentences. Teach them to use the correct prepositions in their sentences. (Examples: *I come by car/by taxi/by bus/on foot.*)

18. Learners complete activity 10 in the Workbook. They look at the graph and answer the questions.

Wrap-up plenary

Talk to the class again about road safety. Talk about wearing seat belts in cars and taxis, wearing helmets when riding bikes and wearing life vests in boats. You can do this in a mother tongue and then write a few simple sentences in English afterwards to help the learners remember. For example: *Wear a helmet. Wear a seatbelt. Wear a life vest. Be careful!*

Quick check

1. Let learners match prompt cards and pictures with the names of types of transport.
2. To test that learners know how to use and spell high-frequency words and other common vocabulary words in the context of simple sentences, write a few sentences on the board. Each sentence should have one word missing (a high-frequency word, one of the spelling words you have given the learners). Learners copy the sentences. Then they listen as you read each full sentence. They fill in the missing words in the sentences.

   Here are some sentences you could use. Leave out one word (or two words depending on the level of the class) in each sentence.

   She is in the boat.

   They come to school by car.

   The ship is in the water.

   There are three boys in the bus.

Unit C Holidays

Resources and materials

- Student's Book pp. 62–63
- Workbook pp. 151–154
- Audio files: Audio 62; Audio 63
- A globe or map of the world (or of your own country)

Key vocabulary

holidays, Africa, China, India

Revise vocabulary that has been introduced this year:

transport such as train, bus, plane, car, boat

activities such as read, play, visit, travel, go, work, swim

Lead-in ideas

Teach the learners a chant about holidays. *Hip Hip Hooray!* is a good example (**Audio 62**).

Script for the lesson

Introducing vocabulary

Introduce and teach the names of a few places (countries/continents) that have relevance to the learners in your class. Revise the names of places already introduced (such as *park, sea, mountains, town*).

Sounds

Revise phonemes that the class find difficult to read or pronounce.

Introducing structures

Revise the following structures:

Let's + verb

Questions that begin with *What, Where* and *Which*

Prepositions of location and position and time (*at, in, near, next to, on*); prepositions of time (*on, in*)

Adverbs of place (*here/there*)

The present simple tense of familiar verbs

Like + verb ending in *–ing*

Previous knowledge

Some learners will know about other parts of the world because they have travelled there.

Activities

Select from these activities depending on the level of challenge needed for different learners, interest levels and what you have time to include. Supplement these with additional activities of your own and/or digital activities from the online resource.

▲ **1.** Have a discussion with the class about the holidays. Talk about what people do during the holidays. As you do this, make a list of activities. Write the words on the board and help the class to make sentences with the words using structures that have been introduced this year. (Examples: *We like fishing. I play with my cousins. We paint the house.*)

▲ **2.** Learners work in groups and talk about all the things they want to do in the holidays. Play or read the following conversation and prompt the learners to use the same structures in their discussion.

A: *Where can we go?*

B: *Let's go to the park.*

C: *What can we do?*

D: *Let's make a house.*

▲ **3.** **Link to social sciences*. Show the learners a globe or a simple map of the world. Show them where they live and introduce the names of a few continents or neighbouring countries. Use sentences such as *This is Africa. Dubai is here. Mumbai is there* as you do this. Let the class talk about countries that they may know and point out those places on the globe or map. Help learners to read the names of a few places.

▲ **4.** Let learners find the story *Around the World* in the Student's Book (pages 62–63). Let them look at the pictures and then say what they think the story is about. Then read the story with them or let them read the story in pairs.

Ask questions about each page. This will allow the learners to use vocabulary that has been introduced during the year. For example:

Where are they? (up in the sky, on the sea, in a plane, in a boat, in the desert, in the snow/ice)

What do they see in Africa? (animals, a river, trees, houses)

What do they see in India? (people, cars, patterns, colours)

What do they see in China? (boats, houses, buildings, kites)

Who do they see at home? (family, cousins mother, aunty)

▲ **5.** Learners complete activities 1 to 4 in their Workbooks.

● **6.** Learners complete activity 5 in the Workbook.

● **7.** Make up a simple story about the holidays. Tell or play the story *Lee and Sue Go to India* to the learners (**Audio 63**) and ask questions to see if they understand the main ideas, such as:

Where are Lee and Sue going?

Who are they visiting?

How long is the trip?

On which day do they leave?

On which day do they arrive in India?

● **8.** Learners complete activities 6 and 7 in the Workbook. They should read or reread the story *Around the World* on pages 62–63 of the Student's Book before they do this.

● **9.** Learners can write a holiday diary. Before they go on holiday, let them write down a few things that they want to do.

● **10.** Learners complete activity 8 in the Workbook.

● **11.** Use some of the prompt cards you have made this year. Choose about 20 words and make duplicates of these cards. Let learners work in small groups and use the cards to play a game. They place all the cards face down on a table. Then each learner has a turn to pick two cards. The aim is to find two matching cards.

The learner has to read the words on the cards that he or she picks up. The other learners can help. If the words are not the same, the cards are put back in exactly the same place and the next learner gets a turn. If the cards do match, the learner who matched the cards gets another turn. The learner with the most pairs of words wins the game.

12. **Link to art*. Talk about special celebrations that may occur during the school holidays. Focus on a celebration that many learners will take part in. This could be a religious or cultural celebration or, perhaps, a birthday celebration. Talk about what everyone will do, what they will wear and what they will eat and drink. Learners can work in groups and make a poster about the celebration. Help them to give the poster a heading. Each child in the group should contribute a picture, poem or a few sentences to the poster. Display the posters in the class afterwards and let the groups talk about their posters.

Wrap-up plenary

Talk about the year you have had together in Stage 1. Ask learners what they have enjoyed doing and what they have learnt.

Review Activity Guidelines

There is a Review Activity on pages 121–123 of this Teacher's Guide which you can use at the end of Stage 1 to monitor progress in an informal way. (Please note that there is no allocated mark scheme and it is not intended that performance in this review activity equates in any way with Cambridge grades or levels.)

Print out some copies of the review activity for the learners. Permission is granted by the Publisher for the photocopying of these pages.

- **Part 1** (the listening section) requires you to read out instructions as supplied below.
- **Part 2** (the reading and writing section) can be done individually, or collaboratively if you feel learners are not ready to work individually.
- **Part 3** (the speaking section) needs to be done in small groups of learners, with you guiding them through it orally.

Use the guidelines below to prepare for each section. We would recommend that the review activity should be kept informal and enjoyable so learners don't feel anxious. It is not intended that this review activity should be used for summative assessment, but only as a tool to gauge general progress. Depending on the class, you may decide to go through the review activity and to discuss the answers together, so it becomes a collaborative activity.

Part 1: Listening

- Ask learners to listen carefully and then tick one of the boxes in question 1.

  Read out sentence (a): The ball is under the table.

  Repeat it once. Give the class a minute or so to tick the correct box (the second one). You may like to demonstrate how to tick inside a box, so they clearly understand what to do.
- Read out sentence (b): The ball is in the box.

  Repeat it once. Give the class a minute or so to tick the correct box (the first one). If they still don't understand what to do you could demonstrate.
- Give the learners colouring pencils. Tell them to look at the picture and listen carefully. Read the following text two or three times: The house has a green roof and a blue door. There is a red heart on the door.

  Let learners colour the items to match your description. Monitor them as they start to colour to ensure every learner is using the right colour for the roof, door and heart. Support them as needed so that they get this right.
- Allow learners to finish off the rest of the colouring using whatever colours they like.

Part 2: Reading and writing

Give learners 10–15 minutes to complete this section. If learners are not ready to complete this part individually they can work together in pairs, or this section can be done collaboratively as a class, led and directed by you.

Answer key:

1 a) yes b) no c) no d) no e) no f) yes

2 a) He is jumping.

b) They are cooking.

c) He is kicking a ball.

d) They are reading.

Part 3: Speaking

Use the picture to have a question and answer session with learners. If possible, work in small groups with the learners. Make sure you go around and include everyone in the discussions and keep the atmosphere fun, relaxed and collaborative so that they have natural curiosity and interest in the activity, and so they don't feel stressed or worried. Start by pointing to objects in the picture. Ask learners to say what you are pointing to. Encourage them to help each other if some cannot remember words. Also name some items yourself and ask learners to point to them.

Ask questions which include numbers, activities/games and prepositions (position of objects) as well as to elicit preferences from learners. Some suggestions for questions include:

- How many people are sitting on the bench? (two)
- How many children are in the tree? (one)
- Point to the boy behind the bush and ask: What is this boy doing? (hiding behind a bush)
- Where is the boy with the cap? (next to/behind the bin)
- How many children are playing hide and seek? Which game would you like to play?
- Do you play any of these games?
- Tell me about your favourite game. How do you play it?

Audio scripts

Topic 1

Audio 1

Song: ***Hello***

Hello [Ali]. Hello [Ali].
How are you? How are you?
Very well, thank you.
Very well, thank you.
How about you?

Audio 2

Rhyme: ***Two Little Dicky Birds***

Two little dicky birds
Sitting on a wall
One named Peter, one named Paul
Fly away Peter, fly away Paul
Come back Peter, come back Paul.

Audio 3

Song: ***An Alphabet Song***

A B C D E F G
Can you do this? Look at me!

H I J K L M N
This is my bag and that's my pen!

O P Q R S T
These are things I take to school you see.

U V W X Y and Z
And this is my favourite colour - red!

Audio 4

Story: ***A Game***

Teacher: What is on the table?
Boy 1: A book.
Girl 1: A ruler.

Teacher: Yes, Well done. And …?
Boy 2: A cat.

Teacher: No! Try again.
Girl 2: A pen, a pencil and a box of crayons.
Boy 3: A clock, an eraser and a lunchbox.

Girl 1: Scissors and glue.
Teacher: That's right, Well done.

Audio 5

Song: ***This Is the Way We Go to School***

This is the way we go to school,
go to school, go to school.
This is the way we go to school
early in the morning.

First we smile and say hello,
say hello, say hello.
First we smile and say hello
as we go into the classroom.

Then we work and sing and talk,
sing and talk, sing and talk.
Then we work and sing and talk
with our friends in the classroom.

Then at break we play outside,
play outside, play outside.
Then at break we play outside
with our friends on the playground.

Audio 6

Story: ***Time for School***

Time for school, so here I come.
Hello teachers. Bye-bye, Mom.

Hello friends - another day
Hours and hours to work and play.

Books to read and sums to do.
Stories, painting pictures too.

When the bell rings, we go out.
Run around and laugh and shout.

Then back in through the classroom door.
We're quiet again. We work some more.

We sing, we clap, we stamp our feet.
And then at last, it's time to eat.

More play, more work, all afternoon.
I'm tired. Is it home time soon?

Half past three. Home time has come.
Bye, bye teacher. Hello Mom.

Topic 2

Audio 7

Song: ***This Is Me***

I am special. I am special,
Yes, I am. Yes, I am.
A very special person, a very special person.
Yes, I am. Yes, I am.

You are special. You are special.
Yes, you are. Yes, you are.
A very special person, a very special person.
That is you. That is you.
Yes, you are. Yes, you are.

(Also: *He is special. She is special. We are special. They are special*.)

Audio 8

Chant: *A Family*

This is a family *[hold up one hand, fingers spread]*

Let's count them and see,
How many there are,
And who they can be? *[count 1, 2, 3, 4, 5]*
This is the mother *[touch pointer finger]*
Who loves everyone
And this is the aunty *[touch big finger]*
Who is lots of fun.
This is my sister *[touch ring finger]*
She helps and she plays,
And this is my cousin *[touch little finger]*
He's growing each day.
But who is this one? *[touch thumb]*
He's out there alone,
Why it's my brother, Sam
And he's eating as usual – bread and lots of jam!
[wiggle thumb]

Audio 9

Poem: *This Is My Family*

This is my mother, kind and dear. *[make a fist and point to your thumb]*
This is my father sitting near. *[show each finger in turn]*
This is my brother strong and tall.
This is my sister, who plays with her ball.
This is the baby, littlest of all.
See my whole family large and small. *[wiggle all the fingers]*

Audio 10

Song: *The Father's in the House*

[sing to the tune of *The Farmer's in his Den*]

The father's in the house
The father's in the house
Hi-ho, the derry-o
The father's in the house.

The father marries a wife
The father marries a wife
Hi-ho, the derry-o
The father marries a wife.

And the wife has a child
The wife has a child
Hi-ho, the derry-o
The wife has a child.

And the child gets a sister
The child gets a sister
Hi-ho, the derry-o
The child gets a sister.

And the children get a cat
The children get a cat
Hi-ho, the derry-o
The children get a cat.

And the cat gets a mouse
The cat gets a mouse
Hi-ho, the derry-o
The cat gets a mouse.

Audio 11

Poem: *What I Can Do?*

I can tie my shoelaces
I can brush my hair
I can wash my hands and face
And cross the road with care.

I can read a story
I can climb up any tree
I can skip and I can run
I know how to have fun!

Topic 3

Audio 12

Song: *What's in the Bag?*

What's in the bag?
A blue book.
A blue book?
That's cool!

What's in the bag?
A red pencil.
A red pencil and a blue book?
That's cool!

What's in the bag?
A yellow ruler, a red pencil and a blue book?
That's cool!

What's in the bag?
A green pen.
A green pen, a yellow ruler, a red pencil and a blue book?
That's cool!

Audio 13

Following instructions: *Draw pictures.*

Find block 1: Draw a ball. The ball is red.

Find block 2: Draw a ruler. The ruler is yellow.

Find block 3: Draw a school bag. The bag is green.

Find block 4: Draw a pencil. The pencil is red.

Audio 14

Story: *I Don't Like Green!*

Anna and Ben are painting their play room.

"Let's paint the play room," says Ben.

'Yes," says Anna.

"Let's paint the room red," says Ben.

"No, I don't like red," says Anna.

"Let's paint the room blue," says Ben.

"No, I don't like blue," says Anna.

"Let's paint the room black," says Ben.

"No, I don't like black," says Anna.

'What colour do you like?" says Ben.

"I like green," says Anna.

"No," says Ben. "I don't like green!"

Audio 15

Song: *The Colour Purple*

I have a purple hat
I have a purple bag
I have a purple T-shirt
And my skirt is purple too.

I have some purple socks
I have some purple shoes
I have some purple jeans
And I wish my hair was purple too.

Audio 16

Song: *Colour Action Song*

Pairs or two groups:

Red, red, red,
Touch your head.

Blue, blue, blue,
Touch your shoe.

Black, black, black,
Hands behind your back.

Green, green, green,
Shout and scream!

Audio 17

Chant: *Do You Know That?*

I'm a bear – **round** and **fat**
I can fish – do you know that?

I'm an ostrich **big** and **tall**
I can't fly – do you know that?

I'm a cat – **soft** and **small**
I like to sleep – do you know that?

I'm a lion – **scary** and **big**
I can ROAR – do you know that?

(By Daphne Paizee)

Audio 18

Story: *Rat-a-tat-tat*

Rat-a-tat-tat, who is that?
Open the door and see.
It's a cat in a yellow hat,
And she wants to play with me.

Rat-a-tat-tat, who is that?
Open the door and see.
It's a fox in blue and white socks.

Rat-a-tat-tat, who is that?
Open the door and see.
It's a goat in a coat … and a dog and a frog
And a bear in pyjamas eating bananas.

They all want to play with me.

Rat-a-tat-tat, who is that?
Open the door and see.
It's a dinosaur. ROAR!
You can't play with me.

Audio 19

Song: *One Two Three Four Five*

One two three four five
Once I caught a fish alive
Six seven eight nine ten
Then I let it go again.
Why did you let it go?
Because it bit my finger so!
Which finger did it bite?
This little finger on the right.

Audio 20

Clapping song: *Beads in a Ring*

Here are beads all in a ring
We will count them while we sing – 1
Here are beads all in a ring
We will count them while we sing – 2
Here are beads all in a ring
We will count them while we sing – 3
Here are beads all in a ring
We will count them while we sing – 4
Here are beads all in a ring
We will count them while we sing – 5
Here are beads all in a ring
We will count them while we sing – 6
Here are beads all in a ring
We will count them while we sing – 7
Here are beads all in a ring
We will count them while we sing – 8
Here are beads all in a ring
We will count them while we sing – 9
Here are beads all in a ring
We will count them while we sing – 10

Audio 21

Song/Chant: *Ten Little Ducklings*

One little, two little, three little ducklings
Four little, five little, six little ducklings
Seven little, eight little, nine little ducklings
Ten little ducklings in the water!

Topic 4

Audio 22

Rhyme: *One Potato, Two Potato*

One potato, two potatoes,
Three potatoes, four!
Five potatoes, six potatoes
Seven potatoes – and more!

Audio 23

Chant: *Munch and Crunch*

Apples red and green
Apples red and green
Crunch them
Munch them
Apples red and green

Carrots small and sweet
Carrots small and sweet
Crunch them
Munch them
Carrots small and sweet

(You can add verses to this chant. For example: Strawberries small and pink, Cucumbers green and long)

Audio 24

Recipe 1: Summer fruit salad

To make this salad you need:
two bananas
ten strawberries
one big mango
a small pineapple
one orange

Peel the fruit. Cut the fruit. Squeeze the orange juice on to the fruit. Eat the summer fruit salad.

Recipe 2: Winter vegetable soup

To make this soup you need:
three carrots
one onion
two pieces of celery
four potatoes
a cup of green beans
salt and pepper

Audio 25

Chant: *I like Bananas*

Voice 1: I like bananas.
Voice 2: Me too!
Voice 1: I like apples.
Voice 2: Me too!
Voice 1: I like spinach.
Voice 2: Me too!
Voice 1: I like potatoes.
Voice 2: Me too!
Voice 1: I like pumpkin.
Voice 2: Oh no! I don't!

Audio 26

Story: What Would You Like?

Girl 1: Would you like a plum?
Girl 2: No, thanks.

Girl 1: Would you like a carrot?
Boy 1: No thanks.

Girl 1: Would you like a mango?

Boy 2: Yes, please. I love mangoes!
Girl 1: Me too!

Audio 27

Rhyme: *Pat-a-Cake*

Pat-a-cake, pat-a-cake baker man
Bake me a cake
As fast as you can
Pat it and prick it and mark it with *B*
And put it in the oven for Basi and me.

(Change the letter and the name as you say the rhyme. Use names of learners in the class.)

Audio 28

Song: *Put the Kettle on*

Polly put the kettle on
Polly put the kettle on
Polly put the kettle on
Let's all have tea.

Cut the cake or make some toast
Cut the cake or make some toast
Cut the cake or make some toast
Let's all have tea.

(Change the name as you practise this. You can also add more verses to the song to practise the new vocabulary you are introducing in this unit.)

Audio 29

Story: *What's for Breakfast?*

Children: What's for breakfast, Dad?
Dad: Cake.

Children: Yuk! We don't like cake.

Children: What's for breakfast, Dad?
Dad: Chocolate.

Children: Yuk! We don't like chocolate.

Children: What's for breakfast, Dad?
Dad: Apple.

Children: Yum! We like apple. … Thanks, Dad.

Children: What's for lunch, Dad?
Dad: Zzzzzz

Audio 30

Story: *Fox and Stork*

Fox: Come and eat with me, Stork.

Fox: I'll play a trick on Stork. Tee Hee!

Fox: Yum!

Stork: Come and eat with me, Fox.

Stork: I'll show Fox. I'll play a trick too!

Stork: Yum!

Audio 31

Rap song: *Do You Like Them?*

Group 1: We like apples and red plums.
Do you like them?
Group 2: Yes, we do./No, we don't.
Group 1: We like pasta with a sauce.
Do you like them?
Group 2: Yes, we do./No, we don't.
Group 1: We like swimming and PE.
Do you like them?
Group 2: Yes, we do./No, we don't.

(*You can add to this rap song quite easily. Add different categories of things to like. Help learners to add their own words (with the same number of syllables). Individual learners in a group can sing their own lines, starting with "I like ______".*)

Audio 32

Poem: *What I Like*

I like mangoes
And I like plums
I like painting
But I don't like drums.

I like chocolate
And I like chips
I like cheese
But I don't like ships!

Topic 5

Audio 33

Conversation: *Play with me*

Girl 1: What are you doing, Anna?
Girl 2: I am reading.
Girl 1: Can you play with me?
Girl 2: No. I'm reading.
Girl 1: What are you doing, Dad?
Dad: I'm working.
Girl 1: Can you play with me?
Dad: Sorry! I'm working.
Girl 1: What are you doing Mom?
Mom: I'm watching TV.
Girl 1: Can you play with me?
Mom: Yes. Let's play snakes and ladders.
Girl 2: I can play with you.
Dad: I can play with you.
All: Lets all play snakes and ladders.

Audio 34

Poem: *Let's Play!*

I like wrestling
And I like swimming
I like playing football
And I like playing golf.
I don't like cycling
And I can't play tennis.
But sport is fun
Come on, let's play!

Audio 35

Song: *This Is the Way*

This is the way we go to school,
go to school, go to school.
This is the way we go to school,
early in the morning.

This is the way we play with our friends,
play with our friends, play with our friends.
This is the way we play with our friends,
early in the evening.

(Add verses such as: *This is the way we eat our lunch … in the hot afternoon.*)

Audio 36

Story: *I Am Bored*

Girl: I'm bored.
Boy: Me too. What can we do?
Boy: Let's play football.
Girl: No. It's raining. I have got a game. Let's play.
Boy: I'm bored!
Girl: Me too. What can we do?
Boy: Let's go to Sam's house. Come with me.
Girl: No. It's six o'clock. She's at her Gran's.
Boy: We are bored, Mom. What can we do?
Mom: You can help me. You can wash the dishes.

Topic 6

Audio 37

Poem: *Put on Your Shirt*

Put on your shirt
Put on your shorts
Put on your shoes
Now you are dressed!

Take off your shoes.
Take off your shirt.
Take off your shorts.
And go to bed!

Audio 38

Story: *Where Are My Jeans?*

Sandi is angry. She wants to go to a party but she can't find her clothes.

"Where are my jeans?" she says.

"They are there!" says her brother.

"Where?" says Sandi.

"Under the bed!" says her brother.

"And where is my scarf?" says Sandi.

"Here!" says her brother.

"Where?" says Sandi.

"On the chair!" says her brother.

Sandi's brother helps her find her socks and her T-shirt.

"Oh! There's my dress. It's in the cupboard," says Sandi. "I like my dress. I'm wearing the dress. I'm not wearing jeans."

"Really!!!" says her brother. "You must tidy up your room."

Audio 39

Conversation: *Is that for me?*

Voice A: Knock, knock. Hello. I have a parcel.

Voice B: Is it for me?

Voice C: Is it for me?

Voice A: It's for Nina Green.

Voice B: I'm Nina!

Voice A: Here you are. It's for you.

Voice B: Thank you. Look. It's a parcel for me!

Voice C: You are lucky.

Audio 40

Rhyme: *Days of the Week*

Every week has seven days,
Seven days, seven days
Every week has seven days
Do you know them all?

Monday Tuesday Wednesday
That's three, there are four more -
Thursday Friday Saturday
And Sunday – that's all!

Audio 41

Song: *Colours of the rainbow*

Red and orange,
yellow and green,
blue, and purple, and violet, too.
I can see a rainbow,
I can see a rainbow.
Look up there! So can you!

Audio 42

Song: *I Hear Thunder*

I hear thunder,
I hear thunder,
Oh! Don't you?
Oh! Don't you?
Pitter, patter, raindrops,
Pitter, patter, raindrops.
I'm wet through.
And so are you!

Topic 7

Audio 43

Rhyme: *There Was a Crooked Man*

There was a crooked man, and he walked a crooked mile,
He found a crooked sixpence against a crooked stile;
He bought a crooked cat which caught a crooked mouse,
And they all lived together in a little crooked house.

Audio 44

Story: *A New Home*

My name is Sam. I'm six years old. We are moving to a new home. My mother is a doctor She has got a new job in Canada. We are going by plane to Canada.

I live in my new home now. It is a small apartment with two bedrooms.

I like my home and it has a big garden, but I feel sad because I haven't got friends here and I miss my grandparents and my cousins.

I have got a new bed. It's big – I like it!

One day I make a new friend. His name is Jo. We like playing football. Now I feel happy here but I still miss my cousins and grandparents.

Audio 45

Story: *The Little Red Hen*

The little red hen lives on a farm. She lays eggs and she makes good bread. She grows the wheat to make the bread. She works hard. The other animals on the farm don't work very hard.

One day she goes out in the field to cut some wheat.

"Who can help me cut the wheat?" she asks.

"I'm busy," says the dog.

"Me too," says the horse.

"Me too," says the duck.

So the little red hen cuts the wheat.

The next day the little red hen goes to the shed to pound the wheat.

"Who can help me pound the wheat?" she asks.

"I'm busy," says the dog.

"Me too," says the horse.

"Me too," says the duck.

So the little red hen pounds the wheat.

The next day the little red hen makes the bread.

"Who can help me make some bread?" she asks.

"I'm busy," says the dog.

"Me too," says the horse.

"Me too," says the duck.

So the little red hen makes the bread. She puts it in the oven. It smells good.

"I'm hungry," says the horse.

"Me too," says the dog.

"Me too," says the duck.

"Me too," says the little red hen. "It's my bread. But here you are. You can have some."

"Thank you,' says dog. "Next time I can help you!"

"Me too," says horse.

"Me too," says duck.

"Let's see!" says the little red hen.

Audio 46

Story: *Jack and the Beanstalk*

Jack and his mother are very poor.

They have to sell their cow.

Jack gives the cow to a man.

The man gives Jack some beans.

The man thinks Jack is a silly boy.

Jack's mother is very cross.

She throws the beans out of the window.

The beans grow into a big plant.

"Look at the beanstalk!" says Jack.

Jack climbs up the beanstalk.

He finds some gold at the top of the beanstalk.

A big giant sees Jack.

"That gold is mine," says the giant.

"I have special beans," says Jack.

"Let's swap," says Jack.

"Okay," says the giant.

The giant is happy.

Jack is happy!

And of course Jack's mother is happy too!

Audio 47

Story: *The Very Big Carrot*

Mr and Mrs Brown are farmers. They grow carrots, beans and pumpkins. They plant the seeds. They water the seeds. The seeds grow into big vegetables.

"Today, we'll pick the carrots," says Mrs Brown.

She pulls up three carrots. But the next carrot is big. She pulls and pulls but the carrot stays in the ground.

"Please help me, Mr Brown," she says.

So Mr Brown helps. They pull and they pull but the carrot stays in the ground.

"Please help us," they say to the son.

So the boy helps. They pull and they pull but the carrot stays in the ground.

"Please help us," they say to the daughter.

So the girl helps.

They pull and they pull but the carrot stays in the ground.

"Please help us," they say to the cat.

So the cat helps. They pull and they pull but the carrot stays in the ground.

"Please help us," they say to the goat.

So the goat helps. They pull and they pull but the carrot stays in the ground.

"Please help us," they say to the horse.

So the horse helps… the carrot comes out of the ground. It is very big. They all fall over!

Audio 48

Non-fiction text: *The life cycle of a bean plant*

The seeds of a bean plant grow in a long green pod. We plant the seeds in the soil. The seed starts to grow. The plant grows bigger and bigger. Flowers grow on the plant. Bean pods grow from the flowers and new seeds grow inside the bean pods.

Audio 49

Rhyme: *Row Your Boat*

Row, row, row your boat
Gently down the stream,
Merrily, merrily, merrily
Life is such a dream!

Row, row, row your boat
Gently down the creek
If you see a crocodile
Don't forget to shriek!

Row, row, row your boat
Gently down the river
If you see a polar bear
Don't forget to shiver!

Row, row, row your boat
Gently to the shore
If you see a lion there
Don't forget to roar!

Topic 8

Audio 50

Song: *Head and Shoulders*

Head, shoulders, knees, and toes,
knees and toes.
Head, shoulders, knees, and toes,
knees and toes.
And eyes and ears and mouth and nose!
Head, shoulders, knees and toes,
knees and toes.

Audio 51

Instructions: *How to clean your teeth*

You will need:

a toothbrush
toothpaste
a cup of clean water

1. Put some toothpaste on the toothbrush.
2. Wet the toothbrush.
3. Brush your teeth softly for a few minutes.
4. Brush all the teeth in your mouth.
5. Rinse your mouth with the water.
6. Rinse your toothbrush.

Questions

1. What do you need to brush your teeth?
2. What do you put on the toothbrush?
3. What do you do when you are finished?
4. What do you use to rinse your mouth?

Audio 52

Instructions: *Rules for keeping healthy*

Listen to these rules for keeping healthy.
- Wash every day.
- Brush your teeth.
- Eat healthy food.
- Drink clean water.
- Do exercise.
- Get enough sleep.

Audio 53

Chant: *What's the Matter?*

Voice 1: What's the matter? What's the matter?

Voice 2: I have a headache, a horrible headache.

Voice 1: Get better soon. Get better soon.

Voice 1: What's the matter? What's the matter?

Voice 2: I have a cold, a horrible cold.

Voice 1: Get better soon. Get better soon.

(You can substitute *headache* with other ailments such as *tummy ache, fever*.)

Audio 54

Conversation: *What's the matter?*

Voice 1: What's the matter?

Voice 2: I don't feel well.

Voice 1: Is your head sore?

Voice 2: Yes. I have a headache.

Voice 1: Do you have a fever?

Voice 2: No, I don't.

Audio 55

Story: *In the Hospital*

Boy 1: Where is Raj?
Teacher: He is in hospital.
Girl 1: Is he sick?
Teacher: No. He had an accident.

Girl 2: Let's make a card for Raj.

Girl 3: Can we visit Raj?
Teacher: Yes, of course!

Children: Hello, Raj. How are you? This is for you!

Boy 2: (Raj): Thank you very much! My leg is sore but I feel happy now. Thank you everyone!

Audio 56

Story: *Sam the Big, Bad Cat*

Tom had a big, bad cat called Sam. One day Sam didn't feel well.

Tom said, "I'll take you to the vet."

Sam didn't want to go to the vet.

He ran away and hid under his bed. Tom found him.

Sam hid under the table.

Tom found him.

Sam hid in the cupboard.

Tom found him.

Sam hid in the shower.

Tom found him. Tom got very wet.

Tom said, "I don't feel well at all. I'm going to bed."

Sam was feeling much better.

Topic 9

Audio 57

Song: *Getting Around*

The swimming pool and the hairdresser,
library and school, library and school.
Take the bus!
Ride a bike! Take the bus! Ride a bike!
To the swimming pool and hairdresser, library
and school.

Audio 58

Story: *Joy and Her Aunt Go to Town*

Joy and her aunty are in town. It is Saturday. They go to many different places. First, they go to the dentist. Joy has a sore tooth. Then they go to the library to get some books to read. After that they go to the hairdresser. Joy's aunty gets her hair done. That takes a long time. Then they go to the supermarket to get some food. They walk past the school on the way home.

Audio 59

Story: *Sanjay Goes to the Museum*

One day it is raining. Sanjay goes to the museum with his aunty and cousins. First they go to see all the big animals. Sanjay likes the dinosaurs. Then they go to see the small animals and insects. Sanjay likes all the beetles. There are yellow beetles, red beetles and purple beetles! After that they go and look at some statues. Sanjay doesn't like the statues. "I'm bored," he says. So aunty takes the children out into the garden. They walk over a bridge. Then they sit down and have a soft drink.

'This is good!" says Sanjay. "I like this place."

Audio 60

Rhyme: *Stop! Look! Listen!*

Stop! Look! Listen!
Use your eyes
Use your ears
Then you can cross the street.

Stop! Look! Think!
Use your eyes
Use your head
Before you use your feet.

Audio 61

Story: *At the Bus Station*

Boy: We are packing.
Girl: We are going to visit our cousins.

Girl and Boy: We are going on a bus. The bus station is very busy.

Woman (Mom): Where's Ana?
Boy: I don't know. She is here somewhere.

Mom: Is she here?
Boy: No.

Boy: Is she over there?
Mom: No. Oh no – she is lost.

Mom: ANA! There you are!
Girl: Sorry! I'm coming.

Audio 62

Chant: *Hip Hip Hooray!*

Hip hip hooray
Holidays are here
Hip hip hooray
Let's laugh and play.
Where will we go?
What will we see?
Let's go, let's go, just you and me!

Audio 63

Story: *Lee and Sue Go to India*

Lee and Sue are going to India to visit their cousins. They are very excited.

Lee and Sue pack their suitcases. It is Friday. They go to the airport by taxi. They are going by plane. They get on the plane. It is a long trip. It's six hours. They get to India on Saturday. Then they go by bus to their cousin's house. They are all very happy and very tired!

(Topic 1 Unit A)

- Cut out the names.
- Say the beginning sounds.
- Put the names in groups.

Ben	Bella	Sara	Sam	Kim	Kit
Anna	Ali	Pedro	Peter	Jenna	Jay
Temba	Tess	Nina	Nick	Tony	Tara
Diego	Don	Daria	Mo	Mina	Zara
Zak	Lee	Linda	Lucky	Pilar	Pete
Penny	Rosie	Raj	Vicky	Vish	Jo

(Topic 1 Unit A)

Write the first letter of each name. What new name can you write with each letter?

Jay	J	Jenna
Anna		
Nina		
Nick		
Andy		
New name:		

(Topic 1 Unit B)

her	name	is	Mary	Ali
his	this	these	that	a
book	pen	table	are	are
pencils	bags	rulers	is	is

Write two sentences.

1. ______________________________

2. ______________________________

(Topic 1 Unit C)

Poem: Time for School

(Topic 2 Unit A)

Listen. Tick ✓ the correct pictures.

1. a)  ☐ **b)**  ☐ **c)**  ☐

2. a)  ☐ **b)**  ☐ **c)**  ☐

3. a)  ☐ **b)**  ☐ **c)**  ☐

4. a)  ☐ **b)**  ☐ **c)**  ☐

5. a)  ☐ **b)**  ☐ **c)**  ☐

(Topic 2 Unit A)

1. Listen. Underline the correct answers.

a) Do you like art? Yes, I do. No, I don't.

b) Do you like maths? Yes, I do. No, I don't.

c) Do you like writing? Yes, I do. No, I don't.

d) Do you like singing? Yes, I do. No, I don't.

2. What else do you like doing? Draw a picture.

(Topic 2 Unit C)

Listen. Tick ✓ the correct pictures.

1. a)  ☐ b)  ☐ c)  ☐

2. a)  ☐ b)  ☐ c)  ☐

3. a)  ☐ b)  ☐ c)  ☐

4. a)  ☐ b)  ☐ c)  ☐

5. a)  ☐ b)  ☐ c)  ☐

6. a)  ☐ b)  ☐ c)  ☐

(Topic 2 Unit C)

Story: Dad, Gran and the Cat Take a Nap

- Cut out the pictures.
- Put them in the correct order.
- Retell the story.

(Topic 2 Unit C; Topic 3 Unit A and Unit C; Topic 4 Unit B; Topic 5 Unit B; Topic 7 Unit A; Topic 9 Unit A)

Bingo

(Topic 3 Unit A)

Story: I don't like green!

- Colour in the pictures.
- Cut them out.
- Put them in order.
- Tell the story.

(Topic 3 Unit A and Unit B)

Listen and colour in the animals.

(Topic 3 Unit B)

Listen. Tick ✓ the correct sentences.

1.

☐ A bat and a frog.

☐ A bat and a cat.

2.

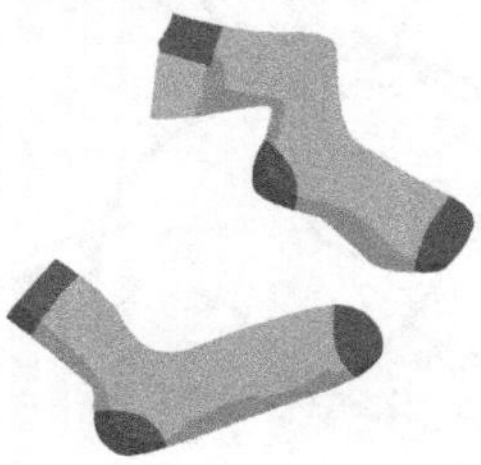

☐ The fox has two socks.

☐ The socks have a fox.

3.

☐ The bird is small.

☐ The bird is big.

4.

☐ The mouse is sad.

☐ The mouse is bad.

(Topic 3 Unit C)

Listen. Tick ✓ the correct boxes.

1. a)  ☐ **b)**  ☐ **c)**  ☐

2. a)  ☐ **b)** 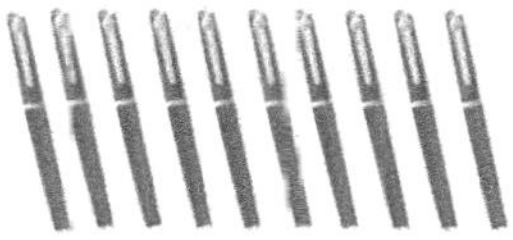 ☐ **c)** 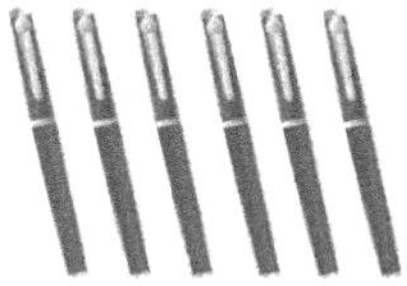 ☐

3. a)  ☐ **b)** 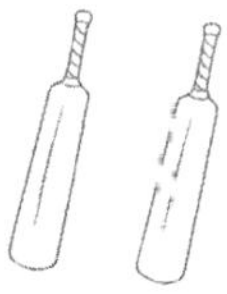 ☐ **c)** 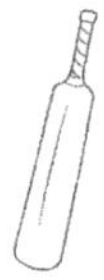 ☐

4. a) 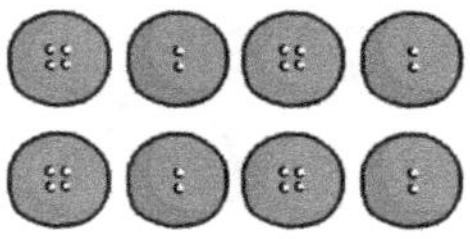 ☐ **b)** 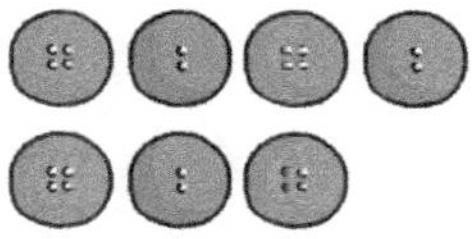 ☐ **c)** 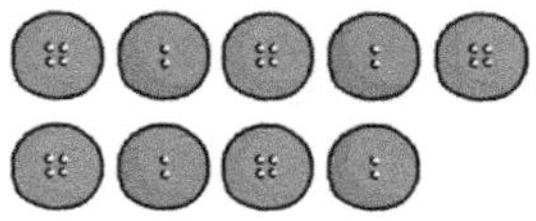 ☐

5. a)  ☐ **b)**  ☐ **c)**  ☐

6. a)  ☐ **b)**  ☐ **c)**  ☐

(Topic 3 Unit C; Topic 5 Unit A)

1–6 Spinner

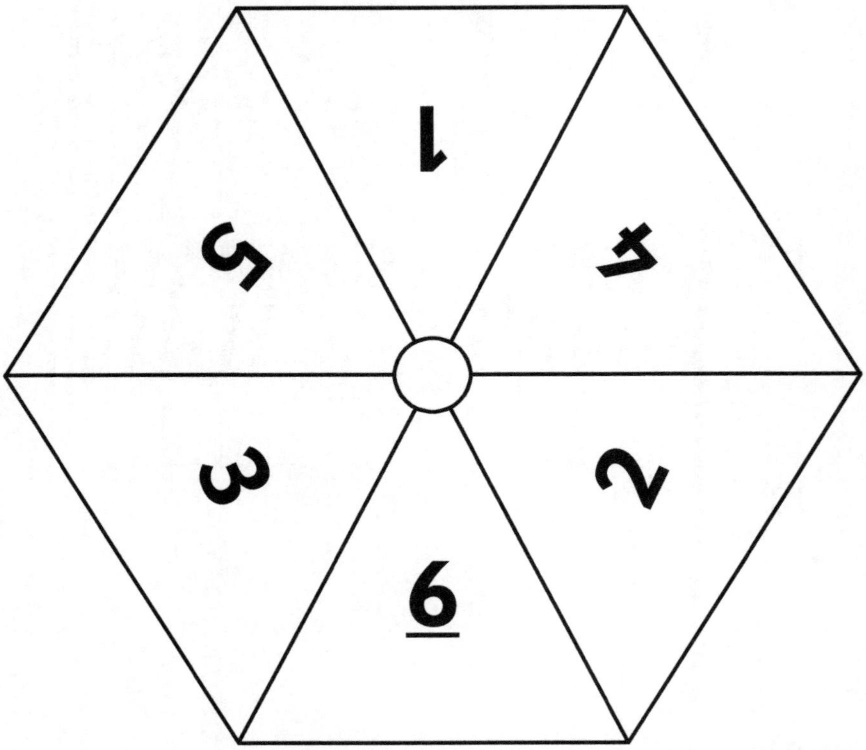

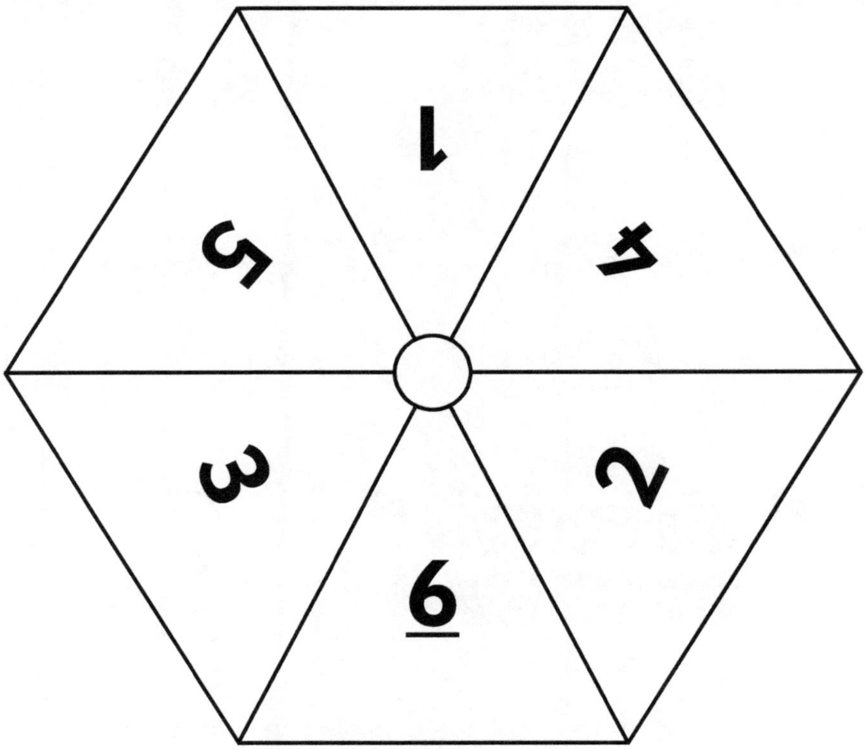

(Topic 4 Unit A)

Listen and tick ✓ what you need.

Then listen again and fill in the number that you need.

Recipe 1

Fruit	✓ or ✗	How many?

Recipe 2

Vegetables	✓ or ✗	How many?

(Topic 4 Unit B)

Listen and tick ✓ the pictures.

1. Benji has ... for breakfast.

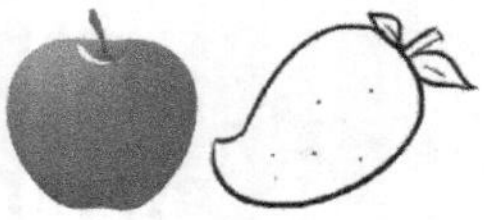 ☐  ☐  ☐

2. Linda has ... for lunch.

 ☐  ☐  ☐

3. Tim has ... for tea.

 ☐  ☐  ☐

(Topic 4 Unit B)
Story: Fox and Stork

- Listen to the story *Fox and Stork*.
- Cut out the pictures.
- Put them in order.
- Tell the story.

(Topic 4 Unit C)

Jo's Restaurant

Menu

Pizzas:

Pizza with cheese and tomatoes

Pizza with cheese and mushrooms

Pizza with mixed vegetables

Pizza with chicken and vegetables

Salads:

Green salad

Mixed salad (lettuce, tomato, cucumber, onion, carrot)

Cheese, tomato and cucumber salad

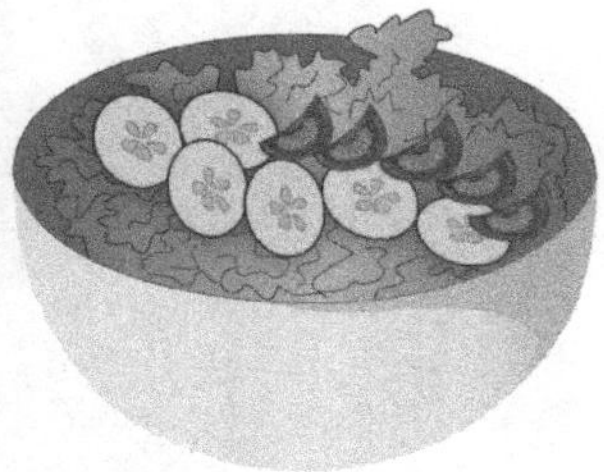

Drinks:

Chocolate milkshake

Orange juice

Water

(Topic 5 Unit A)

1. Read the instructions.

How to play:
Spin a spinner.
Move around the board from 1 up to 30. Take turns!
Go up the ladders when you land on the bottom of the ladder.
Go down the snakes when you land on the head.

2. Play the game.

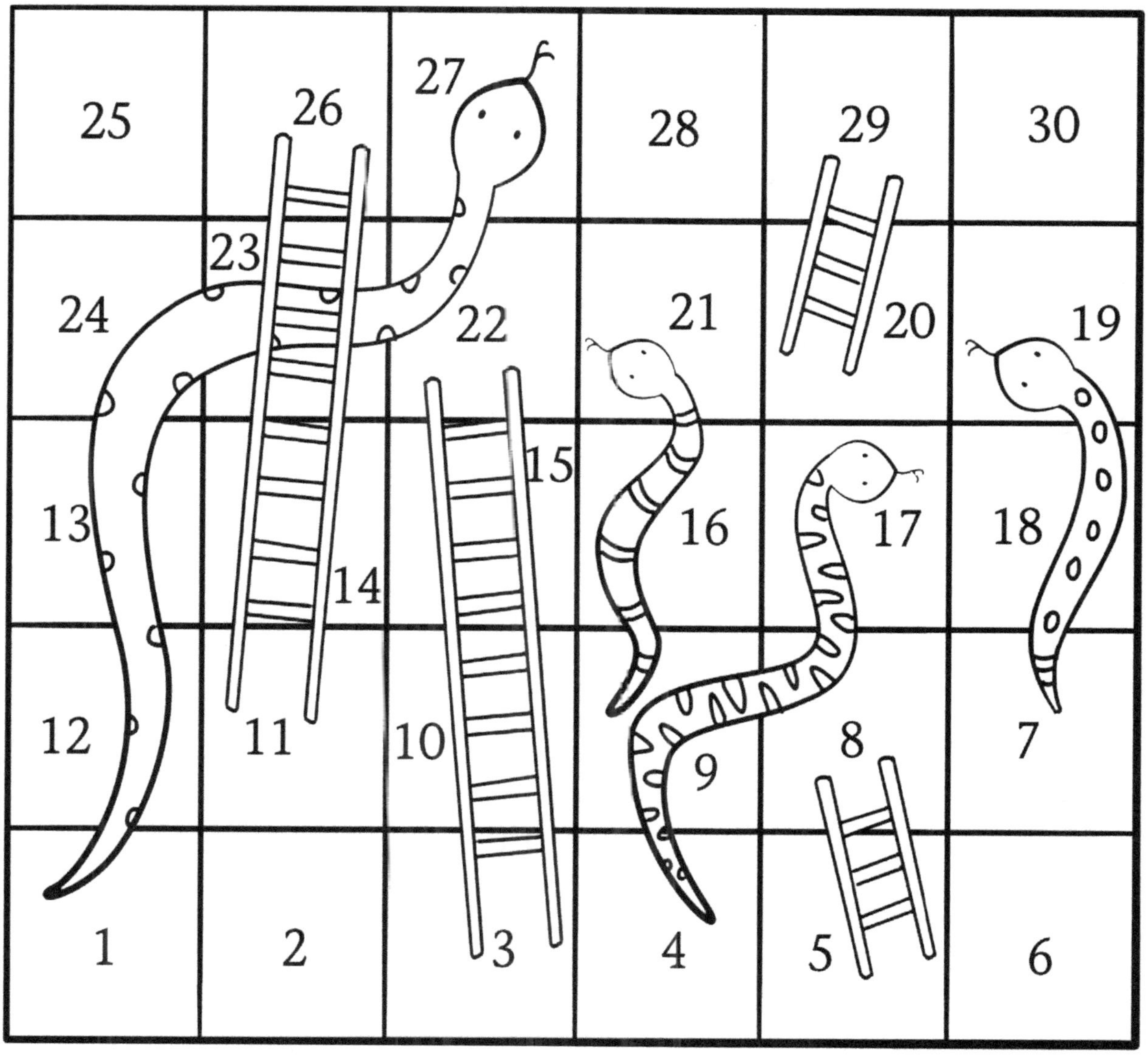

(Topic 5 Unit A)

1. Listen to your teacher and circle the words you hear.

a) in on up

b) at up on

c) near next to under

d) up down off

e) behind near under

f) under next to down

2. Listen to your teacher and write the vowel sound that you hear in each group of words.

a) ____________________

b) ____________________

c) ____________________

d) ____________________

e) ____________________

(Topic 5 Unit A)

Make an origami frog

1. Fold in half twice and fold back.

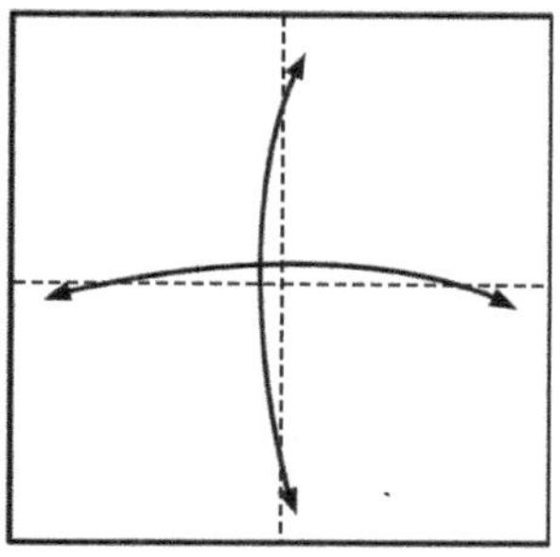

2. Fold top down at dotted line.

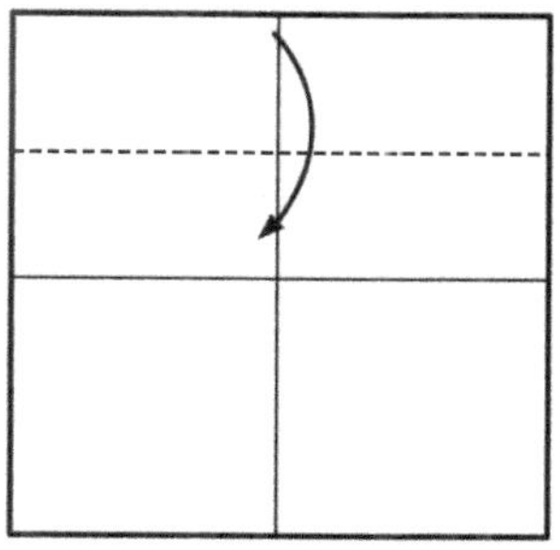

3. Fold corners in.

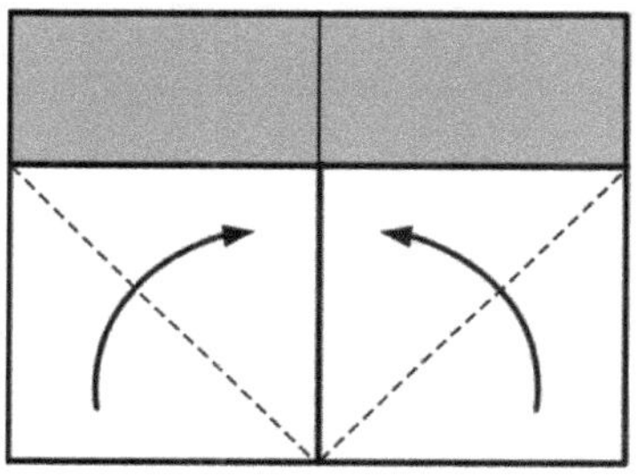

4. Fold both sides in.

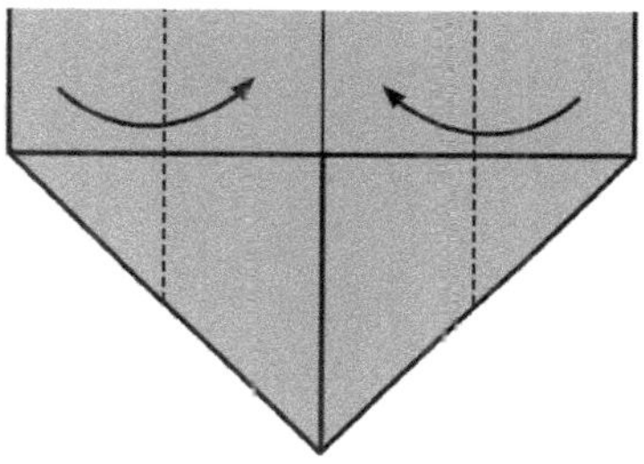

5. Fold down at dotted line.

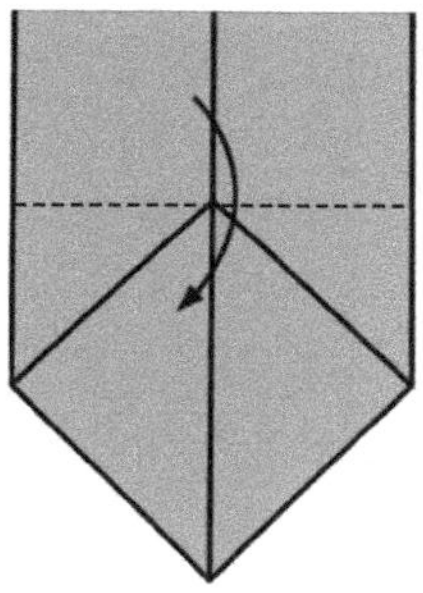

6. Fold at the dotted line.

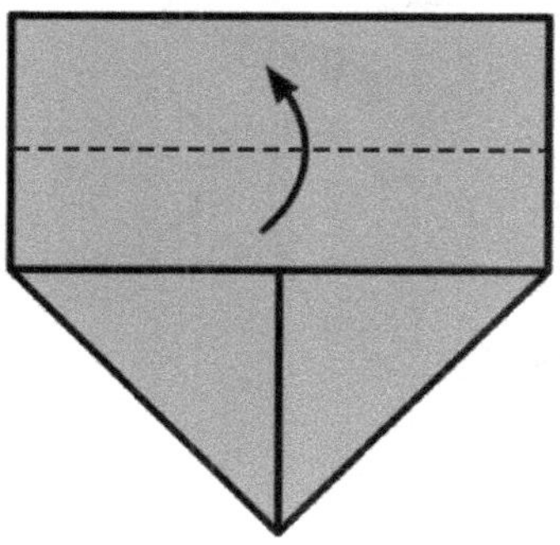

7. Turn over.

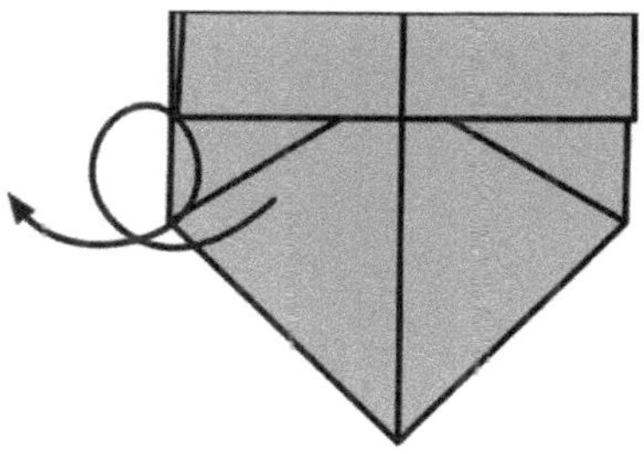

8. Add some eyes.

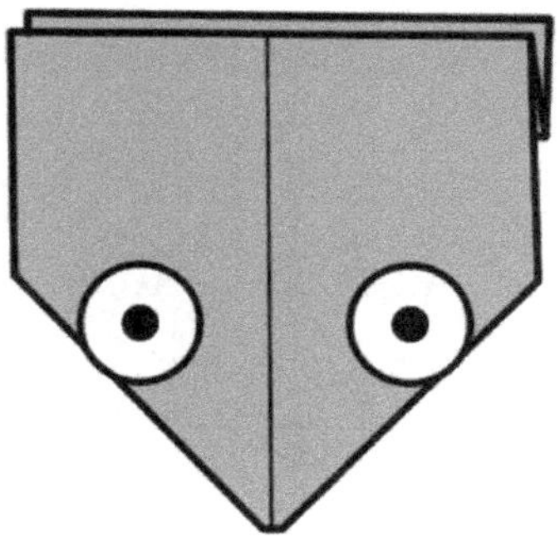

(Topic 5 Unit B)

Make a papier-mâché ball

You will need:

a balloon newspaper glue water

What you do:

1. Blow up the balloon.

2. Tear the newspaper into strips.

3. Put glue and water on the strips.

4. Paste the strips on the balloon.

5. Let the strips dry.

6. Pop the balloon.

7. Paint your ball.

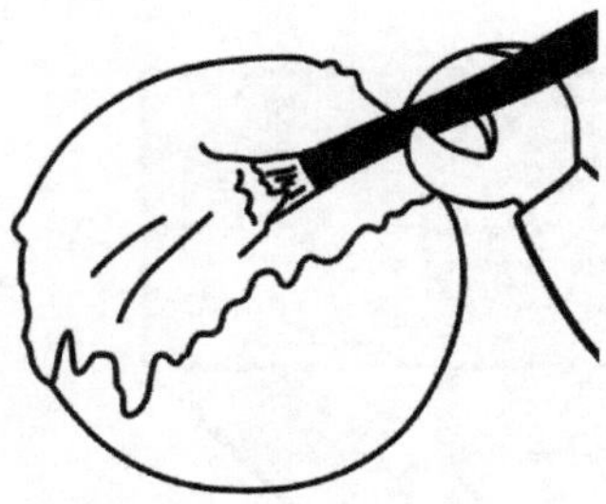

(Topic 5 Unit C)

Fill in the times.

(Topic 6 Unit A)

Look at the picture and colour it in.

(Topic 6 Unit A)

Listen to your teacher. Colour in the pictures.

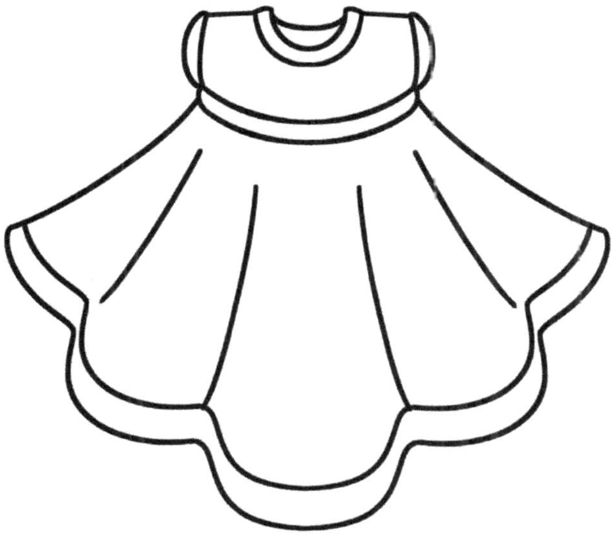

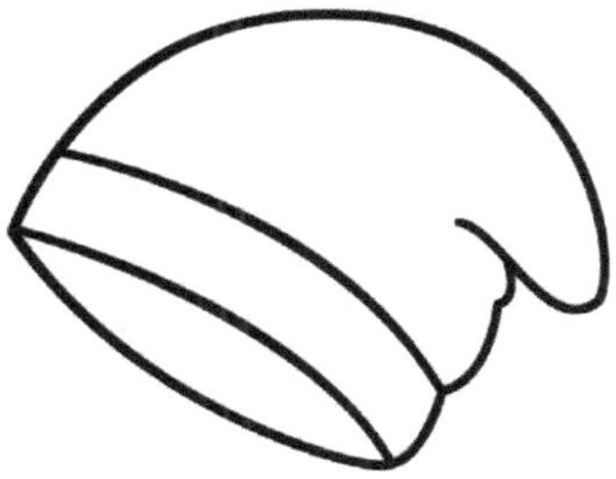

(Topic 6 Unit A)

1

2

3

4

5

6

(Topic 6 Unit B)

Collect information. Record it here.

Question

What do you do on ____________________?

Answers

1. ____________________
2. ____________________
3. ____________________
4. ____________________
5. ____________________
6. ____________________
7. ____________________
8. ____________________
9. ____________________
10. ____________________

What do most people do?

____

(Topic 6 Unit C)
Story: Bob's Secret Hideaway

(Topic 7 Unit B)

Story: Jack and the Beanstalk

- Cut out the pictures.
- Put them in the correct order.
- Tell the story.

(Topic 8 Unit A)

(Topic 8 Unit B)

- Cut out the pictures.
- Put them in the correct order.
- Tell your partner how to wash hands.

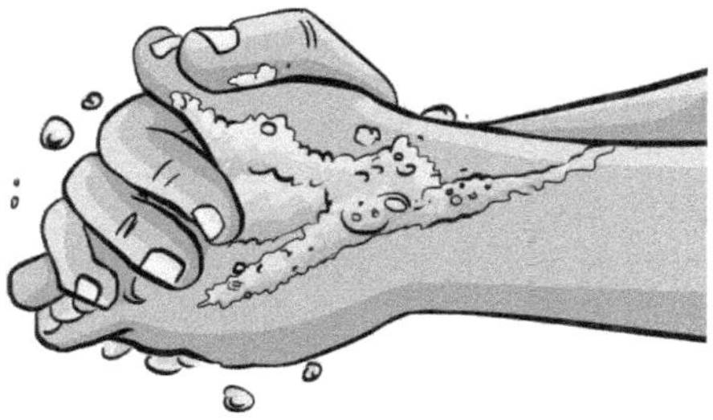

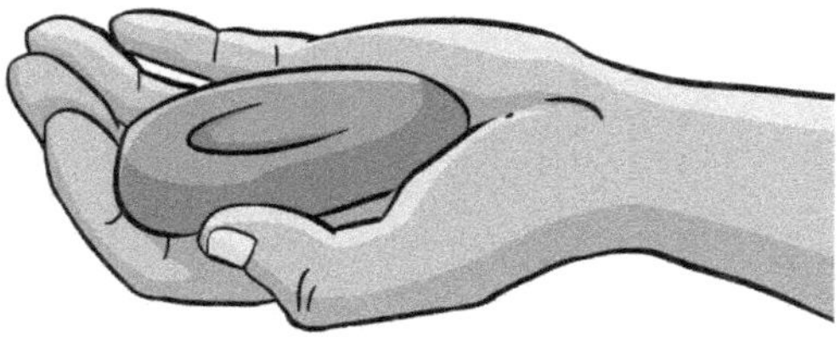

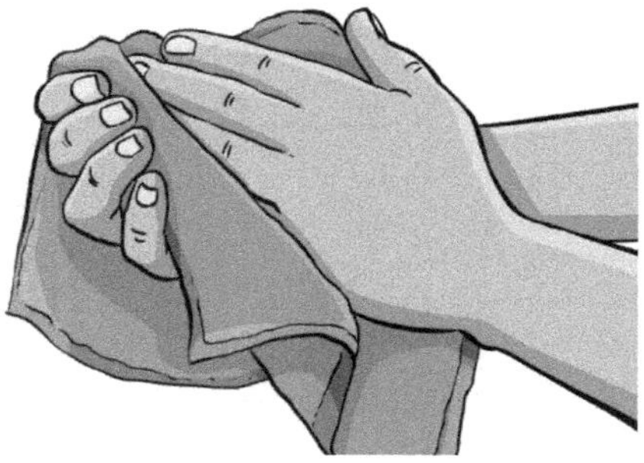

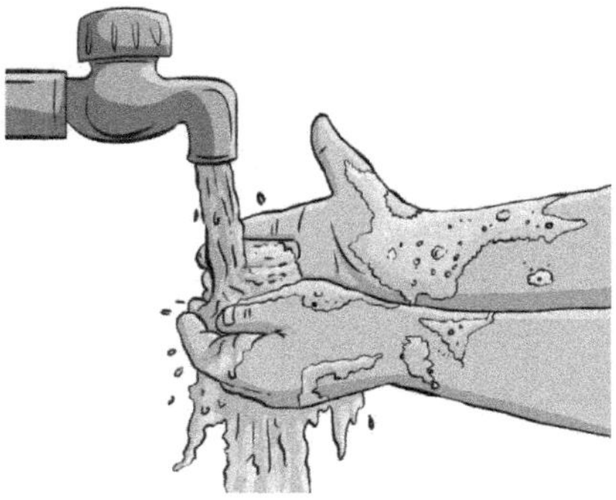

(Topic 8 Unit B)

- Choose pictures which show healthy activities.
- Colour in the pictures.
- Make a poster.
- Use words from the box to label your poster.

drink clean water
eat fruit and vegetables
eat cakes and sweets
drink dirty water
play with my friends
get exercise
go to the clinic
wash my body

(Topic 9 Unit A)

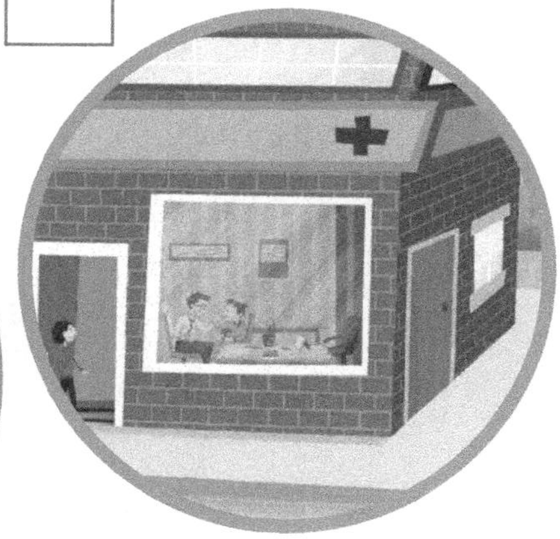

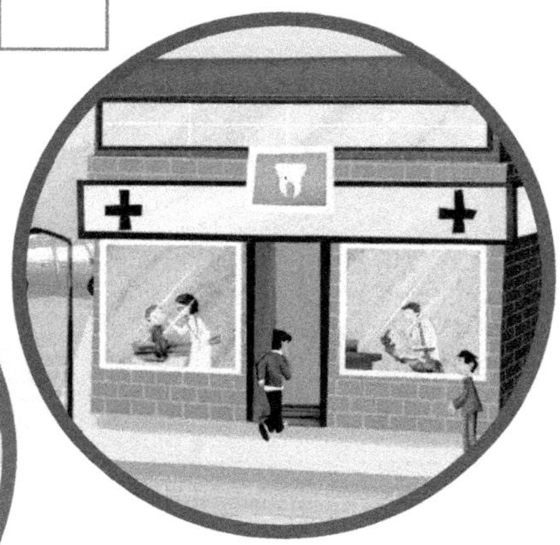

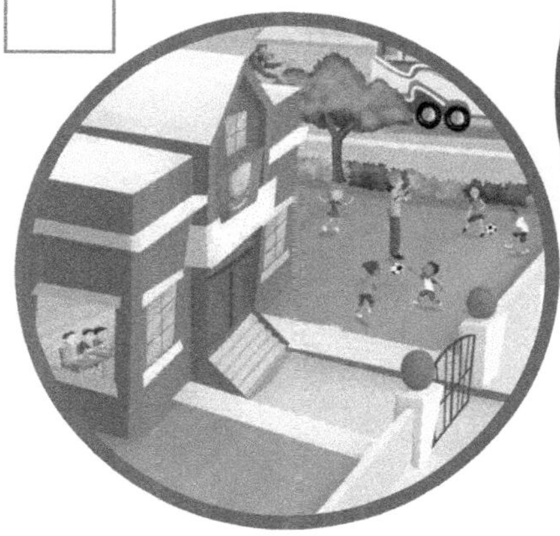

(Topic 9 Unit B)
Make a boat

1. Fold in half.

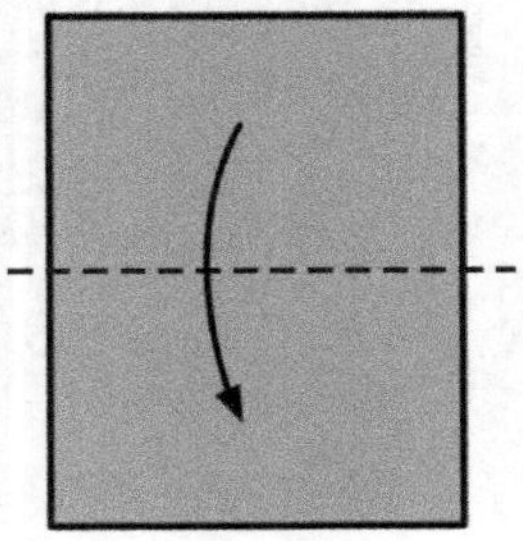

2. Fold in corners.

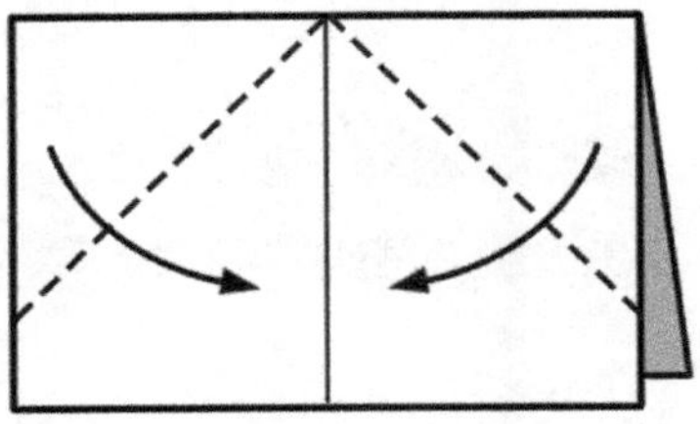

3. Fold up on both sides.

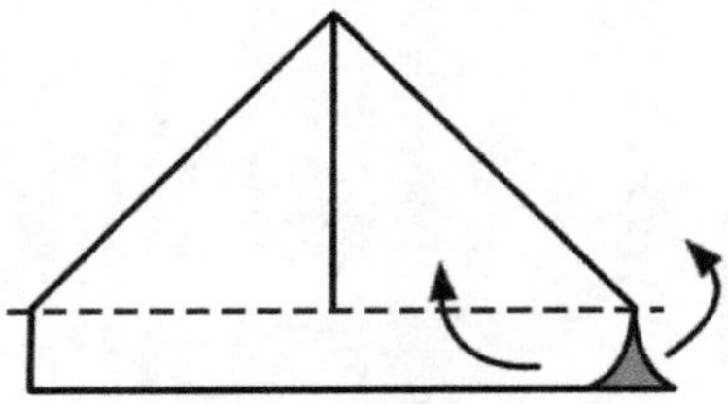

4. Pull out middle and push sides together.

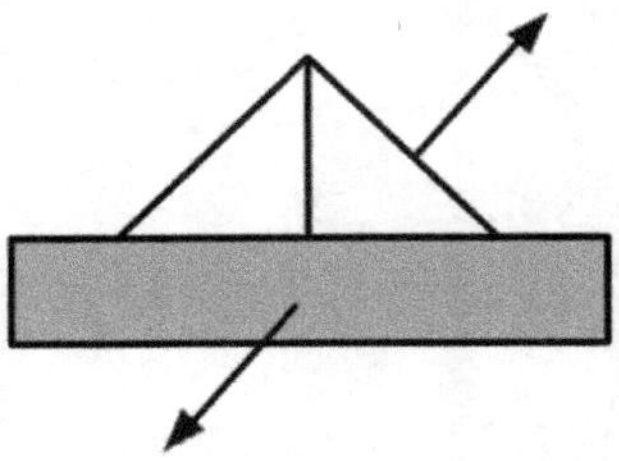

5. Fold up both sides on dotted line.

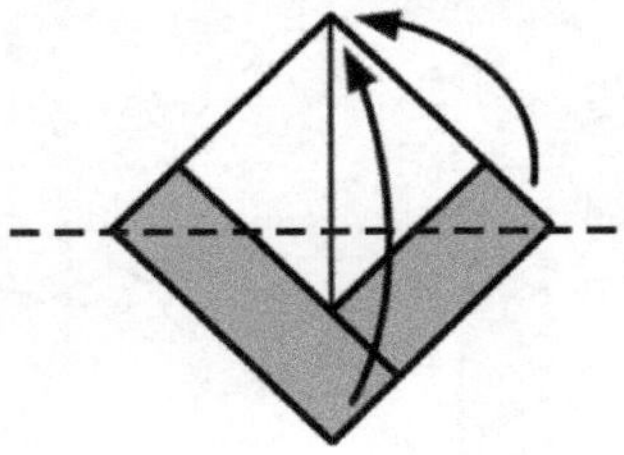

6. Pull out middle and push sides together.

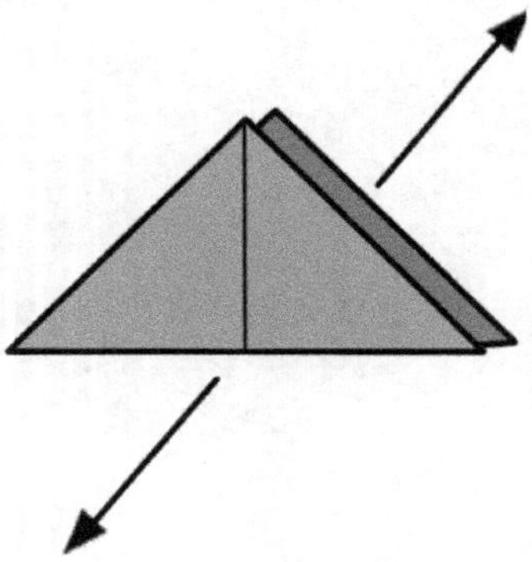

7. Pull the sides apart.

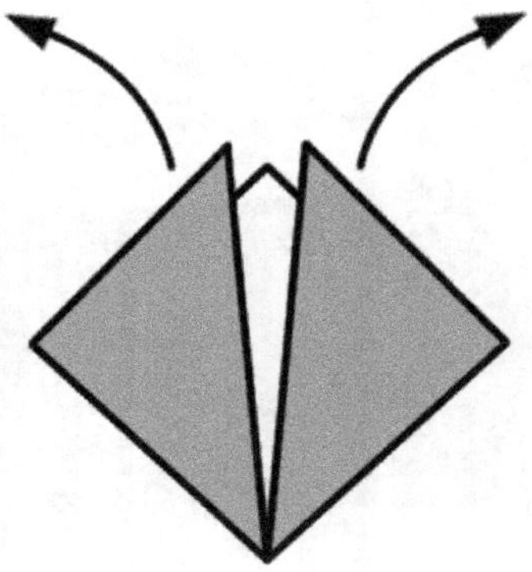

8. Pull sides up into a boat.

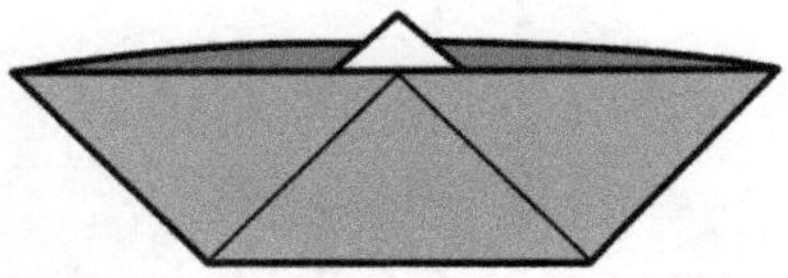

Name: Today's date:

Part 1: Listening

1 Listen and tick the correct picture.

a Where is the ball?

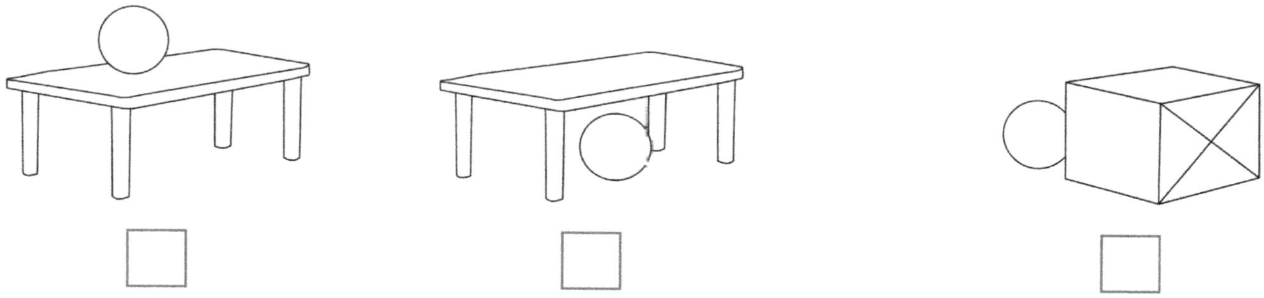

b Where is the ball now?

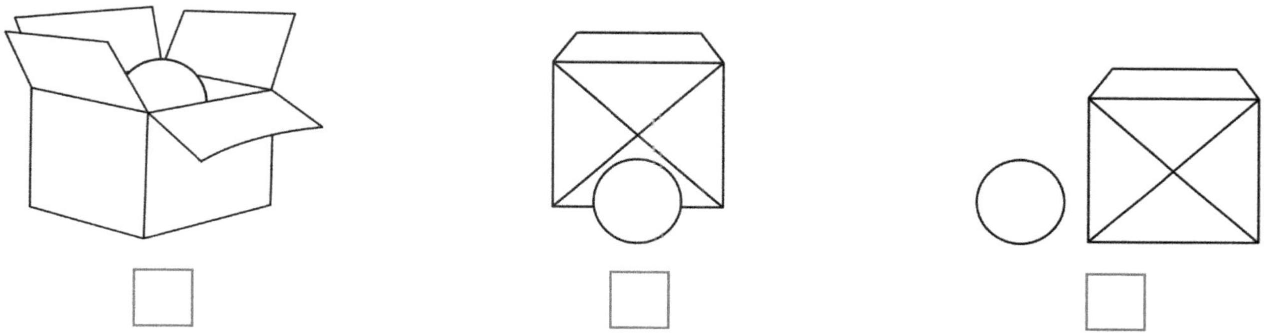

2 Listen and colour.

Part 2: Reading and writing

1 Look and read. Write yes or no.

a The boy is in bed. ________

b It is raining outside. ________

c The boy is writing. ________

d He has three pillows. ________

e The boy is sleeping. ________

f The boy is reading. ________

2 Use words from the box to complete the sentences.

cooking	jumping	kicking	reading

a

He is ________.

b

They are ________.

c

He is ________ a ball.

d

They are ________.

Part 3: Speaking

Do this part of the review activity with your teacher.

Notes

Notes

USBORNE

WHERE'S THE SPY?

A SPOT & FIND PUZZLE STORY

ILLUSTRATED BY
Colin King

DESIGNED BY
Claire Thomas

WRITTEN BY
Alex Frith and Laura Cowan

Who's who?

Meet Simon Horatio Wilberforce, or Si the Spy for short. Your mission is to help this hard-working hero with his latest assignment at the Secret Intelligence Agency (SIA) – to uncover a plot by their sworn enemies, the odious TWINDICATE OF CRIME.

SPECIAL AGENT USB 83629 **SIA** SECRET INTELLIGENCE AGENCY

AGENT NAME: Si the Spy

Height: Average
Age: Between 18 and 80
Birthday: Once a year
Likes: Spying (obviously)
Dislikes: Butterflies (reason unknown)

Agent ID: USB 83629

SIA CONFIDENTIAL MATERIAL
For SIA agents' eyes only

Mission file # 19642

MISSION APPROVED

SIGNED: Z Head of the SIA

You'll find Si the Spy on every double-page scene in this book. Sometimes, you'll be able to spot his spy friends, too – as well as his spy enemies. On other pages, Si will need your brainpower to solve fiendish puzzles and decipher complex codes.

Cast of characters

Spymaster Z
Head of the SIA

"Flawless" Gem
Si's trusted partner

Professor Nyota
Science genius

Teal McBeal
SIA spy

Amy
A teenage coder caught up in the chaos

Twindicate agents
Faithful followers of the Twindicate

?
The Lord High Commander of the Twindicate

This is the only known photo of the Twindicate's mysterious mastermind. No one has ever seen their face...

Si the Spy feels safest in his signature red outfit – but he doesn't always wear it. Friends can pick him out of a crowd by spotting the black belt, and black hat-band, that he does ALWAYS wear.

Special Agent "Flawless" Gem has a signature look, too. She ALWAYS wears sunglasses, a bow and a pair of sturdy boots. She changes clothes often, but NEVER wears pink.

Can you spot Si the Spy and "Flawless" Gem hiding in the grid below? They both appear four times each.

You can check your answers to this puzzle – and all the puzzles – on pages 42–48.

Briefing at HQ

It's a typical Saturday morning in the SIA Headquarters – no one takes the weekend off when they need to save the world! Si the Spy and Teal McBeal are here to be briefed by their boss, Spymaster Z. Can you find them? The mysterious organization known as the Twindicate of Crime is plotting something...
As usual, it'll be up to Si to stop them.

Carnival of chaos

Si's first task: rendezvous with "Flawless" Gem in this city square – but they've forgotten about Carnival Day! Can you help our two agents find each other in the crowd? Their mission is to track down robotic birds, carrying coded messages from Twindicate HQ. There are seven of them, disguised as pigeons – with a few modifications...

ETZELS

Robot feather

Those pesky pigeons managed to get away! Luckily, one of them dropped a metal feather. Help Si match the feather to its owner to discover its radio frequency. He might be able to intercept the pigeon at its next stop...

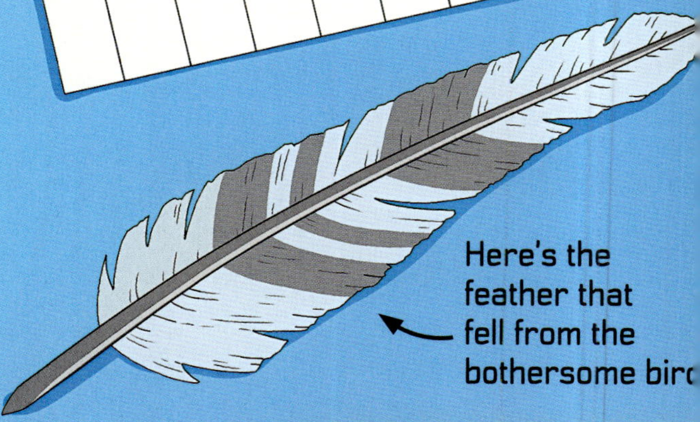

Once you have identified the pigeon, make a note of the frequency it uses to communicate with Twindicate HQ.

Homing in on the pigeon

With a groundbreaking new frequency detector, Si can track down the robotic message-carrier. Use the key to find its final destination, then use your finger to trace a clear path for Si to get there.

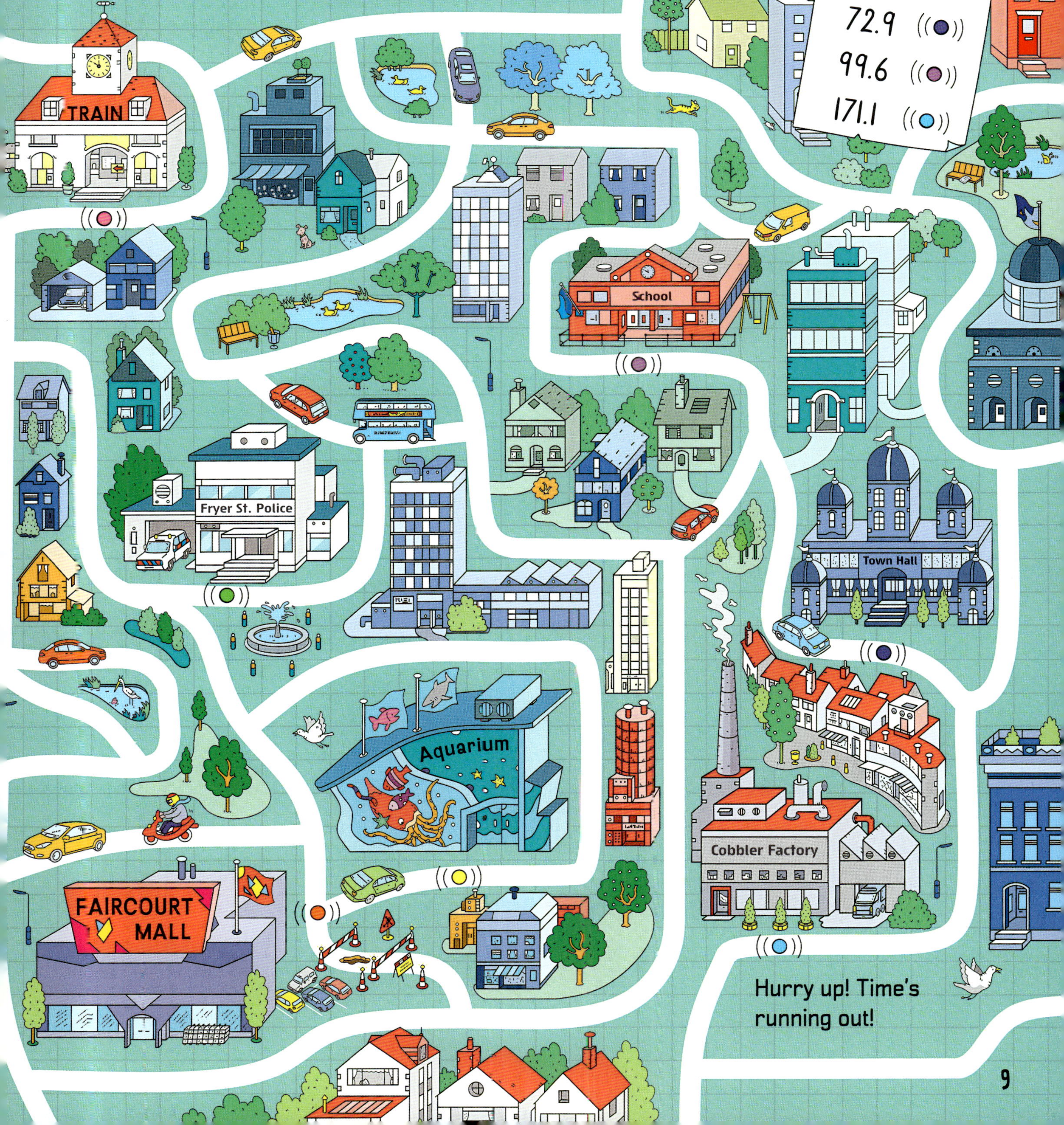

Aquarium pursuit

Si has tracked the robot pigeon down to the city aquarium, but it won't be easy to spot among the swirling sea beasts and hordes of curious visitors. Find Si, the pigeon, and the pigeon's handler – a suspicious man in purple. (Wearing all purple is the Twindicate's way of identifying each other.)

CORAL ZONE

Railway rendezvous

Robot pigeon secured, Si is on his way to meet "Flawless" Gem at the train station. Can you spot them both? The Twindicate isn't far behind though. Keep your eyes peeled for two enemy agents on their trail – in purple outfits, of course!

Ludlum Station
2.52pm Fleming-on-Sea XX Delayed XX
2.56pm Upper Deighton Boarding Platform 3
2.59pm Little Walsingham Boarding Platform 4
3.04pm Orley Farm On time Platform 1
Exit to Chubb Street
Usborne Rail

Carrier of clues

Plugging the robot pigeon into her decoder, "Flawless" Gem has discovered a series of beeps, which Si instantly identifies as Morse Code. Decode the messages, and maybe you'll finally discover what the Twindicate is up to. Look, Si has already cracked the first clue...

- Morse Code Decipher Sheet -

A •—	B —•••	C —•—•	D —••	E •	F ••—•	G ——•	H ••••	I ••	J •———
K —•—	L •—••	M ——	N —•	O ———	P •——•	Q ——•—	R •—•	S •••	T —
U ••—	V •••—	W •——	X —••—	Y —•——	Z ——••				

There's no time to lose – our heroes will have to split up. Gem will check the library, while Si puzzles over another file hidden on the pigeon. To decode that one, he's going to need his code-breaking scientist pal, Professor Nyota.

Top-secret science

Oh no! Those secret messages revealed that Professor Nyota is in trouble! Si will have to run (carefully) through the SIA's experimental weapons lab to find her. Can you spot Si? And what's he holding? It looks familiar, but Si can't quite remember where he saw it before...

Lost at the library

Meanwhile, Gem has gone to the library – and taken the time to change her outfit! See if you can spot her, and the clothes she left behind. Agent Teal McBeal is here too, and, just like Si, he's found one of the power crystals described by the robot pigeon. Si's not here in person, but perhaps you can spot his face...

My spy, my guy
A secret romance

Caught on camera

Back in the lab, Si was too late to rescue Professor Nyota. But all is not lost! While checking the security camera, our hero spies a clever clue the professor left in her office at 6:51pm. She must have found the pigeon's final message – and figured out a whole cipher sheet to translate it.

SECURITY ROOM

Using the cipher sheet will tell Si where to go next. But there's more! It seems the plucky professor had another message to share on her way out. Can you figure out what she was trying to say?

...And did she leave a *third* clue too?

Suspicious slopes

"Hmm," thinks Si, "Why did Nyota send me skiing?" *Ping!* goes a radio in Si's pocket. It's a message from Gem. "I found a clue in the library – there's a Twindicate hideout disguised as a ski slope, and secret plans in a red briefcase." Can you spot it? And signs of Twindicate activity too?

LEGITIMATE SKI SHOP
NO ENTRY

Baffling briefcase

Si has found the red briefcase. There's a power crystal inside, and a bundle of old newspaper clippings and cut-up pieces of paper. Maybe they mean something? Read the article carefully to see if you can spot a secret message. And those cut-up pieces of paper seem to be part of a puzzle worth solving.

CODERS WORLD

Issue #83,629

Spy hunters Now After Top Coders Houjin And Makena, Youth Finalists at last year's tournament. Reports Of Mischief at their lab suggest kidnappers Are Responsible. Coders Are advised to keep a low profile. "Don't Even Try to find me," says Open University programming and Robotics Network leader and pro-gamer Amy. "My Exceptional stealth skills mean you'll find No Trace of me."

Makena (left), Amy (middle), Houjin (right), pictured at last year's Arcade Awards.

...of Crime
...re world,
...r's totally
...an to set
...ation and
...ake news.
...e messages
...e to give all
...e industries.

New super-laser fires up for the first time. Scientist sent to hospital for burnt bottom. See page 16.

1) Scorpio
2) Taurus
3) Aquarius
4) Gemini
5) Leo
6) Cancer
7) Virgo
8) Sagittarius
9) Aries
10) Libra
11) Pisces
12) Capricorn

You will go on a VERY long journey.

"Hmmm," says Si, "there's not much time left to save the day! If I catch a plane, I should just about make it..."

Shopping mall mayhem

One plane trip and a never-ending taxi ride later, and Si has made it to the mall. Can you spot him – and locate the arcade holding the tournament? You might also spot a flawless friend of Si's, who has changed from one outfit into another...
...and watch out for two enemy agents!

We Got Sole
TOYS 4 ALL
SUGAR! SUGAR!
Fancy Bits
Poppy and Sam's Big Adventure

Arcade antics

Si has found the arcade, where the video game tournament is in full swing. The Twindicate is already here, looking for Amy, the top coder from the newspaper clipping. Can you help Si spot Amy before any Twindicate agents snatch her? And what about "Flawless" Gem... where IS she?

ARCADE TOURNAMENT
TODAY!
GRAND PRIZE TOURNAMENT
Sign-up today!
SPIN to WIN
WIN
LOSE
ARCADE
PING!
ARCADE TOURNAMENT
Teach your monster
Galaxy fighters
Jungle jam
BLAST OFF!
BLAST OFF!
PRIZES

The chase is on

Oh, no! Si wasn't quick enough – a Twindicate agent has taken Amy, and Gem is with them too! Hot on their heels, our hero races out of the mall and into the city. Can you find them all?

MONEY
HOTEL
HOTEL

Hot air getaway

The chase has moved up, up and away... into the middle of a hot-air balloon festival – uh-oh! Find the balloon with Amy and Gem inside, and see if you can spot the one Si is using, too.

Track and trace

A *ping* from Si's pocket brings new hope. Amy has found a way to send a signal to his pocket radio. Use the clues to help Si identify their final destination.

3 → 2 ↑ 4 → 3 ↑ 6 ←

1 ↑ 1 ← 4 ↓ 2 → 1 ↑

Secret Island HQ

Si has made it to Twindicate Island. Will he be the first spy to get a good look at the Lord High Commander's face? Only if he can disguise himself. Find him, and a spare purple outfit. Then find the entrance to the jail cells to rescue Amy, Nyota and Gem. And look out for Agent Teal McBeal – he's found another power crystal and is close behind.

d High
mander
JAIL
CELLS

Prison block breakout

Uh-oh... piranha-infested waters and a fiendish puzzle stand between Si and the cells. But our super spy quickly figures it out. He must plot two paths across the pressure-plated floor to unlock Amy and Nyota's doors. There's a code to operate each door – but which codes will rescue his friends, and which will release an angry enemy agent?

DOOR CODES

Hang on a minute – Gem's not here. So where is she?

The final countdown

Our heroes emerge on the far side of Twindicate Island to discover a rocket launch! But who's that about to board the rocket? Why, it's the Twindicate Lord High Commander, with Gem, and they look VERY similar... could they be identical TWINS? Gem was a double agent all along!

Crystal conundrum

At the control desk, Teal McBeal wonders why no one's there to operate the rocket. Nyota explains the controls are pre-set – and can only be changed by someone holding all four power crystals. Good thing Si and Teal found them all then! But what do they DO with them?

First, identify the correct slot for each crystal. Then, figure out which order to press the buttons in. Finally, can you enter a new destination for the rocket?

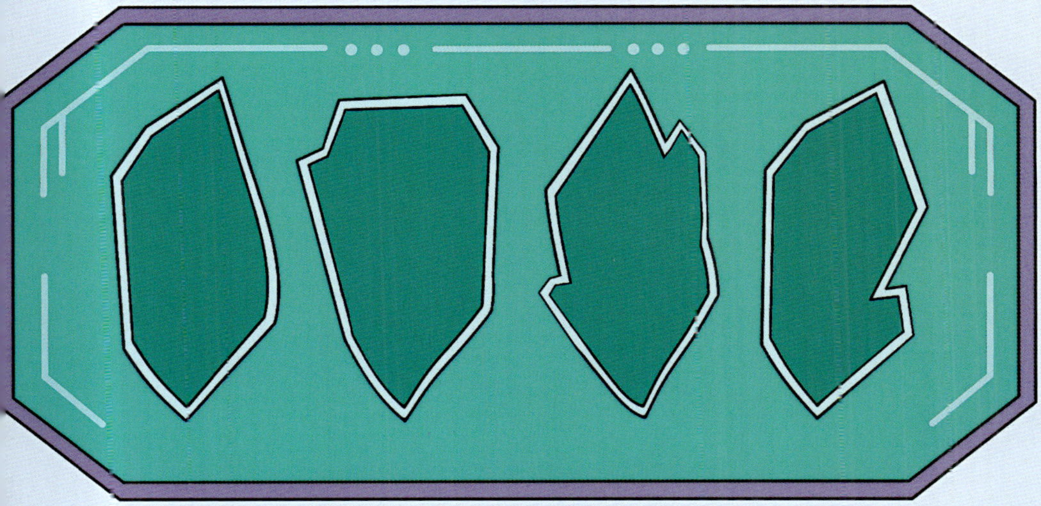

"Hmm," wonders Si the spy. "Where did we find each of these crystals? Which did we find *first*?"

M	E	G	A
O	O	Z	E
A	T	O	M
N	E	O	N

Amy says, "I can see the name of a place that's REALLY far away..."

Mission accomplished!

Si the Spy breathes a huge sigh of relief. The Twindicate leader is stuck on a rocket to the Moon – it'll be a while before she causes any more trouble. Even better, the SIA has uncovered a dangerous double agent: "Flawless" Gem. Who saw THAT coming?*

*Professor Nyota did actually, as you will know if you solved her extra puzzles on pages 20 and 21.

Back on Earth, Spymaster Z thinks everyone deserves a break. Si, Teal McBeal, Professor Nyota and Amy jet off to a tropical island where they're treated to ice-cold coconut drinks, water sports and beachside fun.

No rest for our heroes! Can you help Si and Teal find their phones, to answer the call to action?

Answers

Who's who? Pages 2–3

Briefing at HQ. Pages 4–5

- A spy on skis
- A mouse in a drawer
- A cat trying to sleep
- A fake orange beard
- A spy following a trail of sticks
- A vending machine selling hats
- A spy disguised as a tree
- An airplane dropping hats
- An enemy agent climbing a window
- A spy dressed as a pirate

Carnival of chaos. Pages 6–7

- A clown on a unicycle
- A pigeon wearing headphones
- A pigeon with a pretzel hat
- A spy mailing a letter
- A pigeon stealing a sandwich
- Someone snorkling
- Someone juggling lemons
- A mermaid with a pearl
- A bursting balloon
- A dog on the loose

Robot feather. Page 8

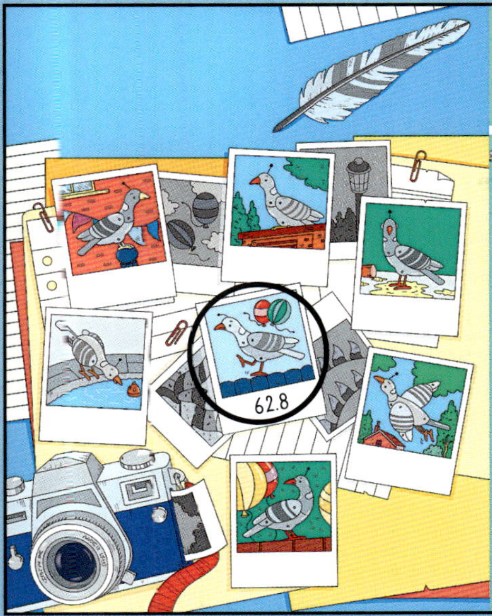

Homing in on the pigeon. Page 9

Aquarium pursuit. Pages 10–11

- A spy eating his lunch
- A stingray wearing a hat
- A lost teddy bear
- An octopus with a shovel
- A mermaid photo shoot
- Three fish balloons
- A crab with a fork and spoon
- A sandcastle
- A man with a mop
- A fish wearing sunglasses

Railway rendezvous. Pages 12–13

- A group camping trip
- A dog with a bone
- A hamburger restaurant
- A very heavy suitcase
- A trapped bag in a ticket gate
- A one-man band
- Two boy wizards
- A discarded umbrella
- Two workers enjoying their lunch
- A toppling stack of suitcases

Answers

Carrier of clues. Pages 14–15

Top-secret science. Pages 16–17

- A spilled barrel of toxic waste
- A slime explosion
- Someone hiding in a box
- A game of ping pong
- A robotic dog
- Someone flying off a treadmill
- A scientist burning some toast
- A paper plane
- A robotic hand stealing lunch
- A gigantic banana

Lost at the library. Pages 18–19

- A snooping detective
- A fishbowl
- A visitor from ancient Rome
- A magical door to a snowy land
- A loooooong book
- A book balanced on a plant
- Someone wearing a very tall hat
- A rodent reading group
- A game of chess
- Spymaster Z visiting the library

Caught on camera. Pages 20–21

Did you spot Nyota's two extra clues?
1) Nyota scribbled a message on the whiteboard. Using the cipher sheet, it reads "Gem is a d..."

2) Nyota arranged her science beakers in a particular order! Match the beakers to the code below the screen, and they spell out the phrase *double agent*.

Suspicious slopes. Pages 22–23

- A reindeer on a ski lift
- A snowman catching a fish
- A red bird box
- A snowboard-eating deer
- Two dogs riding sleds
- A bear on skis
- A rocket-powered skier
- An ice skater stuck in the snow
- A deer wearing sunglasses
- A skier drinking tea

Baffling briefcase. Pages 24–25

Answers

Shopping mall mayhem. Pages 26–27

- Someone slipping on marbles
- A pile of popcorn
- Two children playing tennis
- A runaway vacuum cleaner
- A very tall burger
- Someone floating away
- A teddy bear with a red bow
- Two frogs
- A fake nose for sale
- Someone stuck to a giant lollipop

Arcade antics. Pages 28–29

- A GIANT toy rabbit
- An agent hiding behind a plant
- A child stuck in a claw game
- A dancer in a twist
- A spy-themed arcade machine
- Two dangling donuts
- A slice of pizza
- A tangle of tickets
- A cat climbing a machine
- Spilled gumballs

The chase is on. Pages 30–31

- A broken bicycle
- A falling sock
- A kayak
- A spy with a telescope
- A dog stealing some groceries
- A spy in a manhole
- Ducks taking a bath
- A flyaway suitcase
- Two beehives
- A dog chasing a cat, chasing a rat

Hot air getaway. Page 32

Track and trace. Page 33

- A mouse in a window
- An underpants balloon
- A swiss cheese balloon
- Someone waving a carrot
- Two people eating ice cream
- A balloon filled with balloons
- A parachutist
- A trumpeter
- A wizard hat
- A dog dropping a bone

Secret Island HQ. Pages 34–35

- An agent stealing gold bars
- A pink balloon
- A guitar
- A yoga class
- Someone sawing a giant bone
- A superhero cat in space
- A giraffe plushie
- A cafeteria food fight
- An unearthed fossil
- A volleyball game

Prison block breakout. Pages 36–37

Answers

- An agent holding moon boots
- A falling sandwich
- A yellow cat
- A dangling spider
- A toy rocket
- Workers falling down the stairs
- A kite
- A very long hose
- A nest of bees
- A stowaway mouse

The final countdown. Page 38

Crystal conundrum. Page 39

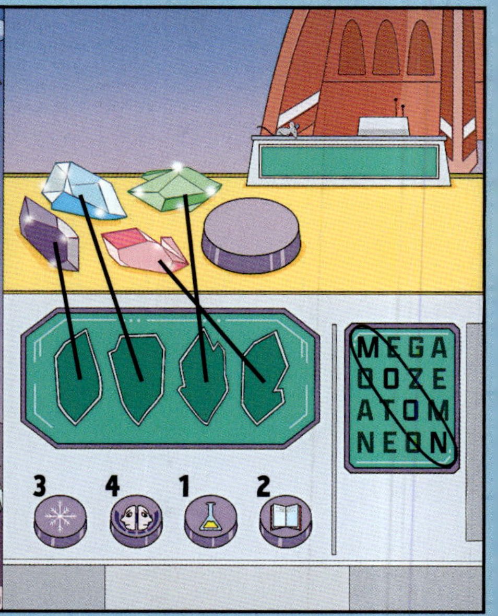

The sequence matches the order the crystals were found in the adventure: the science lab, the library, the ski slope and the Twindicate HQ.

Mission accomplished! Pages 40–41

Cover

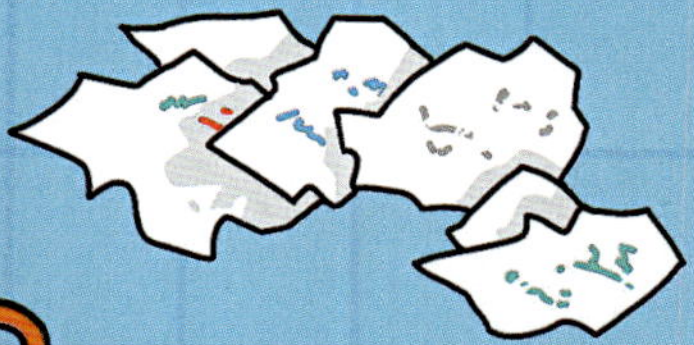

Edited by Sam Taplin

First published in 2025 by Usborne Publishing Limited, 83–85 Saffron Hill, London EC1N 8RT, United Kingdom. usborne.com

uccess (released in December 1993, reached Number 62 and was in the harts for three weeks) inevitably got e boys thinking about a full-time career in the music business.

The expertise to turn the dream into reality was supplied by Nicky Graham, the man who'd guided another pop twosome – Bros – to fame in the late 1980s. As well as experience that would prove invaluable, he added his production and songwriting skills to the boys'

"I've been thinking a lot about how people see us recently, and I think they see up as a pair of mickey-takers. Two little boys who haven't got a clue about what we're doing. But I don't think they could be more wrong" **Dec**

"I sericusly thoug it was going to be doddle when we first started. I thought 'Tonight I'm Free' Top 20 first week! Easy. Everyone warned us abcut what we were letting our-selves in for, but nobody ever tells you hcw to deal with people looki at you in the stree or signing auto-graphs. People said, 'There are going to be a lot c sharks who want make money out you and they're going to be really nice to you', but t amount of people who are out to make a couple of quid from us is frightening. They got pcund signs their eyes when they talk to us" **D**

vocal and performing talents. The result, unleashed on a writing world in the spring of 1994, was 'Psyche'. And, though they but knew it, the PJ and Duncan story was entering an amazing new phase.

The reason wasn't difficult to hear. The taster for the Top 5 album was 'Why Me?', a catchy little single which reached Number 27 in April 1994 and spent four weeks in the charts. But the boys' biggest hit was yet to come.

"Dunno what sort of women I fancy. The Kimberley Davieses and Pamela Andersons don't do anything for me. They're like what me father used to say when I was a kid, 'I'm going to get myself a dolly bird.' That's how I used to picture dolly birds – like them" **Ant**

"We don't get much time to ourselves, so if we do get a spare minute we just relax in the bar and have… a lemonade. We were relaxing in the bar till three in the morning last night… having lemonade! But I love going to parties. It's just that we're usually too busy – working and stuff. But if we grab half an hour in the bar to ourselves just for a quick drink and a chat then that's nice. It's nice to wind down" **Dec**

eleased in July, 'Let's Get Ready to humble' was without question the ummer hit of 1994, staying in the harts for 11 weeks and breaking into the Top 10 for the first time.

Ant and Dec had clocked up other TV appearances – Dec in an episode of *Harry* as "second motorbike thug", and Ant in an educational film about homelessness. But nothing gave them quite as much pleasure as appearing on *Top Of The Pops*. And it would prove to

"Ant got on with everyone on *Byker Grove*. He took the mickey out of everyone, but he didn't do it through malice. A few of the girls used to get on his nerves, but most of the girls got on everyone's nerves at some time" **Dec**

"Dec's most trea-sured possession is either his car or his mobile phone. His phone annoy me when it rings the train. But I'd g for his car, his MG It's a mess and it keeps breaking down. But it's stil his pride and joy" **Ant**

"Dec would most like to go out on a date with Claudia Schiffer: he really likes her. He's quite short so he prefers smaller women… he was just saying he liked Kate Moss the other day" **Ant**

be something of a second home to them as the year went by and hit followed hit. Two more followed in October and December: 'If I Give You My Number' peaked at Number 15, while 'Eternal Love', the lads' suitably slushy Christmas single, climbed three places higher and encouraged much merry munching beneath the mistletoe

That wasn't the end of the story. 'Our Radio Rocks' brought the hit single tal to a Jacko-esque five in a row. And

since the album also included an updated 'Tonight I'm Free', 'Psyche' could have been retitled 'Greatest Hits'. Whatever, it would go on to sell half a million copies – not bad for a first try...

The dynamic duo had embarked on their first UK tour in April 1994, and despite their experiences in the world of television nothing could have prepared them for the sheer effort involved. Said Ant: "touring is really hard work, I'm knackered." Acclaim

was quick to follow, though, and the ecstatic audience reaction encountered when they played dates in their native north-east would have put East 17 to shame. These two snappy rappers proved they were more than just actors cashing in on their small-screen fame, covering every inch of the stage and playing the audience as if they'd done this all their lives.

Not that their musical career spelled the end of the *Byker Grove* connection

"I remember when I first got me car, any girls I'd see, I'd beep and go 'All right girls!' The first time Ant was in the car, I went 'beep, alright girls!' and he went 'Oh no! I know them!'" **Dec**

"I worry about what I throw away in hotel wastepaper baskets! I was in this hotel last week, and the bloke who'd been in the room before had left behind a *Playboy*. I was really paranoid about having this porn mag in the room! I was thinking, 'What if someone finds it?' Did I read it? Course I did! I've had a girl in my room and it's really embarrassing because the hotel receptionists suss it out! You can see them smirking behind the counter going 'aye-aye!' I'm also conscious about how me room looks to people, like room service and stuff. I'm a real worrier, though, whereas Ant always says 'bollocks' to everything" **Dec**

"Ant's ideal holiday would be somewhere hot and sunny with lots of cheap beer. He'll be there with his Union Jack shorts. We go on holiday together but I hardly ever see him, 'cause he always scores with some girl and stays at her chalet all the time" **Dec**

When the boys quit the show they were "sad" but didn't have time to miss it what with their new musical venture. But even with their recording and touring schedule, they couldn't stay away. In 1994 Declan returned to the *Grove* to take part in a competition.

"I was really nervous," he admitted. "Going back was like being the new boy again. I felt as if everyone was watching and thinking 'I wonder if he's changed?' I was determined to show them that I

“Ant has a really short attention span. When we have meetings with our manager he just sits there and then asks me what was said afterwards! The most common phrase on his school report was probably ‘is too easily distracted’ ”
Dec

producer,” explained Ant. “His name is Ray Hedges, and he’s worked with Take That, Boyzone and, er...Russ Abbott. He’s been great for us because he understands the way we want our songs to sound – and, most importantly, he lets us do whatever we want, heh, heh, heh!” Reading between the laughter lines, it was clear this would in no way be ‘Psyche Part II’. “Each track is totally different from the last we did,” summed up Ant. “And that’s what we

"I was alright as a child. A bit cheeky, I think, but that's not bad, is it? Sure, I used to kick around my younger brothers and sisters, but that always happens doesn't it? It's to be expected, isn't it?" **Ant**

"Ant's first job was as a paper boy. He was doing that when I first met him, 'cause a mate of mine said that they'd seen him doing it when he was obviously late for school. He was running round with all these papers and really red cheeks" **Dec**

ant. I can't bear it when you listen to n album like R Kelly's and each song ounds exactly the same."

Ritchie Wermerling, who'd had great success with Let Loose since he last collaborated with the boys, was brought in again to add the finishing touch to 'Perfect', while Ant reckoned 'Love And Devotion' inspired his best-ever vocal performance. He wouldn't say, though, if it was aimed at anyone in particular. And despite the tough studio

"We've grown up. We're not as naive as when we started. There are so many types of people to meet, and it's all so much more stressful than being in *Byker Grove*. I get really worried and paranoid that people will think we've changed and become pretentious" **Dec**

"Why does every one say I wear a don't-mess-with me expression? Everyone says th when they first meet us! When w the last time I go into a fight? Probably the yea before last. I got black eye out of I knew as soon a I walked past thi bunch of arseho that they were lo ing for a fight. Th said to me, 'Give your trousers.' They weren't aft me clothes, it wa like one of those lines like,'Did yo spill my pint!'" **Ant**

regime they didn't hold back on their partying. "We do our best vocals when we have hangovers," Dec claimed.

The first single 'Stuck On U' emerged in July 1995, and the next 'U Krazy Katz', three months later. "It was originally called 'The Rhumble Killer'," Dec insisted. "We decided we wanted to write a song that would be better than 'Let's Get Ready To Rhumble', because we're sick to death of it!" The words of this song were created rathe

"We never argue about who sings which bits in the songs. It's usually quite obvious. Our voices are different, so one line might suit Ant and one line might suit me" **Dec**
"...and it just so happened that most of 'U Krazy Katz' suited me!" **Ant**

nusually, Ant revealed, "were written while playing football. We kept thinking f stupid lines and stopping to write hem down." The singles were, naturally, hot chart items, peaking at Numbers 12 and 15 respectively.

As for an album title, the lads were undecided. "I wanted to call it 'Cats And Dogs'," revealed Ant, "because of 'U Krazy Katz' and the dog on a lead in 'Stuck On U'. But when I suggested it everybody just looked at me and then

"I don't use chat up lines. I've got my set piece: when you see someone you fancy, you catch their eye and hold it for just half a second longer than is comfortable. If she smiles, you're in!" **Dec**

"We've been work ing on a song called 'It's Gonna Be Alright', and it has a real 1960s feel to it. When yo record a song you can have up to 24 different tracks on it, and we've had laugh working out which ones to put on this. There are bassoons and tubas on it at the moment" **Dec**

"The thing with the 'Psyche' album was that we'd go into the studio, sing the songs and go home. It's different now, as we've learned all about how everything works" **Ant**

carried on talking." Dec's suggestion of 'Caviar And Chips' – "because the songs are classier but we aren't" – went down equally badly, so the compromise was 'Top Katz'. As for their feelings as they prepared to take the PJ & Duncan show back out on the road for the second time, they could agree on just one thing: "We're more tired than we've ever been." Dec stayed awake long enough to pass his driving test, so keep an eye in your rear-view mirror for a

ouped-up sports car…and a very amiliar fringe! And there seemed little oubt that PJ & Duncan, those two efugees from *Byker Grove*, were once again in the fast lane to success. As for the future, Ant has his trainers firmly on solid ground. "We realise we're not going to be pop stars forever," he says. "Eventually people'll move on and go back to acting."

Until then…let's Rhumble!

PJ & Duncan discfile

Singles...

Tonight I'm Free
Telstar STAS 2706
Released December 1993
(Highest UK chart position: 62)

Why Me?
XS STAS 2719
Released April 1994
(Highest UK chart position: 27)

Let's Get Ready To Rhumble
XS CDANT/CDDEC 1
Released July 1994
(Highest UK chart position: 9)

If I Give You My Number
XS CDANT/CDDEC 2
Released September 1994
(Highest UK chart position: 15)

Eternal Love
XS CDANT/CDDEC 3
Released November 1994
(Highest UK chart position: 12)

Our Radio Rocks
XS CDANT/CDDEC 4
Released February 1995
(Highest UK chart position: 15)

Stuck On U
XS CDANT/CDDEC 5
Released July 1995
(Highest UK chart position: 12)

U Krazy Katz
XS CDANT/CDDEC 6
Released October 1995
(Highest UK chart position: 15)

Albums.

Psych
Let's Get Ready to Rhumble / One Look
Why Me? / She Scores A Perfect Ten / Tonigh
I'm Free 94 / Eternal Love / If I Give You M
Number / Talk About It / Girlfriend / Our Radi
Rocks / I Want You / Free As A Bird / Psych
Telstar/Ronco TCD 274
Released November 199
(Highest UK chart position: 5

Top Kat
U Krazy Katz / Perfect / Stuck On U / You Are Th
One / Love And Devotion / Stepping Stone
Always My Love / By Your Side
Gonna B Alright / Somewhere I
The Rain / Easy Riser
U Krazy Katz (Clock Remix
Telstar/Ronco TCD 279
Released November 199

Video..

Psyche: The Vide
Telstar Video TVE 106
Released October 199

Top Katz: The Vide
Telstar Video TVE 107
Released November 199